7.82 Kuseell + Kuseell 11-67 (Sweaninger)

AN AFRICAN PEOPLE IN THE TWENTIETH CENTURY

AN AFRICAN PEOPLE
IN THE TWENTIETH
CENTURY

By

L. P. MAIR

M.A., Ph.D., Lecturer in Colonial Administration,
London School of Economics

NEW YORK

RUSSELL & RUSSELL · INC

1965

FIRST PUBLISHED IN 1934
REISSUED 1965 BY RUSSELL & RUSSELL, INC.
BY ARRANGEMENT WITH ROUTLEDGE & KEGAN PAUL LTD., LONDON
L. C. CATALOG CARD NO: 65-18526

Printed in Great Britain

TO

YOKANA M. WASWA

CONTENTS

NOTE ON ORTHOGRAPHY AND PRONUNCIATION

The spelling of Luganda words is that agreed upon by
a committee set up by the Uganda Education Department in
1931. Vowels are pronounced as in Italian, except that *i* is
always short, consonants as in English, except that *c* represents
ch. An apostrophe after *ng* indicates that it is a single sound, as
in *sing* ; otherwise it is always pronounced as in *finger*. The
sign · before a consonant—e.g. ·*siga, ama·zi*—means that the
consonant is doubled. The accent is on the antepenultimate
except when this syllable is a prefix.

ILLUSTRATIONS

PREFACE

THIS book is the outcome of nine months' study on the spot of the effect of European contact upon the village life of the Baganda people. The period of investigation was divided into three parts of roughly equal length spent in different parts of Buganda Province. In each of these districts I lived in native villages, my first three months being spent in a rest-house lent me by the C.M.S., on the site of one of their early mission stations, and the other periods in huts built for me by the natives. During the first month I worked in English through an interpreter. After that time I used no more English ; at first I had with me when interviewing informants a boy to whose voice I was accustomed and who could repeat slowly what was said, but at the end of three months I was able to dispense with this help except in the case of old people who spoke very indistinctly.

My object has been to describe native life as European influences have modified it, and to estimate the degree of success or failure with which the newly introduced elements have been assimilated and the reasons for this success or failure. Such a study does not involve any comparison on ethical grounds of the merits of different civilizations. Fundamentally it consists in determining how the basic needs of society were served by the institutions of the indigenous culture and how far modifications in those institutions, necessitated by changed conditions, have or have not dislocated a working system of social co-operation. That such modifications have in general been made in the past without consideration of their effect upon the social mechanism as a whole, few would deny. If, therefore, we are to envisage the government of native races as a process of scientifically controlled adaptation, it is of the first importance to discover what the results of such changes have been.

I have accordingly given as full an account as possible of the indigenous social organization, describing the salient modifications each in its place. This treatment of the subject has meant that organized European activities, administrative, educational, and religious, are dealt with at less length than is usual in books on colonial territories and from a rather different point of view. But while it has been an inevitable part of my task to indicate the points at which those activities have created problems that they have not yet solved, I should not wish it to be thought that I do not appreciate the work of the many missionaries and administrators who have devoted their lives to the service of native advancement.

It would have made this volume too bulky to include in it a historical account of the penetration of Uganda by European civilization, and there is the less need for this as there is a rich literature dealing with the early days. I have, therefore, assumed some knowledge of the historical background on the part of the reader, but append a bibliography on the subject for those who wish to pursue it further.

There is in existence already a very full anthropological account of the Baganda by the Rev. John Roscoe. This account, published in 1909 by one who had been in the country from 1884, only seven years after the arrival of the first missionary, contains a mass of detail, particularly in the spheres of mythology, folklore, and ritual, which but for his work would have been lost irrecoverably.

His book contains a full account of the native court ceremonial, especially that which accompanied a king's accession, of the titles, precedence, and duties of the chiefs and the areas under their control, of the names of the clans into which the tribe was divided, with the legends of their ancestors, the special duties which they performed for the king, and the names and position of their lands. It includes a large number of the myths told of the various gods, with several accounts of religious ceremonies which are now completely forgotten. It also contains a complete and accurate list of kinship terms, and very complete descriptions of technical processes, some of which, such as canoe-building, are to-day almost obsolete.

Nevertheless it is not altogether satisfactory to the modern anthropologist, for it does not include many data which are now thought indispensable for a sociological study. It does not envisage Baganda society as a mechanism of co-operation, and the links which should connect the structure of kindred and clan, of political and religious authorities, with the normal organization of daily life, are missing. It describes, for example, very fully the ceremonial connected with marriage but does not analyse the system of co-operation within the household. It does not connect the kinship terms with the obligations recognized between relatives, nor the technical processes with the organization through which they were carried out. It is most inadequate at those points at which the student of economic contact most requires accurate and detailed information—in such questions as the system of economic co-operation, or of land tenure, or the relations between people and chiefs.

Moreover, the disadvantage of working largely on the basis of native statements detached from their context is apparent in certain serious distortions of fact. The political organization, for example, is represented as no more than a system whereby a few tyrannical chiefs preyed on the common people and were in turn preyed on by the king. The summary nature of justice and the arbitrary exercise of power by the king and the most important chiefs are exclusively emphasized, while their obligations towards their people, their place in the maintenance of order, and the checks upon abuse are overlooked.

Again, a highly sensational colour is given to the description of the indigenous religion by the over-emphasis of human sacrifice, which is made to seem its central feature. Not only is the aspect of religion as a means of recourse in times of danger or difficulty barely considered, but offerings of human victims to the gods are confused with murders for magical purposes, with political executions for crime, and with the wanton slaughter which was indulged in by some of the kings, so that their total is made to appear enormous.

For these reasons the attempt to make a new reconstruction of the past of Baganda culture seemed to me necessary. In the event I felt it to be justified beyond my expectations, for the number of old men who remember the days before the influence of Christianity and British administration had effectively penetrated the country, and whose accounts, given at places many miles apart, corroborate one another, is surprisingly large. I have indicated in the text the points at which my informants differed positively from Roscoe's, those in which they simply denied knowledge of customs which he describes, and those in which I differ from him for reasons of evidence other than that of native statements which contradict those made in his book. In some cases these differences may be due to the falling into disuse of old customs ; in others, for the reasons which I give in each context, I think they cannot be.

I owe a debt of gratitude for practical assistance in carrying out my work both to the officials of the Uganda Administration and to the Church Missionary Society, who made the difficult period of first contact with the natives easier for me by lending me a house in a Native Anglican Church village and recommending me to its leading members. To Bishop and Mrs. C. E. Stuart my especial thanks are due for their constant hospitality, kindness, and encouragement. I should like also to record my appreciation of the help given me by the native authorities in each place where I stayed.

I have to thank the editors of *Africa* for permission
to reprint, in my chapter on " Land Tenure ", part of
an article which appeared in that journal. For suggestions
and criticisms at many points I am indebted to Dr. Meyer
Fortes, Dr. Raymond Firth, and Dr. H. I. Hogbin.

The Geography Department of the London School
of Economics were kind enough to draw a map of
Uganda to illustrate my account. The officials of the
Colonial Office Library have also given me much help
in consulting documents.

What this book owes to Professor B. Malinowski
in its theoretical approach will be obvious on every
page. My training in field-work I also owe to him.
No one who has not had the privilege of working with
Professor Malinowski can appreciate the extent of the
debt, and anyone who has will understand the difficulty
of adequately acknowledging it. If my work is of any
value the credit is due to him alone.

LUCY MAIR.

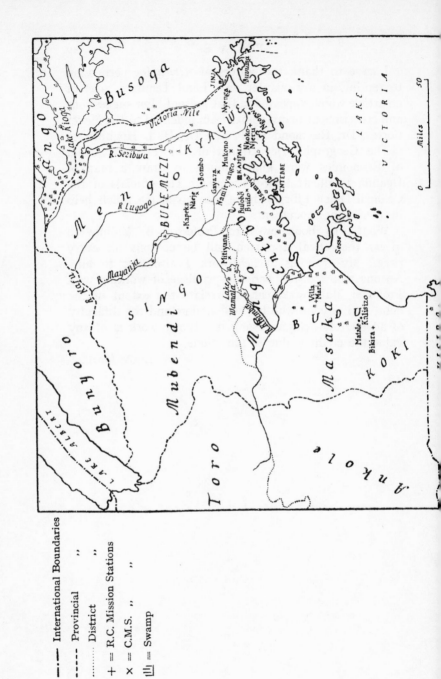

International Boundaries
Provincial   ,,
District   ,,
+ = R.C. Mission Stations
× = C.M.S. ,,   ,,
⊔ⁿ⊔ = Swamp

AN AFRICAN PEOPLE
IN THE TWENTIETH CENTURY

CHAPTER I

THE PROBLEM OF NATIVE POLICY

THE last few years have seen a remarkable growth of
public interest in the policies pursued by various European
governments in the tropical territories under their control,
and a considerable change of attitude towards the ethics
of imperialism. Complacent pride in expansion has
given way to the conviction that it can only be justified
by benefits resulting to the subject peoples and to the
world at large, and the axiom that such benefits result
automatically from the domination of a superior civilization is beginning to be discredited. The system under
which the former German colonies are now administered
lays down as a legal principle that the duties of the government are that of a trustee, and his trust the well-being
and development of the native subjects ; and the scrutiny
to which their affairs are subjected has resulted in an
intensive comparative study of the various policies
which purport to secure this aim.

From this increased interest is resulting a com-
prehension that the difficulties which have been
encountered in the introduction of European civilization
to primitive peoples are not due to mere unreasonableness
on the part of the native, which time and patience will
overcome, but are inherent in the situation in which the
European government finds itself. Even to those who
hold that there is no respect in which European
civilization is not superior to every other, it is becoming

B

patent that its introduction to the coloured races has been attended everywhere with friction and disappointment and often with disaster.

THE SOCIOLOGICAL PROBLEM

The conflict which confronts colonial governments is one not to be solved by methods of trial and error, by mere firmness or even by mere good-will. It calls for scientific study as a basis for rational planning—social engineering, as it has been called. It is a conflict whose roots lie in something much deeper than differences of point of view—in the disorganization which is produced in a primitive culture when it is suddenly confronted with a more complex civilization whose alien elements are almost forcibly imposed upon it—and it can only be dealt with through a full understanding of the nature and effects of this contact. It is here that the science of Social Anthropology—the study of primitive culture as a living and working reality—can render an indispensable service in its application to the practical problems of colonial policy.

Through the understanding of native society that anthropology brings it is possible to see where European innovations have subjected it to the severest strain, where their effect has been positively harmful, where the indigenous culture provides that foundation on which alone can be securely built the new institutions which modern circumstances require.

The problem of contacts is fundamentally one, for European penetration among primitive peoples is directed everywhere to essentially similar aims, and it is these aims that determine the points at which the impact will be strongest. Roughly speaking, the main streams of contact may be classified as religious, political, and economic, and their representatives as missionary, administrative, and settler. Each of these has as its avowed object the development of native life in one direction or another, and in the initial stages the result of each, sometimes deliberately produced, sometimes inadvertently, has been mainly the destruction of native institutions.

European Contact—Religious

Christian missionaries have set their faces against all the patently " uncivilized " aspects of native culture, whether or not they were directly forbidden by the Scriptures : they have opposed polygamy, slavery, the payment of bride-price, initiation ceremonies, dancing, wailing at funerals, and the belief in magic, along with human sacrifice and the exposure of twins, as all being equally repugnant to a civilization in which mechanical warfare is a recognized institution. Yet, to the anthropologist who sees culture as an organic whole, even those institutions which seem in terms of human suffering most cruel will be found to have some place in the maintenance of the society, such that their uncomprehending destruction must carry with it the loss of essential elements in the social structure ; while the condemnation of others will prove often to be due to mere failure to recognize their positive value. On the other hand, the new elements which mission influence has introduced into native society have, in the main, been such as to contribute to satisfactory adaptation— schools and hospitals, and the introduction of new forms of cultivation—and in many territories the missions have courageously championed the natives against the injuries of the other elements of contact.

Contact—Administrative

Administrative contact, too, involves the abolition of native institutions, and the government is able to penalize breaches of the new laws which it introduces. The establishment of an alien government means first and foremost a curtailment of the powers of native authorities. Everywhere they have lost the right of making war, their position as the final arbiter of justice, and such special prerogatives as the right to punish offences against themselves by mutilation or death ; the sanction for their authority becoming instead the support of the alien power. In the sphere of economic organization the chiefs' rights to labour and tribute have often been taken from them. Feasting is discouraged as wasteful, slavery is abolished, men are sometimes compelled to do work which the native division of labour assigns to women, and pastoral peoples forced to cultivate food-crops. The practice of magic is penalized as a form of fraud, while that of sorcery—in native eyes the most heinous of all crimes—cannot be dealt with because European justice refuses to punish a man for something which he cannot possibly have done.

On the positive side a government must introduce taxation, which may be a new element altogether, and in any case has the revolutionary characteristic of being paid in cash. It introduces an army and police force, organized, recruited, and rewarded on European lines, and, in most colonies, on a basis of conscription. It necessitates also the creation of a class of subordinate administrative officials. Administrative contact has meant also the introduction into native society of European institutions, not as a necessary element of efficient government but with a view to the advancement of the natives. Of these the most popular is individual freehold tenure of land. Next to it, though less common in the early stages, is the machinery of representative government.

CONTACT—ECONOMIC

It is in the sphere of economic contact that the gravest problems arise, for here the aim of the European is absolutely irreconcilable with the desires of the native.

The European wishes to acquire all the best land and cultivate crops for export by means of native labour ; the native wishes to remain in his village and cultivate his own food-crops. At the moment of initial contact he is not interested in growing crops for export and definitely unwilling to leave his home and work for wages.

For the moment, however, we are concerned with the new elements of culture which this form of contact brings with it. Of these the first is the idea of work for its own sake or " the dignity of labour " ; the conception that there is something inherently desirable and virtuous in working continuously at one monotonous job which does not produce any obvious advantage to the worker. Quite apart from their natural bias in favour of a principle which will increase the labour supply, white people in the tropics are genuinely shocked at the apparent idleness of the native.

The assumption that wage-labour would have an uplifting effect upon the native is based very largely on the theory that the man of a family should be the bread-winner. But there are a number of reasons why this conception does not work among many primitive peoples. It presupposes not only a money economy, with the whole system of indirect satisfaction of wants which it implies, but very complicated organizations for the division of labour and for exchange ; it also presupposes a fairly dense population. In a small community, whose products are practically limited to needs and where every individual has his allotted task in the joint work of production, you cannot take away a large proportion of the adult males for a long period and expect that a money payment will enable them to replace the loss to the community which their absence has caused. They cannot buy food to replace that which has not been grown, for nobody else has grown a surplus of food to sell to them. Since European crops are export crops, the net result of the plantation system is to decrease the native food supply.

It introduces a further disadvantage, arising, paradoxically enough, out of the one safeguard that the native has against its dangers. In any area where European economic penetration is going on it has been found essential that, in some way or other, the native shall be assured of at least a modicum of land and to a certain extent freedom to live in his own way, and the reserve system has been usually adopted to this end. But this means that he is obliged to go a long distance to his place of labour ; in many parts of Africa this journey must be made on foot, and it sometimes puts as much as two or three months on to the time which the worker is obliged to spend away from home.

European economic contact, even without the plantation system and its demand for labour, has introduced the innovation which has most radically transformed native society—the use of money. In the early stages—and it is so even now among a few tribes whom it has not yet been possible to infect with the European's insatiable desires—money was not appreciated, wage-earning therefore unpopular, and taxation was admittedly regarded partly as a means of obliging the native to produce something for exchange.

But once a money economy begins to be taken for granted, new problems arise. With the desire for money comes the demand for greater individual freedom in the disposal of property and, above all, of land, not so much, as had been hoped, in order that individual enterprise may reap its own reward, but so that money can be easily raised to satisfy individual desires.[1] Thrift and foresight, the planning of expenditure to the best advantage, do not come automatically along with the medium of exchange which makes their exercise desirable.

[1] Cf. the *Report on Land Tenure in Bunyoro*, published by the Uganda Government in 1932. This report points out that while native chiefs have for some years been demanding freehold land in order to grow " profitable trees ", the one use that they in fact make of land over which they have rights is to collect rent from the cultivators ; and that in Buganda, where freehold has been introduced, no landowner has ever taken advantage of this security to raise credit for improvements.

Confronted with an infinite range of new possibilities of acquisition, the native has no idea of money values, and will sacrifice a month's wages for a worthless object. Moreover, the substitution of payments in cash for payments in kind disorganizes the working of systems of distribution which were based mainly on transactions other than the direct exchange of goods for goods ; the chief's economic prerogatives, which in the older economy enabled him to maintain a stock of wealth that could be drawn on by his people in case of need, become a source of oppression when his tribute is paid in money that can be exchanged for European goods. Similarly, the bride-price, which, when paid in cattle, was public evidence of a contract and in many societies was a security reserved to be returned if the contract was broken, when paid in cash becomes a mere source of profit to parents.

THE PROBLEM OF ADJUSTMENT

My object in this analysis has not been to answer the question whether the influence of European civilization on primitive peoples is, in the long run, beneficial or the reverse. Such a question has no relevance to the objective study of a process which is inevitable. I have tried simply to indicate the main problems of adjustment which it creates for the society which is exposed to it and for the authorities who are responsible for the development of that society. The necessity of adjustment is indisputable, and must be faced whatever one's ethical judgment of the new environment or any element in it.

The fundamental question which colonial policy has to answer is along what lines the adjustment shall be made. Three main answers can be seen in practice in Africa to-day. One is the " White Man's Country " policy, advocated openly in South Africa and less openly by the European settler communities in Kenya, Tanganyika, and the Rhodesias—the transplantation entire of a European society, in which the African population only finds a place as a reservoir of unskilled labour. The second is the " assimilation " policy, pursued by France, where the African who has shown himself capable of adopting European civilization is treated, both legally and socially, on terms of equality with the French population, whose citizenship he shares. To a small minority of individuals this system brings privileges which arouse the bitter envy of the corresponding class in neighbouring British colonies, but in terms of the development of African society it means less than nothing. Outside the coast towns the average African has no use for such privileges, and their one effect is to detach from their own people those whose superior intelligence might be of value in carrying out a constructive policy.

The third system is variously known as " association ", " differentiation ", " Indirect Rule ", and " parallel development ". The last of these terms perhaps expresses its object best. It aims neither at making a European society of Europeans paramount in Africa, nor at raising all Africans, by some such process as a literary education, to the lofty heights of European civilization, but at permitting and encouraging the growth of African civilization on indigenous lines. This system has two main aspects, the political and the economic. On the political side it means government by and through authorities recognized by the people concerned ; on the economic it means the exploitation of material resources by the native " working in his own time, in his own way, for his own profit, and with the assistance of his family ".[1]

The degree to which the principle of the preservation and development of native institutions has actually been followed has varied very much between different territories, which all accept it in theory. Which are the institutions worthy or capable of preservation in a

[1] Lugard, " Education and Race Relations," *Journal of the African Society*, January, 1933.

given community is a question that individual judgments answer in different ways ; some champions of native development even go so far as to assert that there are none which meet the needs of modern times, and that the whole theory of Indirect Rule is a mistake, if not a deliberate deception practised in order to prevent the African from attaining to equality with the European.

Differences in the application of any sound principle are essential if it is not to become so rigid as to be value- less ; but who is to decide what they are to be ? Surely we need a decision based on some more valid criterion than the haphazard pronouncements of individual opinion—on a detailed study of the facts, of the nature and functions of the institutions of any given community, the extent to which they can be adapted to meet new needs, or to which, possibly, new influences may have irreparably destroyed them so that something must be improvised to take their place, and the circumstances which, in that case, are likely to favour the success of one innovation rather than another. It is by the provision of reliable material for answering such questions that the use of anthropology can transform colonial administration from an art to a science.

The aim of this book is to examine in the light of the principles set out above the results of European contact in one African tribe—the Baganda. Here, with one or two exceptions, the necessary adaptations seem to have been made with the minimum of disorganization. Though Uganda was not declared a protectorate till 1894, the first missionaries arrived there in 1877, so that the process of contact has been going on for a relatively long time. In illustration of its initial dis- ruptive effects one need only mention the persecutions of native Christians by the king Mwanga and the " religious " wars between Protestants and Catholics. It is now too late to trace the history of the first intro- duction to the native of the European economic system, to follow what would be a most instructive story of early difficulties, and the way in which the present relatively happy solution has been reached.   All one can do is to compare present conditions with what it has been possible to discover about the indigenous system, and note the sum total of change without attempting to analyse the stages through which the changes have passed.   Since changes only have meaning when they are set against the background of past conditions, a good deal of attention will be given to attempting a coherent reconstruction of the Baganda system as Europeans first found it.

CHAPTER II

BUGANDA AND ITS PEOPLE

GEOGRAPHICAL SITUATION AND EXTENT OF CONTACT

THE kingdom of Buganda is situated on the northern and western shores of Lake Victoria, extending from latitude 2° N. to 1° S. The River Nile forms its eastern boundary, separating it from Busoga, and on its other landward sides it adjoins others of the so-called Lacustrian kingdoms—in the north Bunyoro, in the west Toro and Ankole, and in the south Kiziba, from which it is separated by the small tribe of Ba-Koki. All these kingdoms have been formed through the conquest of an agricultural Bantu people by pastoral Hamitic invaders from the north ; but whereas the others are still divided into a pastoral aristocracy and an agricultural peasant class, in Buganda the assimilation has been complete. In pre-European days the Baganda held a dominant position among their neighbours, some of whom are said to have paid regular tribute to their kings, while others were periodically invaded and plundered by them. Baganda tradition contains no record of the reverse process, though doubtless it must sometimes have occurred. Partly owing to their accessible position near the Lake and partly because the native government kept open paths all over the country, European influence spread there very rapidly, and the Baganda are still ahead of the other tribes of the Protectorate in education, have been made administrative chiefs in tribes other than their own, and have generally translated the old sense of superiority into the idea that skilled labour is the sphere of the Baganda and unskilled work that of other tribes.

Politically their kingdom forms one of the four provinces of the Uganda Protectorate, in which they are the largest single tribe and number 870,000 out of a total native population of three and a half million.[1] Their status is regulated by the Uganda Agreement, concluded by Sir Harry Johnston in 1900. This agreement confirms the king and his heirs in their position, assigns to him a share in the revenues of the kingdom, establishes a native council which both administers justice and holds an annual legislative session, and lays down the freehold rights to land of the chiefs found to be in possession of it at the time when the agreement was signed. Though this last provision produced unforeseen results, the general effect of the agreement has been to make it possible to preserve and develop the native system of administration and to keep up a certain element of continuity through the changes that have taken place in the last thirty years.

Economically what has changed the face of Uganda within that time is the cultivation of cotton, which was introduced in 1904. From the cotton crop the vast majority of the population now supplies its every want beyond bare necessities and meets its obligations to the Government and to landlords : " Go and grow cotton !" is the stereotyped exhortation of those in authority to anyone who fails to do so. It is mainly due to the wealth brought to the country by cotton in prosperous years that education and health services have been developed by the Government and by missions, and utilized by the natives to such a remarkable extent ; while on the debit side of the account, cotton has been the crux of the problem of landlordism created by the introduction of freehold tenure.

There are no large continuous tracts of land alienated to Europeans as there are in Kenya, and in the census figures of 1921 the number of planters in the whole Protectorate is given as only 106. In Buganda the total

---

[1] Estimated census returns, 1931.

European population is 1,200,[1] all but 130 of whom are accounted for by the three towns of Kampala, Jinja, and Entebbe. Entebbe is the headquarters of the Protectorate Government ; Jinja is mainly commercial ; and Kampala, besides being a commercial centre and the terminus of the Kenya and Uganda Railway, contains the royal palace and seat of the native government, and the headquarters of both the Church Missionary Society and White Fathers' missions. In the province of Buganda there are two other Government stations, at Masaka and Mubende, as well as the headquarters of the King's African Rifles (who are mostly recruited from other tribes than the Baganda) at Bombo. European-staffed schools and hospitals of the C.M.S. and both Catholic missions (the White Fathers and Mill Hill) are scattered all over the country.

By 1928 only 76,000 acres of land had been alienated for European settlement in the whole country, and many plantations have since gone out of cultivation. A considerable proportion of the total alienated land is in Buganda, but the plantations are largely localized by the fact that the area considered as Crown land is limited ; the majority are in the county of Kyagwe in the east. In this county there is one large Indian estate where sugar is grown and refined on the spot. The great majority of the labour employed in all these enterprises is drawn from tribes other than the Baganda.

The Indian population numbers some 7,000, the majority of whom are concentrated in the towns. Outside them Indian enterprise is mainly confined to cotton ginning and retail trade ; there is a group of Indian shops at every cross-roads, where natives buy such things as cotton goods, pots and pans, soap, paraffin by the cupful, tea, sugar, and salt. The motor-buses which run from Kampala to every part of the country are almost entirely owned by Indians.

These are the main ways in which the non-native

[1] Estimated census figures, 1931.

populations play their part in the life of the country. But there is no remote village where European influences have not penetrated into the very stuff of daily life, and that not only in the form of increased material desires and the need to earn money to satisfy them, but in the adoption of institutions whose existence has already come to be taken for granted. The very appearance of the villages has been changed by the modern fashion of building houses, still with local materials but on a European design. Every village has its church—sometimes two churches, Protestant and Catholic—which on week-days is the school where the children learn their prayers and their letters, and usually next door to it an almost invisibly small " football ground ". In the Protestant churches a service is held every Sunday, though of course there is not an ordained priest in each village. The itinerant priests are mainly native in the Native Anglican Church—the church founded by the C.M.S.— and increasingly so in the Catholic. Central schools run entirely by natives form the backbone of the educational system. No native village is very far from a government dispensary or one of the maternity centres organized by the C.M.S., where simple dispensing is also done ; these institutions too are entirely staffed by natives—in the case of the maternity centres, by women. Nor is any village more than a day's walk from a main road along which motor-buses run daily to the capital.

THE BAGANDA VILLAGE

In position and general plan the Baganda village is very much what it must always have been. Each village is built on the slopes of one of the innumerable little flat-topped hills—so regular in shape that they seem to have been cut out of cardboard—of which the whole country is made up. The hill-top is generally not built on, for the soil there is rocky and in elephant-grass country the short grass which grows there forms the best pasture ; so that in a thickly-populated part of the country the characteristic landscape consists of the expanse of broad, dark green banana-leaves which indicate native habitations, climbing up the slope but coming to an end in time to leave the clear-cut outline of the ridge with occasionally a clump of trees. Between and below the bananas are cotton patches, deep red when the ground has just been cleared, then showing the neat rows of green seedlings, visible miles away in the clear atmosphere, and finally making rectangles of a lighter green. Below this is a piece of grass-land in which the line of a stream is marked by a dense growth of trees, with here and there the scarlet blossoms of the flame-tree thrown into dazzling relief by their dark background. Somewhere in the landscape the course of a river can be guessed from a great flat mass of papyrus. When actually crossing the river all the water that is visible is a little cleared space, dotted with purple water-lilies, a yard or so wide on either side of the bridge.

The village is not built according to any regular plan ; it has no public open place or any other central point. Each house stands by itself among its own bananas, and two houses are seldom so close that one could shout from one to the other. Even the cultivation is not continuous ; there is often quite a wide stretch of fallow land between two houses. Nor is there any scheme in the lay-out of the fields ; some are near the houses, others higher or lower on the hill-side wherever anyone has seen a patch of good land. Every village has its main road, some four yards wide when properly weeded, by which the lorries come to collect the cotton in the buying season. People like to live near the road, and there are generally houses on both sides of it. They stand some fifteen to twenty yards back from it with a clear space in front, which is not only kept weeded but swept every morning. Here children play, beans or coffee-berries are laid to dry in the sun, barkcloths are spread for the final airing that completes their manufacture, skins stretched to dry, the washing is hung out, and visitors are often entertained. Festivities take place here, not in the house. The word for this yard (*lugya*)—perhaps because in the old polygamous days it was the central point of a group of dwellings—is commonly used to indicate the whole household.

It is the disappearance of this type of household that would probably strike an old Muganda most forcibly if he could come back to life and return to his old village. He would remember a series of large groups of round dwellings, but all that he would see now would be one fairly large square house facing the road, with a smaller one at right angles to it. These would be the main house and the cooking-house ; the latter often contains also a sleeping apartment for older children. If a man makes barkcloths he has a separate shed, both because the work takes up a good deal of space and because of the dust that flies off the bark as it is beaten.

The original native hut was a round dwelling built of a framework of canes supported on posts and thatched with grass. Roof and walls were continuous, so that the thatch reached right down to the ground. Over the doorway was constructed an extension of the same structure which formed a porch. Inside, the raised platform on which the goats were tied up at night took up a good deal of the space. At one side barkcloth hangings curtained off a sleeping apartment. Branches lashed together horizontally and tied to some of the posts made a shelf on which such objects as calabashes were stored, and this, with perhaps a wooden stool for the master of the house, completed the furniture ; skins would be fetched and spread on the ground for a guest to sit on. Sometimes a fire is lighted in such houses, but usually the fire is kept to the cook-house, which may be built in the same way as the dwelling-house or may be a mere shelter without walls.

The majority of houses are now built on an entirely European plan, in a rectangular form with the posts

forming the main framework, while between them canes
are tied to support the mud of which the walls are now
made. The roof is usually still thatched, but the thatch
now falls from the roof-tree instead of radiating from a
central pinnacle as it did in the round house, and is
supported by outside posts making a verandah whose
floor is a little above the level of the surrounding earth,
and wide enough for a person to sit in the shade of the
eaves. A corrugated iron roof is every native's ambition.
These have the advantage of permanency and of reducing
the risk of fire. Natives complain that they make the
house very hot ; yet they rarely have recourse to the
simple remedy of making an inner roof of canes.

Such houses may be finished off with wooden doors
and window-shutters or may simply have the old-
fashioned cane framework outer door and close the
openings between the rooms with barkcloth hangings.
The number of rooms may be anything from two—a mere
division into outer and inner room in the old-fashioned
manner—to half a dozen, with separate rooms for husband
and wife, and a guest-room. Built on at the back of the
house is a small cane-fenced enclosure for washing in,
with a number of stones set in the ground at one spot
for the water to drain through.

A chief's house is a more complicated affair. There
is no special position reserved for it in the village, though
it used to be supposed to be desirable to command a
good view, doubtless for reasons of security, and I saw
one or two right on the tops of hills. The chiefs who
under the modern system are the officials of the native
government have to live close to the main road so as to
be accessible to touring British officials.

The universal mark of a chief's house is the fence
of intertwined canes which surrounds it. Only the
chiefs appointed by the government can nowadays
command enough labour to keep up much fencing, and
even they do not now completely surround their houses.
Nowadays the front of the house breaks the line of the

fence, which is carried sideways and backwards to conceal the back premises and enable such operations as cooking and washing clothes to be carried out in privacy. The supplementary houses may be inside or outside the fence. There is always a special house for receiving visitors, often several dwelling-houses to accommodate the relatives who still gather round the chief, and the boys and girls who are sent to be brought up in his household, sometimes a special house to put at the disposal of guests. Usually there is one large cooking-house, with room for several fires, which the women of the household use in common. If there are many goats a large shed is built to tie them up in at night. Sometimes the bathing enclosure has its own house, and there may be a special building for heating the bath-water. A garage is also a not unknown feature. Close to the house of the government chief are the court-house, prison, and rest-house for visiting officials, British or native ; but these do not form part of the chief's enclosure.

Near any house which has been inhabited for some length of time one will eventually stumble upon a row of graves concealed among the bananas—sometimes covered over with big stones, sometimes simply kept smooth and free from weeds, occasionally with some object laid at the head to placate the spirit. Now that land is owned freehold and is certain of remaining in one family unless they voluntarily part with it, a chief's grave is often made more pretentious. A cement slab may be raised over it, with lettering in a fair imitation of an English tombstone, and over this a thatched roof is sometimes erected.

THE PEOPLE—APPEARANCE AND DRESS

The people who live in these villages are dark-brown skinned, woolly-haired, and reasonably tall. One is struck by their superior physique after the Kikuyu whom one sees on the journey through Kenya ; but

they do not attain to the tremendous stature of the
Hima aristocracy in the other kingdoms. It would
be impossible to describe a " typical " Baganda face.
Some are exactly like the full moon, some have Roman
noses ; my best informant made me think of one of
Dürer's " Four Apostles ", and his brother had a
remarkably triangular face which he had passed on
to all his children. They shave their heads at least
every six months, so that the hair never grows long enough
to hide the shape of the head. A light skin is not taken
as a mark of noble birth or Hima origin, but as a sign
of delicate health ; indeed a Hima woman once came
to me for medicine to make her child darker. By
European standards few of them would be called good-
looking, but their bright eyes and ready smile, the fact
that a dark skin does not show minor defects and makes
teeth look better than they deserve, and, in the case of
women, their dignified walk make them very pleasing
to the eye.

The traditional native dress of brown barkcloth is
still a good deal worn by native women, though the
men have given it up altogether. It is simply a wide
piece of cloth wound round under the arms and reaching
to the ankles, tucked in under the arms, and fastened
at the hips by a wide sash—now usually made of white
or black cloth. The extra width of the cloth is not
fastened, but floats out gracefully at the left side. This
garment cannot be kept in place except by keeping the
left arm close to the side, and needs constant adjusting
under the arms, so when a woman is doing any hard
work she unfastens it and lets the upper part hang
down over the sash. They sometimes wear European
stuffs in the same way, but the stock pattern for a cotton
garment really consists in adding a yoke and short
sleeves to the old barkcloth ; there is a fastening on
the left shoulder, but from this the stuff hangs loose
and makes the same ample sweep as before. The women
like bright colours—particularly scarlet—and a group

of them dressed in their best—a wedding party, for instance, winding its way along the paths from one village to the next—make a charming thread of colour through the rather monotonous green.

Only a few very old men now wear barkcloths. Younger men, however poor they may be, prefer sacking, cotton knotted over one or both shoulders in the style of the old barkcloth, or even the plain black sleeved frock that is the uniform in some girls' schools and is known as a " boarding ". What they regard as " native dress " is the Arab kanzu, a straight flowing garment with sleeves, hanging from neck to ankles, and usually covering a European shirt and shorts. The height of fashion is a European suit worn with the trousers under the kanzu and the coat over it. This is the ordinary dress of chiefs and persons of standing, and very dignified they can look in it. But it would be impossible to describe the endless combinations of styles affected by the younger men. There is no limit to the desires of the Muganda as regards all the items of European dress.

Children, unless they go to school, wear absolutely anything. Up to the age of about five they may play naked at home, clad only in the strings of beads round hips, ankle, and wrists, which they wear almost from birth. But even an infant in arms at once has some garment put on it on the arrival at any rate of a European visitor ; and no child old enough to walk would ever go away from home without clothes. Girls usually have some rag of cloth tied round the hips, and later fastened under the arms. Boys wear either a piece of cotton knotted over one shoulder or at the back of the neck, or a shirt, which reaches to the knees or trails on the ground according to the accident of its origin. Little children sometimes have bells fastened to their ankles, which ring when they move and are supposed to encourage them to walk.

ROUTINE OF VILLAGE LIFE

Work begins in the Baganda household at dawn—children sweep the yards with brooms made of bunches of grass ; girls go to the well for water ; women set out with their hoes, taking with them children old enough to help and others too young to be left at home. Men, too, nowadays are often seen at work in the fields, mainly growing cotton but sometimes also food-crops. At about eight, when the dew is off the grass, goats are led out to pasture. Work goes on till about ten o'clock—later in the planting season, which is a busy time as well as being often cloudy and cool owing to the rain. People do not actually work in the rain, even if it is not very heavy, but come in and shelter from it ; women, particularly, object to getting their clothes wet, even when walking through dewy grass in the morning, and it is actually very bad for barkcloths.

When the morning spell of work is over, the midday meal is prepared, though this is sometimes done by the children left behind. A big bunch of bananas is cut down by means of a knife tied to the end of a long stick, and the women sit down in the shade and peel them. Then they are tied up in a large banana-leaf, carried into the cook-house and put on to boil—or rather steam, for the parcel is kept out of the water by being set on the midriff of the leaf, chopped into pieces. The relish, whatever it may be—mushrooms, wild berries, some kind of vegetable, fish, a fowl or pieces of meat if there is a guest, but seldom otherwise—is tied in its own parcel and stuck in at the side of the pot. Then there is nothing to do but wait till it is ready.

When the bananas are reduced to a moist pulp, they are done. The parcel is carried into the house in a basket, laid on the floor, and unwrapped. Water is brought in a gourd and poured over every one's hands. In Protestant households grace is almost always said ; Catholics are content to cross themselves individually.

The mistress of the house then separates a lump from the mass for each person, using a piece of leaf to protect her hand. The food is eaten in the fingers as soon as it gets cool enough. If the seasoning is liquid, the banana is dipped into it ; if solid, it is grasped with a lump of the pulp. This is so dry that it is not at all a dirty way of eating ; but, in any case, when the meal is over hands are washed again. The children carry out the remains, calling " Koko! Koko! " to the fowls, who gather from all sides to eat them up ; the leaves are kept for the evening meal. In wealthy households the meal is followed by tea, made with enormous quantities of sugar and milk.

Nowadays the extras are often served in enamel plates or bowls ; a plate is usually offered to a European visitor, and chiefs eat sitting at a table, with spoon, fork, plate, and water in a glass. These implements are washed afterwards in cold water and spread out to dry on a table of canes which stands permanently in the yard for the purpose—drying with a cloth being unknown.

Any passer-by who presents himself while a meal is going on must be invited to share it, and the proverbial height of meanness is that of a person who provides against this contingency by eating behind closed doors. As the complement of this rule, it is not etiquette to greet people who are eating unless you wish to invite yourself. No one would deliberately pay a call while a whole household was at dinner ; but if, for some reason, one person is eating by himself he will take no notice of a visitor till he has finished and then come forward and greet him. Whether this claim to hospitality is limited to the obligations of kinship, as Dr. Audrey Richards has shown to be the case among several African tribes,[1] I unfortunately did not discover. It is not universal, in the sense that a complete stranger would not drop in for a meal.

In the afternoon women sit about making mats and

[1] Cf. *Hunger and Work in a Savage Tribe*, pp. 81–3.

baskets, shelling beans or pea-nuts, or picking over cotton. In busy times there is another spell of work from about four onwards. Otherwise people pay calls and prepare the evening meal in the same leisurely way as that at midday. Men's work, such as barkcloth-making or carpentry, not being done out of doors, begins later and goes on all day, with a rather ample midday rest. At six o'clock the goats are fetched in, more water is drawn for the evening ablutions (every one washes all over before going to bed), children are washed, the evening meal is eaten, and at seven the noise of drumming and singing shows in whose house there is beer going to-night. By about nine everything is quiet, unless the piercing "lululu" alarm-cry announces some untoward event, such as a house on fire, a burglary, or, more often, a wifely protest against the exercise of the marital right of beating.

The routine of daily life varies with the seasons. The two rainy seasons are times for planting; the dry seasons for harvesting. In the old days one seed-time and one harvest made a complete "year"; the cycle of economic activities was completed every six months. But now the whole arrangement of work centres round the growing of cotton, which takes nine months from sowing to harvesting. The cotton can be planted any time from the middle of May till the middle of July; the earlier planting runs the risk of being spoilt by the short rains in November or eaten by rats in the house where it must be kept till buying opens, the later of dying in the ground if the dry season is really dry. It needs fresh ground every year, so that, if it is not planted in a field where some other crop has just been grown, the grass must be burnt and cleared away and the ground broken up; and this cannot be done till it is reasonably dry. Once planted, it needs thinning, and then has simply to be cleared of weeds until it begins to ripen, in about nine months. The cotton should be gathered as soon as the bolls burst, so that the gathering extends over a long period. Buying begins about the end of January and may go on till the end of May, though the actual harvesting is over by March. The plants are left to wither in the ground, and pulled up and burnt when the plot is wanted for some other crop ; the government fixes a final date, about the middle of May, by which all plants must be removed.

AMUSEMENTS

It is said that in the old days there was a period of rest at each new moon when no garden work was done ; " they did not take the hoe out of doors." Other periods of rest from cultivation were provided by the mortuary customs, which enjoined that the relatives of an adult who died should do no such work through the whole mourning period, sometimes months, while even for a child there were two or three days of cessation. Sunday is nowadays a holiday with most people. Protestants go, sometimes twice in a day, to the village church ; Catholics walk as much as eight miles to the nearest mission church where mass is said by a priest. Every one wears their best clothes, and all washable garments are washed on the Saturday. In the regions near the Lake, where a good deal of trade is done with the people of the islands, market-day is another variant in the daily routine. Some women go to the Lake to buy fish which they retail at another market farther inland ; this expedition takes up a whole day, even if the distance is quite short, for they go in the early morning and do not come back till the cool evening hours. Apart from this, the main general distractions are the festivities at weddings and when a period of mourning comes to an end ; in the past the rejoicings on the birth of twins ranked equally with these, but they have now died out. The introduction of Christmas is perhaps a slight compensation. I did not witness a native Christmas, but was given to understand that

its main feature is that " every one eats meat ". A few
people collect " informally " in the evenings to drink,
sing, and dance whenever anyone has brewed beer.

For women dancing is really the only amusement.
To the European eye, it is neither interesting nor
beautiful. There are no concerted dances ; individuals
simply get up and perform what steps they please.
They consist in waving the arms, stamping the feet, and
jerking the hips, in various movements combined as the
dancer thinks fit. Children, especially girls, are taught to
dance from their earliest infancy ; even babies who
cannot stand are held upright by their mothers and
jerked in the appropriate movement in time to the
music. They are always accompanied by singing as well
as instrumental music—drums and one-stringed violins
played in a perpetual squeaky tremolando. The songs
are led by one singer while the others reply with a refrain,
clapping their hands in time ; they usually consist of
two or three divisions, in each of which a line is repeated
over and over with a slight variation at each repetition
(e.g. in one of the funeral songs : *Kabaka Suna yebase,
Kabaka Mwanga yebase*, etc.—" King Suna is asleep,
King Mwanga is asleep "). Apart from the funeral
songs, most songs are topical ; they emanate from the
court musicians, who compose new ditties on any event
of interest and sing them with a sense of the dramatic
that would do credit to many a comic-opera baritone.

The traditional Baganda sport is wrestling, and some
chiefs are making efforts to revive it ; one of the administrative chiefs in the county of Kyagwe has a team which
he takes round the country challenging other districts.
This, too, is accompanied by music, including flutes,
which play the same phrase over and over ; the wrestler
who wants an opponent advances dancing and dances
till someone comes up to him. For a fall to count the
man must be thrown on his head, which it seems to be
extremely easy to avoid.

Men's other amusement is *mweso*, the game played all

over Africa in which counters are thrown on a board with sixteen holes, the game being to capture the opponent's men according to various complicated rules.

Wherever there is a school there is football, and boys are never tired of kicking a ball about at odd moments. Elsewhere both boys and girls build play-houses by bending down the elephant-grass canes and tying them together, sometimes even making a framework of cut canes and spreading grass over it. (See Plate II.) Boys also construct go-carts of wood, with scooped-out pawpaws for wheels. (See Plate III.) They play a variant of noughts and crosses with stones on a " board " drawn on the ground with a stick, and another game is to spin two plum-stones on a leaf and see which knocks the other off. I once saw a boy making mud dolls. I have never seen children spontaneously enacting the representations of folk-tales, or playing the singing games, which are encouraged in schools as traditional ; but this does not mean that they are not so. They certainly love any kind of mimicry, whether of notable village characters, animals, or dramatic scenes such as a fight between two warriors.

Three Different Villages

During my stay in Buganda, I lived in three native villages, each with its distinctive characteristics. The first was Ngogwe, a village belonging to the Native Anglican Church, on the site of one of their earliest mission stations, which had a boys' central school with a staff of four or five native masters, a girls' school, a church, and a Mothers' Union. Its leading personalities were all church dignitaries and teachers, for, in addition to the Rural Dean, Samwiri Nganda, a man of some wealth with ten children and a large herd of cattle, there were two deacons resident there, and one or two families of lay-readers or schoolmasters whose work was else-where. Old Nganda was a great autocrat. He allowed no music in his village, and parties which came to his church to be married had to leave their bands outside ; some preferred to go elsewhere. Whether it was due to his influence in denouncing beer-drinking or to some other cause, the houses in the village were in general better built and better furnished than in either of my other centres. Ngogwe was in South Kyagwe near the Lake, where the soil is not very good for cotton and petty trade is more important than in most parts of the country. There was a market every day at some place within easy walking distance of the village, where people sold meat, bananas, butter, chillies, pea-nuts, barkcloths and native mats, and clay pots imported from the islands in the Lake.

Kisimula, my next centre, was on the outer edge of Bulemezi, in the north, on the slope of the farthest hill before the land drops to the immense plain of Singo. The village had been founded " when the miles came "[1] by Bugeza, the seventh Muganda, so the people told me, to be baptized. He had selected a patch of very good soil in an area where most of the land was poor ; the chief in occupation had been turned out to make way for him, and he had taken possession with his followers *en masse*, some thirty years ago. Bugeza had died some nine months before my arrival, and was sincerely mourned by his people, who constantly expressed regret that I had not known him. " He was a man," they said, " too good to recognize evil," and he had appointed as a kind of trustee to look after his affairs till the mourning was ended a man who had proved to be thoroughly unsatisfactory in every way. He had also left his property to Kaiso Musa·jange, the son of his third wife, who had retired some time before from a successful career in the employ of a European trading company to live near his father. But he had neglected to have his will duly witnessed, and it was contested by his eldest son, Kyuma, a drunkard, whom he had forbidden to come

---

[1] i.e. the freehold system. See Chapter VI, pp. 164 ff.

into his sight. Under a recent change in the law, whereby
the eldest son of the first wife inherits in case of intestacy,
Kyuma won his case. When I arrived he had been
duly installed as heir a few weeks before, had insulted
the widows—ten in number—so that they had determined
to leave in a body and did so a few days after I came, and
infuriated Kaiso by having his name only painted as
donor on a large cement tombstone which had been
erected at the general expense. The whole village was
by the ears, and every one eager to offer his own view of
the rights and wrongs of the matter ; Kyuma's son, the
favourite grandson, who had been summoned to comfort
Bugeza's declining years, was the only one who even
half-heartedly defended his father, and even he had to
fall back on the argument that Kaiso was a miser and
a fool. A distant relative of Bugeza's who, as a child,
had been brought up in his household, and had risen to
be clerk to the council of his clan—the Bird—Yokana
Waswa by name, had been summoned to do what he
could to set matters in order. He was looked up to as an
authority on all village matters as well as on questions
of native tradition, and he preached in the little church
so well that it was a pleasure to hear him. He became
my principal informant.

At Kisimula I was lucky in finding what was probably
as near an approach to the old-fashioned type of village
community, in which a great number of the inhabitants
were bound to the chief by individual ties of blood or
marriage and all by personal affection, as could be
found anywhere in Buganda, and doubly lucky in being
able to observe the people's reactions to the change from
the quasi-paternal chief who " knew every one in the
village " to the modern landlord who is only interested
in his land as a source of revenue. In a way which is
difficult to define, Kisimula seemed to be a unity and not
a mere haphazard collection of individuals. Doubtless
the reason was partly that its older members had come in
a body under Bugeza's leadership, and partly that so

many of them were his relatives, who had been brought up in his household and planted out by him when they grew up. They were united by a common past and by a common affection for their chief and pride in the village he had made, as well as by the ties of kinship. Whether it was a mere coincidence that there I found a greater general interest in the discussion of native tradition than elsewhere, I do not know.

My third centre, Matale, was in the Catholic district of Masaka to the south-west. The difference of religion did not seem to have any very marked effect. A more striking difference arose from the fact that here a large landowner had relatively recently sold almost all his estate in small holdings. One old man had acquired a fairly large area—about 125 acres—and managed to make a village of his own ; the others simply grew their own coffee with their own hired labour and paid no attention to one another. Village gossip was almost non-existent, and one's visitors much more interested to ask questions about Europe than to talk of native matters. It was here that I was asked whether the project of Closer Union was designed to provide the Prince of Wales with a private kingdom, and if we were not holding Tanganyika in trust for "its owners, the Germans". Here, too, I was regaled by a young man in his fourth year of the twelve years' course of instruction given by the Catholics to native candidates for the priesthood by readings in Latin from the *Imitation of Christ*.

It is from observation of these three villages and from what their people told me of the old days that I have tried to reconstruct the past life of the Baganda and estimate what have been the principal changes that European civilization has meant to them.

CHAPTER III

AN ORDINARY LIFE

1. BIRTH AND CHILDHOOD

IT is against such a village background that the life
of the Muganda is lived. Here he is born; here, unless
he belongs to the minority which goes to boarding-school,
he spends his childhood; here he sets up his own house
and digs the cotton-patch which enables him to pay
his taxes and buy his luxuries; here he leaves his wife
and children if he takes employment on a European
plantation, under the native government, or as a schoolmaster or parson in a different village; here even a
native who has spent his whole life in European employment hopes to return in his old age; and it is the ambition
of every Muganda to become the owner of a small patch
of land which he will pass on to his heirs. Even to
those who work in the capital this background is not
lost, for in Kampala there is no crowded corrugated iron
"native quarter", but native houses standing in their
own cultivation fill the space between the European
areas, and many native employees come in daily by
bicycle from homes at a distance of ten or twelve
miles.

Here then we can study the native culture, as it was
and as the contacts of modern days have modified it,
in terms of the individual's life—its human as well as
its geographical environment, the interplay of claims
and obligations, ambitions and duties, of beliefs and
standards of conduct, which mould his existence as a
member of society. Against the reconstruction of the
traditional native life we can see the innovations in their
place and estimate their effects. As we trace our

individual's history, always in its immediate setting of family and household, we shall find him constantly the focus of wider relationships. Even the household in the old days extended its membership beyond the limits of a single family ; outside it he was linked to clansmen, to blood-brothers, to a chief, to the king, by bonds whose nature will become clear as we see their connection with the various events and activities of an ordinary commoner's life.

Social Groupings—(a) The Individual Family

From the day of his birth the Muganda was a member of three groups—a family, a household, and a clan. In the household as it used to be constituted, his family was one of a number which were linked together by a common father, but each lived in its own house, that of the mother, where the children slept and were fed. The intimate connection throughout childhood between the child and its parents which we usually associate with the family did not invariably exist, since it was very common for a child to be taken from its own parents at an early age ; but all his life the child was bound to them by the fact that various rites connected with his welfare could be performed by them and by them alone. It is now too late to obtain data which would show conclusively whether the relations between pairs of brothers and between brothers and sisters, which we shall later have to discuss, were closer between the children of one mother than between them and other children of the same father.

(b) The Household

The household comprised not only several such families but a number of individuals over and above them. It might include within it widowed sisters, younger unmarried sisters, or aged relatives of the head, and children of other members of his clan who had been sent to him to be brought up. In a chief's household there would be girls who had been sent to him in the hope of later becoming his wives, and a considerable number of slaves. Even a peasant might have slaves attached to him, although his whole household was on a smaller scale.

These persons fitted into the household in different ways. The older relatives would have each his own house, where a child would probably live with him to help him and keep him company ; such a child might be given him either by the head of the household or by some other relative outside. The younger sisters lived in the houses of the various wives and helped them in their daily work ; the girls designed to become wives of the chief lived mainly in the house of his senior wife, as did small boys who were sent to him from outside. All the older boys slept together in one house, except for the boy-slaves who slept in his court-house. Girl-slaves were allotted to the various wives and lived with them.

Note on Slavery.—A word should be said as to the position of slaves. They were almost entirely captives in war—women and boys, the men having been killed. The essential difference between them and the rest of the household was not that inferiority in economic status and functions which Europeans, thinking of slavery in the sense which it has had in their own past history, usually associate with the word ; it lay simply in the fact that they were not, like the rest of the household, members of the clan of its head. No better illustration of the importance of this distinction could be given than the fact that the word for " slave " is used of any man or woman in the house of a member of his mother's clan. Certain duties, it is true, were specifically allotted to slaves, but, for the greater part, they shared in the ordinary life of the household, were described by the head as " his children ", and a stranger would not be aware that they were slaves unless this was expressly explained

PLATE I

IN HONOUR OF TWINS

The little girl is the one on whose account the ceremony is being held (see pp. 48-9). She is wearing her own cord round her neck.

PLATE II

PLATE III

CHILDREN'S GAMES

A Play-House of Elephant Grass.　　　Mechanical Transport.

to him.[1] Captured women were taken at once as wives, and except that they had no relatives to go to in case of ill-treatment or their husband's death their different status ceased to have much importance. Girls might be married into their master's family or might marry other slaves ; the latter on marriage set up their own houses, described themselves as members of their master's clan, and observed its practices. They differed from " free men " in that they could not leave him and that they could not inherit from a real member of the clan. Their children would be indistinguishable from their neighbours, except that it was the duty of heads of clans, who kept track of genealogies, to know that they had not the rights of genuine members as regards inheritance, and that they were debarred from becoming chiefs—a position reserved for people who could prove that they were Baganda by tracing their ancestry back to the original founders of the clan.

(c) *The Clan*

The clan (*Kika*) was a group of persons regarding themselves as related by descent through males from a common ancestor. The most obvious distinguishing mark of a member of a clan was his name, for each clan had a group of names by one of which each of its members was called ; next to this came the observance of a prohibition against killing or eating the animal or plant which was the totem of the clan. Right up to the time of the Uganda Agreement in 1900 the head of each clan lived on the land which was supposed to have been settled by the first ancestor, and one way of describing a member of the clan, especially on ceremonial occasions, was to say that he came from that place.

The members of a clan were bound together by the

---

[1] The relationship is accurately described in the phrase *mwana wentumbwe*, " child of my calves," which refers to the pursuit in which the slave was captured. This is the phrase used in the Luganda version of the Bible for "thy son that shall come forth out of thy loins " (1 Kings viii, 19).

rule of exogamy, by a general obligation of mutual aid, to a certain extent by collective responsibility for the misdeeds of their members, by participation in the various ceremonies which marked significant events in a member's life, and by the fact that inheritance was kept strictly within the clan. But since there were only thirty-six clans in a population which was formerly considerably greater than it is at present, it is clear that every clan would be far too large for its members ever to act together as a single unit. Each clan was further divided into the descendants of sons of the original founder, who formed a ·*siga*, and again into those of his grandsons or great-grandsons, who formed a *mutuba*, but even these sub-divisions were still very large.

Moreover, the village was not established on any principle of kinship, but consisted of those who had elected to attach themselves to some particular chief, so that there were no such compact local groups bound together by the ties of blood as are found in many parts of Africa. There was a certain tendency for a son on marriage to settle in his father's village—sometimes even on land which had been allotted to his father— but no rule obliging him to do so. The fact that a chief often had the sons of his relatives sent to him to bring up and then established them in his village, sometimes in subordinate official posts, meant that there would be in any given village a group of related persons who tended to take the lead in local affairs.

Outside the village the group within which the ties of kinship were of practical importance would consist for each individual of his immediate relatives—parents, grandparents, brothers, and sisters[1]—and other members of the same *mutuba* who lived within reasonable travelling distance. These are the people who would attend funeral ceremonies, turn up to support a relative in a

---

[1] The word *enda*, of which I never got a satisfactory definition, appears to describe such a group. One informant said that all members of an *enda* are known to one another.

court case, join in attack or defence in a blood-feud, and possibly combine to pay a fine.

Membership of the ·siga was important in practice through the recognition of the authority of its senior member, a direct descendant of the original head, who settled disputes on matters of inheritance or clan status, debts or injuries committed by clansmen, and through whom such questions as a levy on clansmen to pay a fine for one member were settled. The ·siga head had to be present at the installation of a peasant's heir, the head of the whole clan or a representative appointed by him at that of a chief's. There appear also to have been recognized senior clansmen in various localities who exercised authority in matters other than the appointment of an heir, though how they acquired the status I do not know. I shall use the word " senior clansmen " to describe all people who were recognized in this way. Beyond the fact that each *mutuba* had its own lands, this division seems to have had little importance.

There was also a clan council consisting of the head of the whole clan and the ·siga heads, and at the present time there is an inferior council in every ·saza consisting of a representative chosen by the members of the whole clan living in each *gombolola*.[1] The clan council is a final court of appeal in disputes between members ; the local councils appear to serve mainly as a means of promulgating its decisions. Nowadays, these councils keep typewritten records.

Like other primitive peoples the Baganda use the so-called classificatory system of kinship terminology, by which terms that we apply only to biological relationships are extended to relatives outside the family. Thus all brothers of the father are called " father ", all sisters of the mother " mother ", and all their children " brother and sister ", and so on. Anthropological

---

[1] The kingdom of Buganda is divided into twenty ·sazas, in each of which there are a dozen or fifteen *gombololas*.

theory has long rejected the idea that this nomenclature indicates a failure to recognize different degrees of distance in relationships, or a general indiscriminate mingling of clansmen in which the family as a unit has no place. But since it seems to be popularly believed that the Baganda do not make distinctions between members of their own families and other relatives, it is worth while pointing out that this is not the case. The view of Malinowski, that the extension of the terms implies a transference in certain circumstances of the obligations of the closer relationships to more distant kinsmen, is supported by various features of the Baganda system, notably in connection with the education of children and with inheritance.

For the ordinary co-operation of daily life the obligations of kinship outside the household were less significant than they are among many primitive peoples. A single household with its slaves might often be able to provide all the labour required for such activities as building and brewing : where the single household was too small, and outside help had to be called in, this does not seem to have been a duty devolving on certain individuals in virtue of their relationship to the man who initiated the work. Outside the household the one definitely constituted co-operating group consisted in the whole adult male population of the village, who could be called on by the chief to perform specified services for himself or the king.

Individual Life—(a) Pregnancy

Membership of the clan began to be significant even before a child's birth, for among the observances connected with its mother's pregnancy were some whose nature depended upon the father's clan, to which it would belong. Each clan had its own customs too as regards the disposal of the after-birth, and the ceremonial at which the child's legitimacy was tested and he was definitely accepted as a member and given his clan name.

The rules which women were expected to observe during pregnancy were of two kinds, which can perhaps be distinguished as medical and magical. The native conception of the process of gestation, the physical condition which it produced, and the especial dangers to which the unborn child was subject, dictated that she should take certain medicines and abstain from certain foods on account of specific effects which they were supposed to produce. Over and above these precautions were the special clan taboos and universally observed sexual and food prohibitions, which were hardly conceived even to produce a vague positive beneficial effect, but whose breach was supposed to cause a difficult birth or the death of mother or child.

The medical treatment of pregnancy must be considered in relation to the popular ideas regarding the process of procreation. These do not form a logically coherent whole, and are doubtless formulated much more clearly by some individuals than by others. The Baganda do not now believe in any other cause of conception than sexual intercourse, and the ideas to be discussed are those which concern the development of the child in the womb.

The woman's body is thought to contain a mould in which the child is somehow moulded by God.[1] My informant proceeded to elucidate the point by comparison with potter's work. Such of his statement as I recorded verbatim is perhaps worth transcribing. The statements made were as follows :—

" *Katonda atonda abana. Olinga nga bwono·dira e·bumba. Ama·zi gomusa·ja gatabagana nagomukazi. Katonda abumba ama·zi ago. Omusai gu·kung'anira ku ma·zi gomusa·ja, negulyoka Mukama nagutabula nagu·sa mu mwesogwe.*"

[1] This description was given me by Aluizi Zalembekiya, a young Catholic native, who was much interested in old tradition. There is a verb *kutonda*, translated by the dictionary " to create ", and the name used for the Christian God is that of Katonda, a formerly insignificant deity whose name is derived from this verb. It is only in this context that I have heard the verb used. The deity who formerly presided over the supply of children was another—Mukasa.

" God creates children. It is as if you took clay. The water of the man joins with that of the woman. God moulds these liquids. The blood meets the man's water and then the Lord mixes it and sets it in his mould."

Barrenness is caused by the mould being turned over so that it will not hold the ingredients, and the medicines supplied to cure it are supposed to return it to the right position. It is worth while mentioning that although the criterion of legitimacy is the actual physiological relationship of the child to its father, Aluizi did not think this process had any bearing on the question why a child should belong to its father's clan rather than its mother's. Yokana Waswa, however, gave as the reason the active part taken by the father in procreation.

My information on the subsequent developments I obtained from various sources, but it is rather scanty. The embryo is supposed to be " nothing but blood " for the first month, after which it " falls together " (ka·gwamu) or " becomes solid " (kataba) ; this stage is also described as lubuto lu·jula, " the belly is full." No further stages are distinguished, but various beliefs are held which explain the regime which the woman was expected to follow. Through the whole period her body is thought to be hot, and this heat is supposed to be dangerous not only to the embryo but to an older child, who is not allowed to sleep in its mother's bed after she becomes pregnant. Excessive heat is also thought to cause miscarriages, and for this reason hot food is avoided. It is also believed to be very harmful for the mother to eat salt. This is supposed to produce a disease characterized by sores on the head, which may break out at any time during the child's life.

Throughout the period of pregnancy the woman used to be expected to drink medicines every two or three days. Some were believed to strengthen the child and make it " sit on the medicine and not play about " ;

some, which were taken especially during the first three months, to make it safe to eat salt. Medical authorities assert that the effects of these medicines were entirely harmful, but, although all women who go for ante-natal treatment to the village maternity centres are warned against their use, it has by no means died out. A case occurred during my stay in Kisimula of a young woman in her first pregnancy who was seriously ill with a threatened miscarriage, caused, in the view of a European doctor who examined her, simply by native drugs.

Sir Apolo Kagwa's book, *Empisa za Baganda*,[1] gives a list of foods which must not be eaten by a pregnant woman because if she ate them the child would die at an early age. This list includes salt and hot food, the " medical " objections to which I have already discussed. It might possibly prove that similar explanations could be given for the other prohibitions ; but, if he is right in stating that their breach had no direct effect, they deserve to be classed with the purely magical restrictions. The forbidden foods which he mentions are sugar-cane, taro-leaves, onions, a kind of sweet banana (*gonja*), a kind of wild plum, and two types of wild berry which are used as relishes. He also states that eating earth was forbidden for the same reason. Unfortunately I obtained no list myself, so cannot tell if this is complete ; nor do I know how far the prohibitions are still observed.

Complete sexual abstinence was prescribed for the woman during this period, but the husband was not debarred from intercourse with his other wives, nor, provided he did not use the pregnant woman's bed, was there any special taboo on sexual relations with other women. For the woman the central prohibition carried with it a number of minor rules which were always observed by persons between whom intercourse was permanently or temporarily proscribed. She must not take a man by the hand, give food into his hand, let

[1] p. 180.

him pass her in a doorway or step over his feet, nor must she sit on his bed or wash from the same pot. In the case of men other than her husband the two last possibilities could of course only arise in very compromising circumstances. Any breach of these rules might cause the death of the child, while actual adultery would result in a difficult birth and possibly even the death of the mother, and repeated transgression in a fatal disease called *makiro*, in which the woman attempted to eat her child.

As between husband and wife these prohibitions have broken down with the great decrease in polygamy. There does not seem to be a definite rule that a man with two wives should keep to one while the other is pregnant, and Eresi Nalubega, the young widow who gave me most of my information about marital relations, said that nowadays intercourse is continued till the seventh month of pregnancy and resumed a month after the birth. It is also remarkable that Yokana Waswa, my most intelligent informant and the one whom I found in general most reliable, had no recollection of any restrictions during pregnancy. The belief that a difficult birth is a punishment for adultery is still prevalent, but the younger generation, while they will define *makiro* on request as a disease which wanton girls may be expected to contract, are not seriously afraid of it.

The specific " customs " of the various clans consisted in minor restrictions, apparently only one for each clan. There are not now many people who know anything about them, but one may give certain examples in illustration. In the Oribi Clan a pregnant woman might not lift up the leaves of the *ntula*—one of the forbidden fruits—to look underneath for the berries, but if she picked them she must feel for them. In the Wild Rat Clan she had to take a stick with her when walking along a narrow path, and push aside the grass so that it did not touch her. In another she could not walk over the split stems which are spread in the banana-groves for manure. Breaches of these prohibitions were thought to cause the death of the child.

The special rules of his own clan were explained to a young man just before his marriage by some old woman who knew them—either a woman of the clan or a wife of a clansman. Lutaya, one of the schoolmasters at Ngogwe, who was married while I was there, told me that he did not know what these customs were in his own clan, but that as he was about to be married he would probably be told. He evidently did not attach much importance to them. Later he took me with him to see an old woman whose exact relationship to him I did not discover, and asked her to expound "the customs of the clan ".

(b) Birth

The birth took place in the banana-grove if it occurred by day, in the house if at night, the woman kneeling and holding to a banana stem, or a post of the house. The woman was assisted by some female relatives of her husband, though this does not appear to have been the duty of any particular person ; in the case of the only birth which took place near me a sister of the husband looked after the woman and spent most of her time in the house for several days. Different informants said that the cord was cut by a sister of the father, or by his mother, if either was near enough. Since it has always been customary among the Baganda for a young man on setting up house to leave home and go to some other village, it must have been largely a question of chance what woman among his relatives would be near at hand. In case of a difficult birth, some old woman who was believed to be specially expert was called in, while, at the same time, the woman was urged to confess to some adultery, and sometimes even beaten to make her do so.

The cord was cut in the doorway of the house. The

new-born child was then washed all over in warm water in which pounded medicinal herbs were mixed. Medicines were rubbed on its navel, and, if it appeared to be ill, dropped in its mouth, and it was massaged all over to strengthen and warm it. Then it was given to the mother to nurse.

The disposal of the after-birth according to the pre-scribed method was thought to be absolutely essential to the safety of the child. The after-birth is sometimes spoken of as a twin, and said to have a spirit, the same word (*muzimu*) being used which describes the spirit of a dead person. But there is not really any idea of the after-birth having a personal soul which behaves like the spirit of the dead, and the natives sharply distinguish between the way in which an offended spirit causes death and the death of a child through transgression of prescribed observances, which here, as elsewhere, is said to be caused by " the transgression itself ". The method of disposal was another of the distinguishing customs of different clans. The after-birth was always put in a potsherd and buried in some part of the cultivated ground round the house, sometimes under a plantain, sometimes under a barkcloth-tree. Various other methods of disposal are described by Roscoe.[1]

The mother remained for three days in seclusion. Then she came to the doorway of the house with her husband, who took the child in his arms and proclaimed it as a member of his clan, referring to the ancestral lands—" This child is from such and such a hill." Although the child's legitimacy—that is to say its actual physiological relationship with its supposed father—was again tested at the naming ceremony, it was stated that the mere pronouncement of these words over it, if they were not in fact true, would cause its death. When this was over the parents retired into the inner room, the wife sat on the ground with her legs stretched straight in front of her, and the husband stepped over

[1] *The Baganda*, pp. 56–7.

them [1]—a rite which symbolized sexual intercourse. This rite is always described by the verb *kukuza*, " to make to grow," but since the verb is used in contexts where that translation would make nonsense it does not seem possible to call it a piece of " sympathetic fertility-magic ". The verb *kukuza* is used of the duties of a guardian, and the aim of the rite wherever it is performed seems to be to produce a general beneficent effect on the process with which it is connected—here, of course, the healthy development of the child. In this particular case the rite is concerned with the well-being of the whole clan ; it is called *kukuza e·gwanga lye kika*, " to protect all the people of the clan," and is said to be of very great importance. It is also called *kukuza akasiki*, " to protect the cord," for after it the wife wrapped up the cord in a piece of her barkcloth sash and concealed it in her bed in her husband's absence.

If the father did not live in his own parents' village, he made no formal announcement of the birth to them, simply sending a message by the next person who happened to be going. But a formal announcement to the mother's relatives was necessary, because her brother had certain rights over the child which will be discussed later, and this announcement was made by the father himself, taking with him a present of beer.

(c) The Birth of Twins

Thus the actual birth of a child was not an occasion for much public ceremonial, and for most children the moment at which they received the greatest publicity was on their formal recognition as members of their clan. But in the case of twins everything was different. The rejoicing and formalities which followed their birth were more elaborate and prolonged than those which

---

[1] The word which describes this action—*kubuka*—means " to fly, jump, or step over ". It is used, for example, of a person who inadvertently steps over a magical object placed in his path. Roscoe's selection of the translation " jump " for this context is unhappy, as I know from having seen the action imitated.

accompanied a marriage, and their passing is looked upon with regret by all modern Baganda except those whom it has saved from the trouble and expense of carrying them out.

Before going into details of ceremonial it is necessary to make clear the immense importance of the birth of twins in Baganda life. An event which thus arbitrarily singled out certain individuals without any special effort or any particular merit on their part was taken as a manifestation of spontaneous benevolence towards them on the part of Mukasa, the divinity who sent all children. Even now the recipients of this rather ambiguous favour —as we shall find it to be—are singled out for the rest of their days, as are the twins themselves and to a lesser extent their younger brothers and sisters. The father of twins is called *Salongo*—a name used as a term of respectful address to the king himself—and their mother *Nalongo* ; and, at any rate in the woman's case, that name would invariably be used of her unless there was some special need to distinguish her. For the twins themselves special names are prescribed— Waswa and Kato for two boys, Kato and Nakato for boy and girl, Nakato and Babirye for two girls—and there is a series of names for subsequent children. In the past a woman who had borne twins could never be turned out by her husband. Yokana Waswa's mother, a woman who had been kidnapped in childhood and did not know her clan, was discovered after his birth to be of the same clan as her husband ; any other woman would have had to go back at once to her near relatives, but the importance of *Nalongo* over-rode even the laws of exogamy. A girl who bore twins before marriage had at once to marry their father ; the latter had not the usual option of refusal.

Throughout their life twins were marked out by the right to wear ·*bombo,* a kind of creeper which grows wild in every banana-grove and which plays a considerable part in the twin-birth ceremonies. A twin who was ill always tied a piece of this creeper round his or her waist ; women do so to this day. Twins or parents of twins wear it at the burial of twins or their parents, and at the naming ceremony of twins every one ties it round his neck or waist. The grave of a *Nalongo* is covered with long strands of it.

The elaboration of the ceremony itself and the stress laid on the need for its due performance—even now, when all that is left is the small vestige which has not been condemned as obscene both by Church and State—show more clearly than anything else the attitude towards the birth of twins as an event of the utmost significance ; they also show an attitude, which at first seems contradictory, towards the twins as potentially extremely dangerous.

The ceremonial has been described at very great length by Roscoe (pages 64–73). The accounts which were given me differ from his in a number of details and omit a good many points which he gives ; since his version was obtained at a time when the rites were still performed, I should not venture to question his accuracy on points where I have no definite evidence, especially as I suspect that the phallic element in them was deliberately suppressed by some of my informants who remembered it perfectly well. But since a description must be given here, I prefer to give the account which I obtained myself and take the responsibility for such inaccuracies as it may contain. It may be of interest as showing what part of the ceremonial has been most quickly forgotten.

Immediately upon hearing the news that his wife had given birth to twins, the father climbed on the roof of her house and called out " Mukasa has given me offspring ! " for, if any one forestalled him in announcing the news, the children would die. The next rite which had to be done at once was for the father to go out at night to a neighbouring banana-grove, knock down a young tree by hitting it with his elbows, and bring in the fruit, which was kept in the house wreathed with ·*bombo*.[1] A prophet of Mukasa or, if he was not available, some man not a member of the father's clan—probably a sister's son—was sent for to carry away the after-births, which were put in a new cooking-pot wreathed with ·*bombo*, and hide them in the forest. He received two barkcloths for his services.

In the case of twins, the naming ceremony was performed at the end of a month or two (much earlier than was common with other children) and until it was done the parents had to live in a peculiar way. The door of the house was blocked up, and two new openings, one for each, made at opposite sides. The food which they ate was stolen from other people's gardens and roasted instead of being cooked in a pot. The father could not see the children. He wore two barkcloths knotted one over each shoulder and tied at the waist with a grass rope which could not be untied, and he must not wash or shave. No further public announcement of the birth was made, but the father went to the houses of every one who would be interested—his chief, all his relatives within reach, his blood-brothers, and other friends—and thrust into the thatch of their houses near the door a little twist of dry plantain-fibre with a cowry shell in each end to represent " the heads of the twins ". This constituted an invitation to the public ceremonial ; the delivery of all the tokens might take a month or more. Throughout all these rites, and at any other ceremonial connected with twins, the clan drum-beat was played on a " drum " made of a piece of green plantain-bark folded in three and tied together, the outer strip of the top piece being raised on two sticks to make it resonant.

[1] The reason for this is given by Roscoe (p. 69), that, at the naming ceremony, the flower was placed beneath the wife's legs as she lay on the ground and knocked away with his penis by the boy *Salongo* (see below). Since there would be no other reason for selecting a *young* tree than that the flower was required—it drops off before the fruit is ready for eating—I feel sure that some of my informants knew of this, but none would admit it.

The ceremonial falls into three parts—the naming in the house of the twins' own father, the formal visit of announcement to the father's parents, and that to the mother's parents. Throughout the ceremonial, the parents were accompanied by a "little *Salongo* and *Nalongo*"—a boy sent by the father's father and a girl by the mother's—who "helped with everything" and specifically carried baskets in which presents of cowry-shells and coffee-berries were collected. Every one who looked at the children was expected to give them cowries. Rather than complicate this account with a description of the ordinary naming ceremony, I shall leave that to be discussed in its own place. What is peculiar to the case of twins is that even if they died a version of the ceremony was performed at which their cords were produced and tested for legitimacy in the same way as at an ordinary naming. The feast, too, had to be given on a particularly lavish scale, two goats and two fowls being killed and the tongues of the fowls tied up with the children's cords, which were preserved in a peculiar manner designed to do especial honour to the twins.

The visits to the two grandfathers were identical in their ceremonial, which was called *kumenya lukanda*, *lukanda* being a load of sprats hung on a stick, one of the essential elements in the feast. A large party of persons from the father's village—relatives and friends—set out, taking food with them, and arrived in the small hours of the morning at the grandfather's house. Here a barrier of withered plantain-leaves had been hung across the yard, and was defended against the visitors in a sham fight with sticks. When the party had forced their way past the barrier, they set to dancing while the food was cooked along with a share provided by the hosts. The dancers wore bells tied to their ankles and green banana-leaves round their waists. Some informants said they danced naked, and it is certain that the dance is now forbidden on the grounds of its obscenity by a law of the native parliament. The songs which

accompanied them are also said to have been very
obscene.

When the food was cooked it was brought into the
yard and the party ate it there without washing their
hands. The parents of the twins and the husband's
parents each formally handed all the others a helping
of banana, sprats, and mushrooms, passing the food in
the bare hand, not as usual in a piece of leaf. Every one
else was then given food in the same way, and when the
feast was over the remains were stamped into the ground
with more dancing. The visitors then left without
saying good-bye and returned in the course of the day
to pay a visit of the ordinary kind, the father of the
twins bringing a goat to be killed for a festive meal.
His mother washed the children's cords, and each was
wrapped in a piece of barkcloth, which was rubbed with
butter to make it shine, fastened to a sort of hoop of
rope, and adorned with strings of cowries taken from
those which had been collected by the " little *Salongo*
and *Nalongo* ". The rest of these were kept by the
mother of the twins. While this was being done, the
twin-songs were sung and the clan drum-beat was played,
people tied ·*bombo* round their necks and waists, and
there was general rejoicing and consumption of beer.
The finished articles, which are called " twins ", were
taken home and carefully put away.

Every subsequent child of the mother had its cord
preserved, though the others were merely tied up in a
roll of barkcloth with one or two cowries at each end and
fastened to a loop of string ; and whenever this was done
for a new child all those which the household possessed
were brought out, and every person present put them
on round his neck " to honour and please the twins ".
(See Frontispiece and Plate IV.) The same singing,
drumming, drinking, and garlanding with ·*bombo* went
on as at the ceremony for the twins themselves. I saw
this done at Kisimula for one of Bugeza's children.
The presence of the child's father is necessary, and as

PLATE IV

AT A TWIN CEREMONY

Yokana Waswa and Nola, the *Nalongo,* wearing the decorated cords.   Note
the *bombo* round *Nalongo's* waist.

PLATE V

A MODERN WEDDING

The bride is kneeling in the centre while her brother holds her left hand and the bridegroom her right. Note the big drum on the right.

he was dead his place had to be taken by the heir. Such
was the anxiety of the child's mother to have the rite
performed that, although she had herself gone back to
her own family, she made a point of coming to Kisimula
to seize the opportunity of Kyuma's presence on a
short visit to get it done. In the case of a mother of
twins, during the ceremony of concluding mourning,
the " twins " are brought out and worn in the same
way while the songs are sung.

The midnight visit, followed by the feast next day,
was repeated with exactly the same ceremonial at
the house of the mother's parents. The husband had
then to give his wife a goat and to give a goat and barkcloth, and—according to one informant—also two strings of
ninety cowries each to the "little *Salongo* and *Nalongo*".
After this visits were paid, and the dances danced, at all
the houses at which the birth had been announced.

This ceremonial is seldom discussed without some
comment being made on the burden which it imposed
on the father of twins. One old woman even said that
a poor man would obtain medicine to separate twins.
The wife drank the medicine, slept with *bombo* wound
round her, and in the morning urinated on the *bombo* ;
the process was presumably thought to get rid of one of
the twins. Kanywamagule, my next-door neighbour
at Kisimula, whose wife was pregnant, confided to me
that he thought she would have twins and was therefore
going to send her to the local maternity centre for her
confinement so as to avoid the expense of a celebration.

But for a chief even this did not complete the process,
since, in his case, the event had to be announced to
the king, and the latter's permission obtained for the
announcement to his own parents. This could not be
done until he had been to war and killed a man—which
was called " taking the *lukanda* to Bunyoro ". On his
return he went with a large present of goats and cowries
to Mugema, the chief who was described as " the grandfather of the king ", and arranged with him a day for

E

an audience. On this day the king received him in the main gate of his enclosure and handed him a gourd of beer—the usual proceeding at any formal reception—after which he was free to go on with his private celebration.

This meant that, in a chief's case, the period of special observances lasted very much longer than with a peasant ; but this did not inconvenience him seriously because it was one of the duties of his leading subordinate chief to perform rites on his behalf. It fell to the latter not only to announce the birth from the roof of the house and to deliver all the preliminary messages but also to endure the discomfort of going unwashed and unshaven.

All this ceremonial is now very largely obsolete. An increasing number of births take place in the village maternity centres, which makes the rites that followed immediately after the birth impossible, and the general feeling seems to be that this absolves the parents from the necessity of performing any others—or, possibly, makes them useless. In the case of the twin ceremonial, the dancing has been specifically forbidden by a law of the native parliament which prohibits all obscene dances, mentioning these by name ; and most of the other rites have been suppressed by missionary disapproval, made effective by the educated native authorities and genuinely shared by some of the natives who are most attached to old traditions. But some celebration is still thought essential here, though it is confined almost to the actual eating of the feast. It is still the need to have this done by the right persons that makes it important to know the father of an unmarried girl's child. Again, at a wedding which I saw of a girl who was married by missionaries without her father's consent, the joke of all the onlookers was " If you have twins, where will you take them ? To the Fathers ? "

I also saw a naming ceremony of dead twins. There was no dancing, singing, or drumming ; merely a series of offerings of coffee-berries by the guests to the parents and to " little *Salongo* and *Nalongo* "—in this case grown-up persons—who stood in a row outside the door of the house. But even this had gathered together relatives who had not met for years, and the father, who was quite a poor man, killed for the feast three goats and a sheep, which might be worth altogether about twenty-seven shillings.

What is the reason for this elaborate and expensive ceremonial? Roscoe interprets it in two ways—as an expression of thanks to the god Mukasa and as a rite for producing fertility in people, cattle, and crops. Neither of these explanations seems to me satisfactory. There is nothing in the foregoing account to support the first, except the wording of the announcement made immediately after the birth, while the second is expressly denied by natives.[1] The one reason which

[1] Roscoe's version mentions (p. 72) that offerings were made by the father of the twins to the god Mukasa. I should not dispute this, though none of my informants corroborated it, but this in itself would not give the whole ceremonial the character of a thanksgiving to the god. The explanation of it as a form of fertility-magic cannot, in my opinion, be upheld in the face of the persistent statement of the natives that nothing could make crops grow but hard work, with which they countered every attempt to inquire into the existence of economic magic. Magic for the fertility of cattle was left to the alien Bahima who herded them, and human fertility was promoted at need by charms obtained from prophets. Against the suggestion that the sprats were a fertility-symbol must be set the explicit native statement that they are used because they come from Sesse, the island in the Lake which is the home of Mukasa. Here, as in many other parts of his work, Roscoe is clearly influenced by the theories of Sir James Frazer. An even more striking example of this *a priori* approach is to be found in his chapter on totemism, where he not only (p. 137) reports a tradition which describes the division of the different animal species among the clans in order that they should not all be eaten, but even attempts to interpret the rite universally practised on eating grasshoppers as a form of *intichiuma*-ceremony (p. 144). Frazer himself, in dealing with Roscoe's material in *The Golden Bough* (vol. ii, p. 102), describes the twin-ceremonies as " performing dances in the gardens of favoured friends ", and thus conjures up a pleasant picture of some sort of blessing of crops. The origin of this phrase is so remarkable an instance of false reasoning based on etymology that it deserves to be explained. The equivalent given in older vocabularies for the word *kyalo*, which simply means a group of huts with the surrounding cultivation, is "garden". Roscoe himself refers to a village as "a garden (so-called) ". Actually, the dancing was done in the cleared space in front of the house.

they give is to please and honour the twins themselves, and the sanction for the correct performance of the rites is simply the fear of the anger of the twins in case anything is omitted. It was not clear whether this vengeance could be wreaked even during their life-time ; some informants did say that twins share with the father's sister the power of haunting a person while still alive. But it is so common for one or both twins to die that it is probably the fear of the spirit that is really significant. This suggestion is perhaps borne out by the fact that, if the infants were ill, the " drum " described above used to be beaten " to call them back from heaven ",[1] and that it is still considered dangerous to say, in so many words, that a twin has died ; instead such euphemisms are used as " They have flown away " or " They have gone for firewood ". Failure to carry out these, as many other rites, was thought to be visited with death ; but twins were also supposed to be able to burn their successors in the womb. My own boy, Ephraim Musoke, whose father was a very good Christian, showed me a birth-mark which he said some people believed was due to his father's having omitted to perform the ceremonial for twins who were born before him ; he would not commit himself to an opinion. Even if nothing had been done to offend them twins might gratuitously kill their parents, and, for this reason, twins of opposite sexes were preferred, since each was thought to counteract the other's ill-will against the parent of the opposite sex to itself. The fact that the after-births had to be disposed of by a non-member of the clan indicates that they, too, were regarded as dangerous, and even the little tokens which were thrust into neighbours' houses were believed to cause the death of any one who lost one.

Thus, despite the apparent contrast, we have here an attitude essentially similar to that of the many other African peoples who have regarded twins as so dangerous

---

[1] Of course, a modern phrase.

that they put the children, and sometimes also the mother, to death. It would be an exaggeration to say that all the rejoicings and honorific treatment are consciously thought of as a mere deception to placate the unwelcome twins, but it is certainly true that the element of propitiation is very strong. Here, as elsewhere, it is the abnormality of the twin-birth which demands special treatment and not the unusual fecundity of the parents. A woman whom I asked why people make such a fuss about twins replied, as if the answer was obvious, " Well, when most people have one child at a time and someone suddenly has two, isn't that an extraordinary thing? " At the same time, since in the days when the full ceremonial was performed the giver of twins was the god to whom every one used to appeal for children, an indication of his especial interest in a particular couple was regarded with satisfaction ; for it would be pressing the fear of twins too far to argue that he was thought to send them out of malice. That the title *Salongo* should be used in an honorific sense of people to whom it does not strictly apply shows that a father of twins was considered as a distinguished person ; and the respect shown to the parents through the rest of their lives is not directed, like the ceremonial, to please the twins themselves, but is rather the recognition of an achievement. It would be interesting to know whether, in the other cases where twins are hailed with ritual rejoicings, this dual attitude can be traced.[1]

[1] Such cases are quoted by Dr. I. Schapera in his article, "Customs relating to Twins in South Africa " (*Journal of the African Society*, vol. xxvi), where he, too, stresses the essential similarity of attitude which among some peoples dictates the murder of twins and with others the celebration of their birth. Dr. Schapera does not accept an explanation of such customs by the abnormality of the occurrence, arguing that they represent an organized and not an impulsive reaction. But this argument ignores the fact that what may be called normal abnormalities—events which are uncommon and alarming but yet not unprecedented—are dealt with in a ritual manner in most primitive societies : and his explanation by the theory that the "occurrence of two individuals with identical personalities " is an event calling for a peculiar reaction by the society whose structure is affected leaves out of account that some societies have also an organized mode of reaction

(d) Infancy

The treatment of infants has hardly been influenced at all by Europeans. Throughout the first few months they are washed twice daily in hot water, with many medicinal herbs, in a small pot or a broken piece kept for the purpose. At four or five months the medicines are left off, and a washing in cold water in the middle of the day is added, which is supposed to improve the child's appetite. At three or four it begins to be washed in cold water only. Neither children nor plates are ever dried by rubbing with a cloth, and as soon as a child can run about it is simply left to get dry by itself.

The one form of special care which is given to a young infant is that efforts are made to keep it warm. There is hardly any idea of need for careful handling. I have seen a child a week old seized by one arm and swung into position on the back of a small sister of five or so, and one of a month with its head bumping from side to side as its nurse ran. They are held in a standing position at a month or two; at six weeks they are propped sitting on their mother's lap; and at three months sat up with the soles of the feet placed together to balance them, and barkcloths tucked round them for support.

In the old days this was the next ceremonial occasion of a child's life. Its father's mother came to make it sit up, and gave it its personal name. This was the name of an ancestor, and was selected by a sister of the father, or *sengawe*. It was her duty to select a name which was " likely to be lost "; that is to say, it was

to other types of abnormal birth—feet presentations, etc. Indeed a native volunteered the statement that a feet presentation would be treated in the same way as a twin-birth. This is doubtful, but it does suggest that, to the native, the essential feature of a twin-birth is the abnormality. While it is true that only in the case of twins does the ritual reach such a pitch of elaboration and that, therefore, this case perhaps calls for some further explanation, I feel that it is preferable not to hazard any theory which does not rest upon concrete facts of individual behaviour. Such evidence of this kind as I obtained does not lead beyond the conclusions stated in the text.

important that the ancestors should all have their fair share of remembrance. It was thought that a spirit was pleased at having a child called after it, but there is now no idea that the naming constituted it a special guardian of the child, still less that the name indicated a belief that that particular ancestor was reincarnated. The grandmother took home as her reward the barkcloth on which the child was seated.

The mother sometimes took her child with her when she went to work, carrying it on her back in a strip of barkcloth, and laid it on the ground among the bananas or by the edge of her plot. But even the first child in a family often had some older child to look after it— a slave, a daughter of one of its father's brothers sent to him to bring up, or a younger sister of its father. In the modern monogamous household one often finds that the mother has some such relative to help her— frequently nowadays an adult unmarried woman. At present it is as common to see boys looking after infants as girls, since the girls begin very early to hoe and cook, but whether this was so in the past I cannot say.

Roscoe mentions (page 55) the prohibition of intercourse between husband and wife during the suckling period, and from all we know of other East African tribes this is what one would expect. But no modern Muganda has any recollection of such a rule, and Eresi Nalubega treated the suggestion as most unreasonable and answered, " Why ? She is not ill." But what is certain is that, during this period, adultery by the father was considered to be fatal to the child. Its effects were instantaneous ; the father would return from seeing his mistress off the premises to find the child at the point of death, and it could only be saved by fetching her back to perform a rite over it. This consisted in washing it with a decoction of leaves which she had first rubbed over her body, and saying, " My child, I am not killing you, I am your mother ", or, alternatively, in cutting off a small piece of her sash and putting it in the child's wash-pot with the same words. Quite young people still believe in this disease, but it is now thought possible to provide against it in advance by tying a charm to the child's wrist.

Suckling goes on till the child is about three years old, though it begins to be given solid food at a few months. Children are not now separated from their mothers as they used to be, but when this was the practice the separation did not necessarily come at the moment of weaning, since it had to be preceded by the naming ceremony.

(e) Naming

Although the child had been proclaimed as a member of his father's clan on the day of his birth, he was not formally recognized as such till the ceremony at which his legitimacy was tested and his clan name given him. This did not take place until the child was weaned, and in some cases not till quite a long time after. It could not be done unless there were children of both sexes, and of more than one father, present, and, since a group of brothers would wish to have all their children named at the same time, the ceremony might be put off indefinitely because one or other could not come. But, since no person who had not been through it could attend the funeral rites of a member of the clan, the death of a near relative was often an occasion for the hurried naming of a few children. The ceremony was performed at the house of the eldest brother who had a child to be named. Here the parents and children assembled, the mothers bringing with them the children's cords, which had been carefully preserved for the purpose. Before the actual rites began, a feast was eaten which included as essential elements salt, specially prepared by the women of the fathers' clan from the ashes of burnt swamp-grass, and sprats. Then the mothers sat down in a row outside the house, leaning against the posts, each with her child seated quite naked on her thighs, and each husband stood opposite his wife. A large water-tight basket containing water mixed with beer was brought and set on a new barkcloth. The grandmother threw the cords into this. A child's legitimacy was proved if its cord floated, or—according to the theory of some clans— if it pointed towards the father. In some clans it was customary to rub the cords with butter beforehand, and, at the ceremony which I saw, so much butter was used that only a miracle could have prevented them floating. Some clans followed this by yet further tests, but in most cases the floating was considered sufficient, and was hailed by cries of joy, amid which the senior man of the clan present proclaimed the children as members of the clan, enumerating several of their direct ancestors and then the original heads of the *mutuba* and *siga* and of the whole clan.

The really decisive element in this test was not the result of any careful observation of the behaviour of the cords, but the belief that a child which was put through the test, if it was in fact illegitimate, would certainly die. This belief meant that a woman who had committed adultery would generally refuse to bring her child to the ceremony. Moreover, if suspicion rested on any woman, she would be cross-examined beforehand by her husband's relatives, so that little reliance was in fact placed on the mechanical test. If in any of these ways a woman was convicted, or thought to be convicted, of adultery, every effort would be made to induce her to confess the name of the child's father, and it would be sent to him or to his people ; but, if she refused, it took the totem of her husband and was treated as a member of his family, except that it was absolutely debarred from inheriting from a member of his clan.

When the test was over, the husbands' sisters washed both mothers and children all over with the mixture of beer and water, and took the opportunity to splash them severely if they disliked them. Then the grand-mother brought in a meal of *obu·ta*—a kind of porridge made of dried bananas pounded into flour—with sprats mixed into it, and, taking a lump in a banana-leaf in each hand, touched the mothers with them all up their legs and arms, and then held the leaves to their mouths while they ate the food without touching it with their hands. Lumps of the mixture were also thrust into the children's mouths. At the ceremony I saw bunches of taro-leaves and of a native vegetable called *·jobyo* were brought in, but nothing was done with them. I was told that they were shown to the women as suitable food to cook for their husbands, and that there should also have been a piece of banana-root to indicate where they could find food in a famine.

Then the mothers placed the cords along the end of the barkcloth, rolled up the whole cloth, and carried it into the house, while the women of their husbands' clan stood round the door singing a song, and pinched the mothers unmercifully as they went in.

Next day the clan names were publicly given by the *sengawe* of the man at whose house the ceremony was held. The grandmother shaved the children's heads for the first time and preserved the hair in a barkcloth. She gave each daughter-in-law cowries and coffee-berries " to thank her for bearing the child ", and the gathering dispersed.

I saw this done for two children—a full brother and sister—who were taken off immediately afterwards to the funeral rites of their grandmother. It was quite contrary to traditional custom for the rite to be performed for the children of only one man, and—what offended sticklers for the proprieties still more—the father had been in too much of a hurry to fetch " another grandmother ", the wife of one of his father's brothers, who should have officiated, and instead simply called in his own sister, who lived in the same village.

In this ceremony we see the affirmation of the superiority of members of a clan on their own ground to non-members which, in some way or other, marks all clan ceremonies. When it is described the women of the clan are referred to as " princesses " by contrast to their sisters-in-law, a form of speech that we shall meet again in connection with mortuary rites. At the naming of dead twins, which I attended, the distinction was marked by the order in which those present made their gifts, members of the clan having precedence. When we come to funeral rites, we shall see it emphasized even more strongly.[1] Another striking feature of this ritual is the opportunity given to the husbands' sisters to ill-treat their sisters-in-law ; taken together with the showing to the wives of food which they are recommended to cook for their husbands, this perhaps indicates a certain determination of the women of one family to see that the wives of its menfolk do their duty by them and their children, and make them suffer for it if they do not.

This ceremony is nowadays more and more disregarded. Practically every child receives Christian baptism, and both the Christian name—which usually takes the place of the native personal name—and the clan name are given it then. There is no gathering of relatives for the church service. The native rite is specifically condemned by Christian teaching, European and native, because of the beliefs in supernatural causes of death which it involves ; this disapproval has been extended to all beliefs of the kind, so that the moral sanction which they constituted has vanished. To-day one finds educated Christian natives who deplore the fact, but it is too late to re-establish a supernatural sanction once the general belief in its efficacy has been undermined. Children are still sometimes taken to the grandparents for the first shaving of the head, which is celebrated by a feast without any other rite.

(f) Guardianship of Children

Once the child's clan membership was definitely established, there arose the question where it was to be

[1] See Chapter VIII, pp. 213–15.

brought up, for it was common for a child to be sent away from its own parents to the household of some relative of the father. This was done from a number of motives, which are so distinct that it is not possible to give an adequate account of the custom by trying to find a single underlying reason for it.

Children were sometimes sent to a brother of the father, and the reason always given for this is that they were more strictly brought up than by their own father, who was inclined to indulge them too much. Though the natives do not themselves offer this explanation, the practice is evidently connected with the fact that brothers were expected to take an interest in one another's children and that it was thought preferable for a man to select as his heir a son of his brother rather than one of his own, in order " to hold the clan together ".

In the case of boys, another reason was the fact that a boyhood spent in a chief's household was the surest way to advancement in life, and boys might be sent to a quite distant relative if he was a chief. There they would have the opportunity of being sent to court as attendants on the king, a position from which, if they gave satisfaction, they were almost certain to rise to important chieftainships ; while, even if they stayed with their own relative, he might appoint them as his subordinate officials or recommend them to the king to be made chiefs. There was also a quite definite feeling that children learnt better manners in a chief's household.

Then certain relatives had a claim upon the services of children, particularly in their old age. A man could not refuse a request of his parents to send them a child, a request which was made as much from the desire " to have a child about the place " as for the sake of the material advantage of its help in the house ; such a child, if a boy, was very often made the grandfather's heir. Even stronger was the claim of his *sengawe*, of all relatives the one held in greatest respect and awe, for she alone could make a curse effective during her lifetime.

In her home a child would be assured, in theory at least, of a strict upbringing ; but in the home of the grand-parents severity was not even theoretically expected. Here a child was free to behave exactly as it liked, and able to count on infinite indulgence.

Thus one can trace two separate motives for the practice which are not necessarily always in harmony. One is interest in the child's own future and the wish to secure him a sound upbringing and opportunities of advancement. The other lies in the recognition of mutual obligations between relatives and a desire to strengthen the bonds of kinship in a concrete manner.

Girls were sometimes sent as children to the house-hold of their father's chief with a view to becoming his wives when they were old enough. But this was not a regular practice ; it was usually done as a means of soliciting the chief's favour.

Old women talking of this custom never give any sign that they regarded it as a hardship. " The father's brother is the same as the father," they say. " You know he will be kind to the child. And it comes back often for visits of a month or so to see the others." I did inquire into the possibility of the parents getting the child back if they found it was ill-treated, but that was considered so remote that no one had many ideas as to what would be done ; there was simply a general feeling that such a situation would be very disgraceful. Frequently the child was not in fact taken very far from its parents ; in many cases it would still be in the same village. On the other hand, one old man told me that he had been taken from his mother when he was weaned and had never seen her again.

But there was another relative who had a claim on the child of quite a different nature—the mother's brother. The brother who made her marriage arrange-ments and formally handed her over to her husband had the right to take any of her children unless it was " redeemed " by gifts. These gifts were not sent immediately on the birth of the child, but as soon as it was old enough to be separated from its mother he could come at any time and claim his rights. A man who stood on his full rights was disapproved of ; he was expected to waive his claim to the eldest and youngest, and " if he was very kind " might let it pass in the case of every third child. But he was strictly entitled to every child unless it was redeemed by a cow or goat, a barkcloth and 1,500 cowries, or by a slave of the same sex.   This right was called his *ndobolo*,[1] a noun from the verb *kulobola*, " to take one's share," which is used of a chief taking his share of taxation, fines, or spoils in war, and its *raison d'être* was said to be " to thank him for giving the woman who bore the children " and " because the children are a sort of profit ".

The father, even if he had to let a child go, might redeem it later on by sending the appropriate gift ; but the position of a child which was not redeemed was regarded as very unhappy. He had none of the advantages of belonging either to his father's or his mother's family. Of his father it is said, " Neither he nor the mother has any power over him," and " If he has not redeemed them they are not his children "— but, since his clan was determined solely by physiological descent, he was not his uncle's child either, and in the latter's household he had no rights. The mother's brother is the Baganda counterpart of the cruel step-mother.   He was under no obligation towards his sister's child, since only clan bonds carried with them obligations, and there was nothing to prevent his selling it into slavery, though of course this was disapproved just as cruelty in stepmothers is disapproved in the fairy-tales. At the best the child lost touch with his own clan, and this in itself was regarded as a definite misfortune. " He grows up a fool," they say. " He does not know

---

[1] Roscoe quotes this word as used to describe children given by grateful parents to the service of the god Mukasa, but seems to have been unaware of its commoner meaning.

the customs of his clan, he does not know his brothers, nor his fathers, nor his father's sisters, nor his sisters, he only understands his uncles." In contrast to this situation, a child who had been duly redeemed was entitled to ask for anything he liked in his mother's brother's house and, if his request was refused, to help himself.

Christian influence has been directed against a system which, though it separated children from their parents for just about the same proportion of their lives as a public school education does in England, appears to be incompatible with the ideal of home life which the missions are anxious to instil into the natives. This influence has been effective to the extent that the *ndobolo* custom has lapsed altogether and is hardly even remembered, and that very few children are now sent away from their parents for the mere sake of sending them away ; one does occasionally come across such cases. But the claim of the older relatives is still as strong as ever, and it is only the very few natives in close contact with Europeans who feel justified in disregarding it. Sickly children are often sent away, sometimes from a suspicion that somebody is bewitching them, but also because the change in itself seems to be expected to do them good. A young mother sometimes has a little sister living with her to help with the baby. One still sees in a wealthy chief's household a number of miscellaneous children, not necessarily of very near relatives, who have been sent to him partly so that they may grow up in a socially superior environment and partly so that he may pay for their education.

The last reason brings us to the quite new motive which, at the present time, is much the strongest. There is an immense demand for education, and in every village where there is a state-aided school there is hardly a household without one or two relatives' children living in it for the purpose of attending school. The question of fees sometimes presents difficulties. One man gave it as the main reason for the general decline of the custom that nobody was willing to pay for the schooling of some-one else's children, and I knew a native master at Budo, the leading C.M.S. boys' school, who actually refused the offer of two young nephews, made him with obvious ulterior motives.   But, except in the case of persons who are definitely wealthy by native standards, such as administrative chiefs and large landowners, the parents do not usually try to push the responsibility for paying for the children on to their temporary guardians, and those who do are regarded as mean.   The general arrangement is that the father provides the child's fees, clothes, and soap for washing clothes ; the guardian feeds the child, and the child does the same work in the house as the other children there.   There is no longer the same one-sided emphasis on the relationship through the father ;   children may be sent to a mother's sister to go to school, and sick children seem to be sent even oftener to the mother's relatives than the father's.

(g)   Education

The education of children in the old days consisted mainly in learning the various household activities in practice, by imitating their elders but without the help of much deliberate explanation.   In the case of girls, one can still observe it.   At the age of three they are given small hoes and go out to work with their mothers,[1] and at little more handed a knife and told to peel plantains.   By the time they are seven or eight, they are as quick at this as a grown-up person.   They are also given a calabash to scoop out.   Next they are taught how to wrap up food and set it on the fire.   I have seen three children, of whom the eldest was not more than

---

[1] It would be so cumbrous to qualify every reference to the father or mother with some phrase to cover the case of children who did not grow up with their own parents that I do not propose to do so.   In their case, the father's place was taken by the head of the household, that of the *sengawe* by some woman whom he " called sister ", and the mother's by the wife to whose care the child was entrusted.

six, quite competently preparing a meal with no supervision. I met them coming in from the banana-grove,
the youngest rendered almost invisible by the bunch of
bananas on her head, and watched the two elders get them
ready for cooking while the youngest commented on a
previous failure of her elder sister by an impromptu
song and dance to the words " She eats raw food! " At
about seven they begin raffia-work, going from baskets
to mats.

Boys in the pre-school era had to get up early and
sweep the yard in front of the house to be neat by the
time the head of the household was ready to go out,
then to fetch the goats and tie them up in the yard till
the dew was off the grass, when they went off to herd
them. In most cases the only work for which they
needed actual instruction was barkcloth-making ; this
they learnt by working with the father. Specialists,
such as smiths and potters, taught their sons their
crafts. When a boy made his first barkcloth, knife, or
pot unaided, the father gave a feast to celebrate the
event, at which the parents performed the *kukuza* rite.
The object made was given to the mother or grandmother. Nowadays a corresponding feast is held when
a boy leaves school.

Etiquette is still an important element in education.
Children begin to be taught the phrases of greeting and
farewell almost before they can speak, and they are
drilled in the correct gestures—to kneel and put their
hands in the stranger's. Refusal to do this is one of
the few reasons for which I have seen a child beaten.
They are taught to sit down at once on the ground on
entering the house of any person of importance, for to
stand in such a person's presence is disrespectful. Girls,
in particular, begin as soon as they can sit without
support at all to be taught to sit decorously, which means
with the feet together tucked sideways under the body ;
their mothers take hold of their feet and tuck them in
place. The obligation to make presents to a guest is

F

impressed very early on small children. A child is encouraged to go and fetch an egg or two for the visitor, definitely as his own gift. Instruction in general good manners is not left to the parents ; on neutral ground, at least, any grown-up person present may take a hand.[1]

Such general information and advice as children received was imparted in the main by fathers to sons and mothers to daughters ; but the *sengawe*, being both a woman and connected by a particularly close bond to the father, had her say in the upbringing of children of both sexes, and where a girl did not grow up with her own mother it was from her *sengawe* that she received most of her instruction.

For a boy it was considered very important to know his exact position in the clan, his relationship to the other members, and his whole genealogy, so that he might be able to make good such claims as he had to seniority, to prove his membership in case of a dispute, and, above all, to prove that he was a true Muganda and entitled to become a chief. This information was not picked up casually, but formally imparted by the father in the evenings.

Both boys and girls received a certain amount of general advice on conduct. That given to boys was summed up by Aluizi Zalembekiya as follows : " Be sure to know your relatives, so that you need not be afraid to stand up for your rights. Do not refuse to pay a debt ; if you do, you will have no one to lend to you, or redeem you. Do not commit adultery, but love unmarried women who have no husbands [with a view to matrimony, of course]. Do not betray a blood-brother who is hiding in your house. Do not steal, except in war. Do not listen to your wives telling tales of one another, or you will be left alone." Yokana

[1] Unfortunately I had not, when in the field, the advantage of knowing the brilliant analysis made by Dr. Audrey Richards, in her *Hunger and Work in a Savage Tribe*, of the place of eating etiquette in a child's general education in kinship behaviour, and I have no data on this point.

Waswa, dealing specifically with marital duties, added :
" Pay attention to the words of your wife ; do not
introduce customs which will spoil the marriage [this was
explained as meaning that he should lay down a household routine at the outset and stick to it] ; you ought not
to ill-treat your wife by bringing in other women ; you
ought to love the relatives of your wife."

Girls' education was definitely orientated towards
marriage, and in the performance of each household
task they were reminded that this was work which they
would later have to do as wives. Specifically a girl was
told to be agreeable to other wives, not to quarrel or be
jealous if another seemed to be unduly favoured (e.g.
with gifts—clothes or meat), not to steal food from the
others' plots but to work hard at her own, to listen to
her husband and obey him, and treat him and his
relatives with respect, not to go visiting without her
husband's permission, not to commit adultery (almost
implied in the preceding phrase), not to cook food without
a relish, to be hospitable to guests and cook for them,
and to look after children carefully, both her own and
others in the household.

Of all the relatives among whom the child grew up the
one whom he was taught to treat with most respect was
the father's sister. The phrase with which the rule is
explained is always the same : " Because she is the same as
the father " ; and she is even sometimes addressed as
" Sir " by her brother's children. The consequences of
offending her were even more serious than those of
misbehaviour to the father himself ; he could banish
a child from his presence, and could utter a dying curse
which would dog the child's footsteps through life, but
the *sengawe* in her own lifetime could curse a brother's
child so that it died. Some believe still that her spirit
is the only one which is malevolent after death, and
certainly the majority of cases of sickness thought to be
due to possession by a spirit are ascribed to the *sengawe*.
It would be very rare for her potent curse to be used

against a young child, for most natives will say that children do not understand what they are doing and ought not to be visited with such a dire penalty; but, at any rate in the old days, the child knew that he had it to fear and behaved accordingly. This belief is probably ceasing to have much influence with the younger generation, and now that there is so much school education, and so little left of the rites in which the *sengawe's* relationship was formally recognized, her importance in the lives of the next generation must have been much reduced. But the fact that a child is still often sent to live with its *sengawe*, and that the father treats her with the respect to which he was brought up, means that the children of the present day have not altogether lost the traditional attitude towards her.

Perhaps no single innovation has brought such great changes into native life as the introduction of schools. This has affected boys much more than girls, for in the main the mothers simply do not let their daughters be taken from their household duties. As a young lady of about eight said to me, " Boys go to school all day, but we women are cooking in the morning." It is only a very small minority who think that education or anything else should take precedence of these duties. But for boys it has meant that almost their whole education is now given outside the home. It is true that those who do not go away from home still help in odd jobs of building, or pick cotton on Saturday; but they seldom now learn their fathers' crafts, since school education takes them farther than the practice of native crafts can do and, though the schools do not deliberately encourage disregard for native institutions and traditions, their mere existence and the new interests that they create must weaken the old links. The parents themselves are anxious to have their children go to school; there is no question of the children being taken from their influence against their will. The older men follow their children's progress with a genuine, if slightly mystified, interest, while there is already a generation of fathers who have had some sort of schooling, and some teach their own children to read, generally using the Prayer Book as a primer.

The parents do not themselves feel that European education is likely to make their children disrespectful. Indeed I remember one father declaring that children were better kept in order at school than at home. Most children live in a native household even if they are away from home, and have therefore the normal background of native family life. The number who go to boarding school is not more than a few hundred. For them the separation from their normal environment is complete. In the case of boys, the household routine goes on without them, and when at home they seem to spend a good deal of their time paying calls in their smart school uniforms ; they also read anything printed in English which they can lay their hands on. Girls more readily slip back into the old routine, though one told me proudly how she had refused to dig on a Sunday, saying, " I was brought up among Europeans." If the native intelligentsia are successful in the demand that their daughters should not dig while at school—at present all the girls' boarding schools but one grow their own food—it will be interesting to see if they will return contentedly to their household work at home.

As I shall explain more fully later on, kinship obligations did not bulk as large in the life of the Muganda as they do among those peoples where the kinship group is also a territorial unit. A son was not obliged to live in his father's village and was thus, in effect, free from paternal authority as soon as he acquired adult status and set up his own house on marriage. The difference that modern conditions have made is that his independence now comes not from a marriage which required his father's assistance in providing the bride-price but from the ability to earn money, and this is both to boys and parents the principal aim of education. But this change in the relationship of a son to his father is a result of the modern economic system, not an effect either of the boy's absence at school nor of what he is taught there.

(h) Blood-Brotherhood

A step which was taken by every father who could provide for his son's future was to arrange for him to make blood-brotherhood with some friend. The compact by which this relationship was set up involved an unlimited obligation of mutual aid, and every man made such a bond with at least two or three, sometimes as many as six, different people. Once he had attained to adult independence he made the arrangement for himself ; but his first blood-brother, or *mukago*, was found for him by his father. In every case the ceremony was performed in the home of the father or of a senior relative, because it involved a partial assimilation of the blood-brother to membership of the clan.

The father would offer to give his son as *mukago* to a friend of his own, possibly a neighbour, possibly a stranger from another village, or he might further cement the relationship with a *mukago* of his own by suggesting that the compact should be made between their sons. The offer, implying as it did considerable confidence in the person to whom it was made, was regarded as a compliment.

In the actual ceremony the two parties sat side by side on a barkcloth, each with a woman to represent his wife ; when a grown man made the compact his actual wife would be there. The father brought them coffee-berries. In each coffee-berry there are two beans ; each partner opened one berry, made a cut in his body, rubbed both beans in the blood, swallowed one himself and gave the other to his partner. It was the physical act of swallowing the bean with the partner's blood on it that created the relationship ; and it is vaguely conceived as remaining permanently in the stomach, where it was liable to swell up and kill a person who

broke the compact. Any attempt to avoid such consequences by not swallowing the bean was equally
supposed to be visited by rapid death—again thought to
be caused by the bean itself which, in this case, swelled
up in the mouth. Each partner then took a spear and
knife and put them behind him to indicate that he
would protect his friend from violence. A feast, cooked
by the mother, was then eaten by as many relatives as
could be collected. The feast was called *kwalula mukago*,
the verb being the same as is used for the ceremony of
admitting a child to the clan.

This ceremony could not make the blood-brother a
full member of the clan, since he did not cease to belong
to his own clan, but his status was in a certain degree
assimilated to membership. He respected his blood-
brother's totem as well as his own, was prohibited from
marriage with women of his clan, was referred to by other
members of the clan by the same kinship terms as his
partner, and at ceremonies in his partner's clan he played
the same part as a real relative of the same degree. Each
was introduced to as many of the other's relatives as
possible. The relationship was inherited, and, though the
custom is now obsolete, people still respect the relationships created by such a tie between their ancestors,
though they cannot always trace it back to the original
compact.

The value of such a relationship was that it provided
security against all possible risks, including those
resulting from the commission of a crime. A blood-
brother could refuse a man no request of any kind, from
a drink of beer or safe keeping for his cattle to a wife,
the payment of a heavy fine or debt, or the concealment
of a fugitive from justice. The relationship took precedence of kinship, in that a murderer might count on
finding refuge with a blood-brother even if the latter was
a relative of his victim, and one informant said that
the blood-brother might even give himself up to be
killed in the place of his friend.

It was particularly advantageous to have blood-brothers in distant villages or even in other tribes. A man could count on their hospitality when travelling and if, for any reason, he had to run away from home. They were expected to put him in the way of good bargains and to see that he was conducted safely through unknown or hostile country; if two partners met in war they would spare one another, and a man might even secretly warn a blood-brother if his village was to be attacked. Blood-brothers fighting on the same side would defend one another, and a wounded *mukago* could not be abandoned.

The supernatural sanctions which safeguarded this compact were stronger than those attaching to any duty of kinship. Some have already been mentioned. There was also a special procedure by which one party to the compact could bring down vengeance upon the other, and which could be used in the case even of a trivial failure to fulfil its obligations. The offended *mukago* would secretly bring some coffee-berries, a new hoe ("to represent his wife"), and a new knife, and leave them in a new barkcloth in the doorway of the offender's house, stating aloud the injury which had been done him. Merely to look at this parcel might cause the death of the offender or of any of his children. A new door had to be made for them to go in and out by, and either a "doctor" or a man related to the head of the house through a woman was fetched to remove the parcel and throw it into the bush. The offended *mukago* was then summoned to a solemn reconciliation feast, after which both were washed with medicines by the "doctor", and they joined in buying a cow or goat for his fee. It was then possible for amends to be made for the injury if it was a question of repayment, but before this ceremony had been gone through it was dangerous for any goods to pass from one partner to the other.

The compact seems to have been strongly disapproved of by missionaries, as part of their general disapproval of practices implying a belief in supernatural causes of death. Samwiri Nganda, the parson of Ngogwe, also said to me that a ceremony which involved drawing blood was disgusting and only worthy of heathen, and that such private compacts should not be entered into by Christians, who were all brothers in Christ. Nowadays the greatly increased opportunities of getting into debt would make any man hesitate before undertaking unlimited responsibility for a friend ; this is the argument against the custom which was advanced by the hardheaded Kanywamagule. The need for it too has died out in the greater general security of modern times.

(i) Adolescence

While for a boy there was no formal recognition of the attainment of physical maturity, marriage itself marking the entry upon adult life, for a girl there was a definite break at the first menstruation. During this period she had to cook her own food and eat it alone, behind a curtain, and could not touch a boy. When it was over the *kukuza* rite had to be performed by her own parents, to whom she returned if she had been living with some other relative. They then ate a ceremonial meal, which Eresi Nalubega said was not a feast, meaning that outsiders were not invited.[1] Since a grown person might not sleep in the home of his parents, this meant in the girl's case that she lived from that time till her marriage in the household of a married brother, a removal from close contact with the older generation at a period of tension which probably helped to reduce causes of friction. Since all the boys of a household slept together in their own hut, no such change was necessary for them.

---

[1] Eresi Nalubega also stated quite definitely that there were no taboos of any kind during subsequent menstruations, that a woman would do her ordinary work unless she felt too ill, which she said was common, and that there was no reason why she should not, because " You can wash your hands with soap." I unfortunately failed to obtain definite information from older women with regard to the past, but it seems probable that the taboos mentioned by Roscoe and Sir Apolo Kagwa have lapsed with the decrease of polygamy.

Now that the normal household consists of only one house, and that the age of marriage is much later than it used to be, special arrangements have to be made for boys of fifteen or sixteen. Sometimes such a boy builds himself a little reed hut too small to do anything but sleep in ; if the father is fairly well off he may build his son a little house next his own. Girls sometimes sleep in the cooking-house or have a reed hut built for them. In Kanywamagule's family the cooking-house had fallen down, and a daughter of fifteen or more was living in the main house with her parents. This suggests that the rule is breaking down ; but there are also cases where it is so strictly observed that even when the father is dead or living somewhere else his children will not sleep in his house. Bugeza, the old chief of Kisimula, had had a small house built simply for his grown-up sons to sleep in when they came to see him, and Kyuma, even though he had " become his father ", continued to sleep there when he was in the village.

Old women will still tell you that girls should marry as soon as their breasts begin to hang, before they have " learnt wantonness ", and because it is disgraceful for an unmarried girl to become pregnant. This is assumed as the inevitable alternative to early marriage. Of course such cases still occur, and probably increase with all the influences which now combine to make the age of marriage later. It is not at all uncommon for schoolboys to become fathers. The European, seeing how much more childish, both in bearing and general outlook, the Muganda schoolboy appears than an English boy of the same age, can hardly help a certain sense of shock at the idea, and it needs an effort to remember that a generation ago those same boys would have been taking their place without question as adult members of the community, and that it is only against the alien background of European surroundings and ideas that they seem immature.

This is one of the cases where the adjustment of

traditional attitudes to new conditions has been most unsatisfactory. The present attempt at a remedy consists in fixing the school holidays for boys and girls at different times, a very partial remedy at best, since the total number of children who go to boarding schools is so small. A movement is also on foot in the Native Anglican Church to demand that an unmarried father shall be made legally responsible for his child's maintenance.

Native custom does provide a penalty for the seduction of an unmarried girl, and native disapproval of such an action has always been strong. The ritual in connection with it is still carried out. It was described to me by two young men, neither of them over thirty, who had themselves performed it, and it was performed by a man at Ngogwe while I was there. The first essential is to find who is the girl's lover in order that she may be sent to him to give birth, and the proper rites be performed if she has twins. This is regarded as so important that girls usually confess, though some refuse for fear their confession results in the boy being expelled from school. In any case the girl can have no contact with her parents till the child is born, but must cook her own food and eat it alone, living in a temporary hut built for the purpose. If the proper procedure is carried out, her brother, who takes her to the boy, demands a gourd of beer from him and leaves her with him, saying, " Here is your wife. When her child is born, I will fix the bride-price. Or if you do not want to marry my sister, I will take her back and she shall marry some other man."

When the child is born, the lovers go back to the girl's parents, taking the child with them and as presents to the parents a goat, a barkcloth, and a gourd of beer. A meal of bananas and mushrooms is eaten, at which each of the four hands food to the other three ; the goat is left behind for the parents to eat when the couple have gone, in the same way as they eat a goat on a daughter's marriage night after she has left them. After eating it, the girl's parents perform the *kukuza* rite, and this must be done also by the lovers when they reach the man's home. If the couple are to be married, the special rules of behaviour between a man and his wife's parents come into force at once, though the marriage is still not complete until the bride-price has been paid. There is absolutely no feeling that the lover is under an obligation to marry the girl.

If the couple are not married, the girl goes back to her own people after two or three days. The father has a right to take the child when it is weaned, though in the past he could not do this without paying the *ndobolo*, and one of my informants, describing modern conditions, said that he has to bring a goat when he comes to fetch it. In the meantime, he is also expected to provide clothing for the child and give occasional presents of meat or sugar to the mother.

No informant suggested that the fact of her having a child would prejudice a girl's chances of finding a husband. One told me that he had had a child " in the manner of wantonness " by a girl who already had three, but the reason he gave for refusing to marry her—with an air of the utmost self-righteousness—was, " She was a lazy girl and would have spoiled my religion."

In the villages girls simply put in the time till marriage by helping in the work of a brother's house. But a few of those who have been to secondary schools spend the time between leaving school and marriage in wage-earning occupations. There are, for instance, girl type-setters on the staff of native-owned newspapers, and girls are employed to do fancy sewing by the Singer Sewing Machine Company. But the numbers of these are negligible. There are women nurses both in mission and Government hospitals ; and native midwives are trained by the C.M.S. and sent out to the village maternity centres. Women teachers are required for the girl's schools, and the Mill Hill Mission has recently started a native teaching sisterhood. But this does not account for all the educated girls, small as is their number relatively to the total, and various schemes have been set on foot to train them for other occupations. Lady Cook, who, as Mrs. Katharine Cook, inaugurated the training of native midwives, has now started a domestic science course at her own house, where some dozen girls are learning European cooking and house-work. Another plan which, if it succeeds, should bring more direct benefit to the girls themselves is to give a training in infant welfare which will first qualify them for employment as nurses to European children—women are already so employed, but these are usually older women, and are said to be very unsatisfactory—and will later enable them to bring up their own children on more hygienic lines. In so far as this training con-centrates on improvements which would be practicable in a native home it should be very valuable ; but the scheme is not yet in operation and, in any case, will for some years to come be confined to a single school with a very small number of pupils.

CHAPTER IV

AN ORDINARY LIFE

2. MARRIAGE

ALTHOUGH those of the Baganda who like to dwell on the good old days when children obeyed their parents assert that, in those days, marriages were entirely arranged by the elders, their statements are belied by the actual native ceremonial of betrothal, which presupposes an agreement made first between the couple themselves and then ratified by the girl's parents. Girls had actually a good deal of freedom—indeed the tears which they are expected to shed at their marriage are sometimes explained as expressing grief at the loss of it—and many opportunities for making friends with boys at festival gatherings, the commonest of which were the termination of mourning and the rejoicings on the birth of twins, and in casual encounters on their expeditions to fetch wood and water. The festivals probably presented the best opportunity of all, since their main feature consisted of dancing, whose principal object was the display of physical attractions. There was also dancing when a chief gave a beer-drink, say, to entertain a guest, and girls who were known to dance well would be summoned to perform.

Rules of Exogamy

Freedom of choice was limited by the rules of exogamy, which prohibited marriage within a person's father's or mother's clan. This ruled out marriage with almost all the persons among whom a child was brought up. Accidental breach of these rules is often said to be impossible because a person's clan is indicated by the name. But, in fact, people are often called by the personal and not the clan name, and Christians nearly always use the Christian name, so that cases of involuntary breach may occur. The attitude towards it does not seem to vary with the distance of the relationship; it would be unlikely to occur nowadays except between persons who could not trace their genealogical connection, for in these days of letter-writing and motor transport people keep in touch with relatives all over the country. After the upheavals of the religious wars there were many cases where children captured when too young to know their family, and possibly before they had been given their clan name, married into their own clan—so much so that a proverb says it is inadvisable to look for a lost relative. But such a marriage was never believed to be visited by any terrible supernatural punishment. So long as the relationship of the couple was unknown, nothing happened; if it was discovered, they had to separate—but this rule, as has been mentioned, was overruled by the dignity of a mother of twins, who could even go on bearing children to her husband. The cases which were regarded as really serious were where a man turned out to have married his father's sister or maternal cross-cousin. A man who deliberately had sexual relations with either was described as *owe kive*— a phrase reserved for this context and denoting utter abomination—and put to death. But incest with a real sister—which it was admitted might occur—was atoned for in the same way as the seduction of an unmarried girl; while all that happened to a man who knowingly had intercourse with any other woman of his clan was that he was reprimanded for " disowning " her—not recognizing their relationship.

Betrothal

Marriage took place at the age of fifteen or sixteen. The girl signified her approval of a suitor by accepting various small presents, culminating in a new barkcloth.

The first formal declaration—made of course by arrangement with her—took the shape of a present of three small packets of salt, one to herself and one to each of her parents. If the father wished to refuse his consent, he did so at this stage by sending back the salt. It was sent to the girl's own father even if she was living with some other relative. If it was accepted, a date was then arranged for the formal ceremony of betrothal.

The central feature of this ceremony was the presentation of the suitor to the girl's parents. He went first to her *sengawe*, taking her a present of salt, and she led him to the girl's eldest brother, who received a gourd of beer. When some of this had been drunk they went on together, the suitor carrying a second gourd of beer, to the father's house, where were assembled such friends and relatives as could be collected. The girl, dressed in the new barkcloth he had given her, was present, but stood in a corner and did not speak except at the formal greeting. The brother presented the suitor, with jesting statements that he was trying to steal the girl and that his sister was rebelling against him and no longer wanted to cook for him. The *sengawe* knelt before him and said (speaking for the girl), *Nku·ze, ntuse okufumbirwa, nefuni·de obwesenze bwange.* ("I am grown up, my time has come to marry, I have found my master"—or, "my home," *obwesenze* being derived from the verb *kusenga*, to be some chief's man.) Thereupon the father called his wife and said to her, *Omwana wuyo atu·jemyeko, yefuni·de obwesenzebwe.* ("This child has rebelled against us; she has found her master.") The *sengawe*—again as the girl's representative—was then told, if she agreed to the marriage, to pour out the beer, which she and the suitor drank first. The amount of the bride-price [1] to be paid, with the distribution

---

[1] I use the term "bride-price" rather than select one of the alternatives which have recently been suggested, because each of these has been found open to some objection and it seems therefore better to keep to a word which is well established in anthropological literature. By its use I do not mean to suggest that there is any analogy between the marriage contract and the purchase of a commodity.

among his various relatives of that part of it which consisted in beer, was announced to the suitor by the girl's brother, having been fixed in advance in consultation by her father, brother, and *sengawe*. He was also told to produce four " sponsors " (*baza·de*, lit.: " parents "). These were older men from his village, who served in the first place as a guarantee of his respectability and an indication that he had friends who would protect him against violence. If he actually killed his wife they would be held responsible. This completed the betrothal ceremony. No informant knew of any promises as to future conduct, even of the vague kind described by Roscoe.[1] The gourd in which the beer was brought, with the banana leaf with which it was adorned and the head-pad on which it was carried, were kept in a safe place by the girl's parents until the marriage, lest some jealous person should get hold of them and use them to cause the death of the girl by sorcery. After this ceremony only the discovery that the suitor was guilty of sorcery could justify a refusal on the girl's part to go on with the marriage ; and only her flagrant infidelity could justify him in repudiating her. If the marriage was broken off through her fault, all the presents which he had brought were returned.

The Bride-Price

The transfer of the bride-price was, and still is, the essential act which legalizes the marriage. In the old days only slave-women could be married without it. Nowadays among the highly educated natives the girl's father waives his right to fix the amount, leaving it to the husband to give what he thinks fit, but even here there is no question of omitting the gifts. Compared with the bride-price, the ceremony in church is of secondary significance, even to the most religious. Normally the

---

[1] *The Baganda*, p. 88. Nor did I meet with any suggestion that frequent moving from one village to another was thought reprehensible in a husband.

banns are not cried until the bride-price has been paid, the presence of the bride's brother when the names are given to the clergyman being required as evidence of the payment, but occasionally missionaries insist on the legalization of an irregular union by a religious marriage. I witnessed one such case in a Catholic district ; one or two natives upheld the action of the priest, but the majority considered that it made the situation very much worse, changing a mere visit by the girl (which had lasted a year) into her forcible seizure by the man.

The nature of the bride-price has undergone various changes. At one time it consisted principally in beer, though the father could demand a barkcloth for himself or his son and any delicacy which he particularly fancied, such as meat, salt, or tobacco. Later cowries were added, and these presently came to be more important than the beer. At the present day the most important item is a money payment, though the beer is not always dispensed with, and either barkcloths or cotton garments are sometimes given. There were also certain gifts which did not form part of the bride-price proper : these were fixed by custom, not determined by the will of the girl's father, and were not returnable if the marriage was dissolved. Each of the last class of gifts was supposed to be given for some special reason or as a return for some specific action. Thus, on the wedding night, the girl's mother received a garment " to cover her breasts ", in token of the rules of avoidance which she would henceforth have to observe towards her son-in-law, and a parcel of 1,000 cowries called *kasimu*, from the verb *kusima*, to approve, " because he is pleased with her daughter." A large gourd of beer and a goat were also sent on the night itself to provide a feast which was eaten by the girl's family after her departure.

The persons to whom beer was sent were mainly brothers of the father, though he could order it to be given to any relative. Their share of it does not seem to have carried with it specific obligations such as are found among some other African peoples, though it is interesting that a modern native law, establishing a fine for the seduction of a betrothed girl, lays down that the charge may be brought by any of " those who drank the *mwenge* and shared the dowry ". (Official translation.) The cowries used also to be distributed among such relatives as lived in the same village ; nowadays, however, the father keeps the greater portion of the money he receives, only handing on a little to his own brothers and to the son who introduced the suitor to him.

Preparations for the Marriage

The bridegroom had also to prepare his house and furnish it with the simple requisites of Baganda domestic economy—mats, barkcloth hangings and bedclothes, beds, pots, knives, and hoes—and to provide a supply of barkcloths for his wife to wear, since her family were not supposed to give her anything whatever. He could be getting on with this at the same time as he collected the bride-price, and unless he was not ready the preparations for the wedding began as soon as the whole amount had been handed over.[1] He would collect the amount partly by petty trade and partly by the help of his father, who, if necessary, would appeal to his blood-brothers, but only in the last resort to clan relatives. In the case of later wives he could count on no help from his father, but would go to his own blood-brothers if necessary.

Such preparations for the marriage as were made on the girl's side were the concern of her female relatives, the father himself not being informed even of the date which had been fixed. A week before the wedding day the girl was formally placed in seclusion by her *sengawe*.

[1] Two very old men in different parts of the country described a quite different procedure in which the bridegroom first came and fetched his bride, leaving the *kasimu* on her mother's bed, where it was found ostensibly by chance, and that the girl's brothers then went to his house and took the bride-price (consisting in this version of goats) from him ; but nobody else had any recollection of such a custom.

During this time she stayed in one room, eating alone or with her mother, and was washed three times a day with warm water and smeared with butter, on the last day by her mother, on whose lap she sat. On the last morning she cut firewood, and fetched water from the spring and grass to strew the floor of the house ; this was regarded not as a ceremonial of leave-taking— since in many cases she would not in fact have grown up in her father's house—but as a demonstration that she knew how to perform these duties of a wife.

The Marriage Ceremonial

The bridal procession set out by night, the bride walking behind her *sengawe*, who held up a barkcloth by the edge so that it hung down over her head and covered her. For a woman to be seen going to her husband was a great disgrace, since normally this only happened when a girl already pregnant was sent to her lover ; and some old women for that reason still think Christian weddings shocking. She was also expected to weep loudly at losing her freedom and passing into the power of a man who could treat her just as he liked. To this day it is thought extremely immodest for a bride to smile, look about her, or speak ; the weeping is now done in private after the arrival at the husband's house, but it is still definitely expected.

The bride was also accompanied by her brother and by a young girl attendant (*mperekeze*), not necessarily a sister, whom she chose herself from among her relatives. A company of friends and relatives of the family went with them, the female members shouting admonitions to the bride to support her household by her own work, not by stealing from her neighbours. They were met about half-way by a party of the man's friends, who engaged them in a sham fight. If the man's friends won, the girl was handed over to them ; if not, they had to " buy " her with a payment of cowry-shells, supplied, of course, by the bridegroom. He himself was waiting nearer his house. When the procession met him the bride knelt down and her brother took her hand and placed it in her husband's; no word was spoken. This action was the central point of the marriage ceremonial. (See Plate V.)

The bride's party then went home, all except the *mperekeze*, who stayed with her for four days to soften the parting from her own people. She was described as the husband's " second wife ", and if he wanted actually to marry her this was taken as a compliment by her family. It seems to have been quite common for her to become pregnant by him, and such an event was not attended with the disgrace which customarily attached to it.

The bridegroom had to give a number of further presents on his wedding day. The bride's *sengawe* and brother each received either a barkcloth or its equivalent in cowries on parting from her, " to show them what a good *muko* (relative-in-law) they have got "; according to some accounts the procession made frequent halts, at each of which the *sengawe* received cowries; and every stage of the bride's installation in her new home was accompanied by a gift of cowries. She could refuse until he gave her the amount she asked, a proceeding which was supposed to test his love for her; and sometimes it was two days before the marriage was actually consummated. She demanded " payment " for entering his house, sitting down, eating, washing, getting into bed, and letting him join her. The present given to induce her to eat was sent to her mother; the rest she kept.

On the day after the marriage was consummated the girl's *sengawe* and a sister of the husband came to inquire if she had proved to be a virgin. If she was, the barkcloth on which the couple had slept was taken back to her parents, smeared with butter, and a goat was sent to them as an expression of thanks for looking after her properly. There was no question of any refund of the bride-price should she prove not to be a virgin.

On this day also, the couple were washed by the husband's grandmother with water mixed with magical herbs in a large banana leaf, which was then taken away by two children, who carried it off without looking back and threw it away in the long grass.[1]

Four days after the marriage, two of her sisters went to see her, taking a present of plantains and various relishes—mushrooms, simsim, and pea-nuts. This visit was called "taking the butter [with which the bride was smeared] from the road". It was regarded as very important as indicating that the bride had relatives who were interested in her welfare. The *mperekeze* went home with them, taking with her a barkcloth as a return for her services.

The bride remained in seclusion for a period of two or three weeks—longer if her husband was a person of importance. This period was not a time of mourning, as is sometimes stated, but was closely analogous to the European honeymoon. During it the bride did no work and was treated as the guest of her husband and his sisters, who did all the work of the house for her ; it was once described to me as "a time for looking nice ". She might look no one in the face but her husband, and when she went outside for such necessary purposes as washing she was covered with a barkcloth by her husband's sister in the same way as she had been by her *sengawe* on her wedding night.

The conclusion of this period and her entry upon her duties as a wife was marked by two ceremonial visits to her own and her husband's parents. The visit to her own parents was called "taking back the butter ". On a summons from her father, the bride, accompanied by one of her husband's sisters, went back to her parents' house, taking with her the actual package of butter from which her mother had smeared

---

[1] Roscoe's statement that the girl was washed all over *before* marriage by the youth's female relatives, in order to see if she had any disease, is possibly based on a confusion of these two customs. I could find no confirmation of it whatever.

her face on her wedding day, wrapped in a new barkcloth. Here she was provided with all the materials for a feast— bunches of plantains, numbers of fowls, goats, cows if her father was a rich man, salt, simsim, and mushrooms. These were carried back for her by a number of boys and girls, friends and relatives, under the presidency of her *sengawe*. The procession attracted general attention ; the burdens were carried in pairs of baskets as was the custom with presents to persons of importance, and the bunches of plantains balanced upright on the heads of the bearers instead of being tied up in leaves in the ordinary way. People who met the procession clapped their hands and congratulated it. On arrival they knelt and set down their loads, as would be done with an offering to a chief, while the wife gave a fowl into her husband's hands.

The cooking of the feast was a formal demonstration to the bride—though of course at this stage she had in fact nothing to learn about cooking. She herself took no part in it beyond peeling the first plantain, after which she handed the knife to her *sengawe*, who directed the whole of the proceedings. The feast was eaten by the bridegroom and his friends, the bride and her friends taking no part in it. When they had finished their work they returned home, the husband placing cowries in the empty baskets.

Next the bride, accompanied by a sister of her husband, paid a formal visit to his parents. Here she performed the duties of a daughter, fetching water and wood and hoeing in the banana-grove. This visit is sometimes said to be " to teach her to dig " as the other was " to teach her to cook ". At the conclusion of each task she was given cowries ; the hoeing had to go on until they were brought to her by her mother-in-law, and the latter, if she did not like her, might leave her at work a long time. When she left her father-in-law gave her a barkcloth and her mother-in-law a knife for cutting down and peeling plantains ; she was also given a goat to cook for her husband, to emphasize the fact that she should never cook him a meal of plantains only without any kind of relish. Next day her husband gave her a hoe and she settled down to her duties.

These two formal visits were supposed to mark the conclusion of the bridal period and the beginning of her duties as wife, but it seems that even in the past they were sometimes postponed so long that the couple could not wait till then to begin their normal married life. Either the father or the husband might have difficulty in collecting the necessary provisions or cowries. At the present day, when the provisions for the feast are very often bought in the market, postponement for a long time is fairly common. Until this visit has been paid, however, the bride's parents should not come to her house, nor receive presents of food from her; and during this period the avoidances of relatives-in-law, though theoretically these should be respected at all times, are supposed to be observed particularly strictly.

The visit to the husband's parents could be made although the " taking back the butter " had not been done. But this, too, was sometimes postponed or omitted altogether. It could also be made to a brother of the father—who is " called father "—if he happened to live nearer. Sometimes the husband merely took his bride on an ordinary visit to introduce her to his parents, and the whole ceremonial was omitted, while if the real father was dead it was not thought essential to pay the formal visit to his heir. I observed one case where, the father being dead, the visit to the heir was not made till three years after the marriage, and another where, rather than go seventeen miles to see her own father-in-law, the bride paid her respects to " another father ", whose house was only six miles away.

At two stages during the ceremonial the bride's parents performed the *kukuza* rite—after their daughter had left them, and again when the bride " brought back the butter ". Only her actual parents could do this, and to this day if the mother has left her husband she is expressly fetched back for it and may stay with him for the whole period between the two occasions.

Modern Marriages

In modern marriages the ceremonial is losing its importance, while the outlay expected of the bridegroom at every stage has increased. Most men expect to start their married life in debt, or at least having spent their last farthing. The suitor now begins his formal addresses by writing letters to the girl, her parents, and her *sengawe*, possibly also to her brothers and sisters, and each of these letters is expected to contain four or five shillings. The outfit of clothing which he gives the girl now consists of cotton goods, and has to be bought from the Indian merchants. The actual bride-price may be anything from 90 to 300 shillings as well as some cotton garments. Instead of the beer brought on the wedding night, some fathers prefer a tin of paraffin for lamps, which costs about eight shillings. In furnishing the house, the youth is not expected to refuse his betrothed anything which she may ask for—cups, plates, kettles, tea-pots, a basin, a large aluminium cooking-pot, blankets and sheets, and so forth. The soap with which she is washed in the final week and the cheap pomade which is now used instead of butter during that period are provided by him. He has also to pay the musicians without whom no bridal procession is now complete. He is not expected to wait for the marriage before assuming the obligations towards the girl and her relatives which the marriage will make definitely binding. Thus, if she is ill, he must buy her tea and sugar to make the sticky beverage which the Baganda call tea, and which is their principal comfort in sickness, and if one of her relatives dies he should bring a barkcloth to bury him in and beer to console the bereaved. The position as explained to me is that he is under no binding obligation to give such gifts, but that if he did not do so " she would think he did not love her ".

Modern marriages have their definite ritual in which the European elements are already firmly fixed by tradition. All marriages, even if there is no Christian ceremony, take place by day, and when one sees the gay procession of women in bright silk stuffs and men in newly-washed cotton or tussore silk *kanzus* winding along the paths from one village to the next, one cannot help feeling that the change is an improvement. The only blot from the æsthetic point of view is the bride herself, who is invariably dressed in a white dress of European cut, white stockings, and shoes, with a veil which is often made of cheap mosquito netting, and, if she has a long way to go in the sun, is covered by a man's felt hat. For the husband a complete Arab costume used to be the fashion, and it is still hired by those who cannot afford a smart European suit. A white tarboosh is absolutely *de rigueur* in any case.

Most of the minor ceremonies surrounding the actual wedding are now obsolete. The bridegroom still sometimes has to " buy " the bride's consent to enter his house, the payments at each stage varying from about thirty cents to one shilling, and some informants told me that the inquiry as to her virginity was still held ; others, however, said that it would be futile to worry about the point as she would almost certainly not be a virgin. The one thing which is regarded as unpardonable is for a girl to be caught with a lover after she is betrothed. In this case, the marriage is almost always broken off and such gifts as have been given returned. The lover is liable under a native law for damages of 200 shillings, but this is not often claimed.

The wedding-feast is a new development since it became the custom for the wedding to take place by day. It consists of tea or beer, sometimes of pieces of dry bread and occasionally of an iced cake ordered from Kampala. Along with the hire of the wedding-garments

and the payment of drummers and musicians, this feast
may cost as much as the bride-price itself. Friends
sometimes help the bridegroom with contributions of milk
and sugar. The guests sit under a leaf shelter set up
outside the house, the bride and bridegroom sitting in
solemn state behind a table covered with a cloth and
receiving the congratulations of their friends. After a
short time the bride retires within the house and sits
down in a dark corner. No one may now speak to her
without giving her a few cents, and even then she can
only reply to their greetings in a whisper. The female
relatives who have come with her go into the house and
stay for a few minutes ; then they take leave of her and
go home, not staying to share in the festivities. The
bride then goes into the inner room, takes off all her
finery, which is returned at once to the Goanese from
whom it was hired, puts on a barkcloth, and begins the
ceremonial weeping. Her husband joins her at sunset,
but the rest of the party may go on drinking and dancing
till late at night.

While the ritual surrounding the actual passing of the
bride to her husband has thus been modified to suit
Christian ceremonial and European ideas of what a
wedding should be, the customs which complete the
inauguration of her married life are followed as before.
The period of seclusion is now shorter than it used to be ;
in the case of Protestants, the couple are married on a
Saturday and the bride makes her first public appearance
at church on the Sunday week. Though her seclusion
has been described by a missionary writer as " the time
allowed her to bemoan her hard fate ",[1] there has been no
attempt to put down the custom. Its essential function
—the reservation of a period free from the complications
of household duties for adjustment to the intimacies of
married life—is something which is regarded as indispensable to a European marriage, and is even more so
in a monogamous than it was in a polygamous household.

[1] Hattersley, *The Baganda at Home*, p. 214.

The subsequent visits to the bride's and bridegroom's parents contain nothing objectionable by European standards, and to native eyes are an affirmation of the bonds and obligations of kinship whose abandonment would indicate a complete disregard of family ties in the younger generation. The fact that they are now liable to be postponed for so long is certainly a sign that these ties are not as strong as they used to be.

Marriage as Linking Two Families

The marriage contract not only binds husband and wife but links each of them by certain obligations to the relatives of the other. These are of two kinds—those towards relatives of the older and of the same generation. Those of the older generation have to be treated with respect, and, if they are of the opposite sex, with avoidance. The husband and his wife's mother, as well as all women whom she calls mother, call one another *muko*. The rules of behaviour between persons who stand in this relationship are all such as to prevent their coming into close contact, and thus to guard against the friction which seems inevitably to result where a married couple are expected to maintain intimate relations with one another's parents.[1] They may not take one another by the hand, pass one another in a doorway, look one another straight in the face (the woman should cover her head or fix her eyes upon the ground, and if they meet in the road would turn aside), or be left alone in speech together. They may not eat together, nor may one eat food which the other has left. A *muko* may not touch the corpse of a *muko* nor throw earth into his grave. In fact, between such persons the behaviour permanently prescribed is that required of a woman towards all men on occasions when she has to observe sexual taboos.

[1] This explanation of mother-in-law avoidances was suggested by Miss C. H. Wedgwood in a paper read before the British Association for the Advancement of Science in 1931.

These rules hold good even after the marriage is dissolved, and breach of them is believed to afflict the guilty person with palsy. Though I was repeatedly told that they are now disregarded—one reason given being that it was impossible to keep them when travelling by bus—I noticed one or two striking instances of their observance. Thus, at a mortuary ceremony, where I was sitting in the doorway of the cooking-house with Yokana Waswa, a strange woman came up with a bundle of leaves, in which the morning meal had been cooked, to put them away ready for the evening. Half a dozen people called out, " Don't go in. That's your *muko*," and she had to take her bundle somewhere else. Again, at the naming of twins which I saw at Matale, the *bako*, instead of putting their offerings of coffee-berries into the hands of the parents, laid them on the ground for them to pick up. Doubtless the rules are more strictly observed on ceremonial occasions than at any other time. I also remember a conversation in which real horror was expressed at my statement that in Europe a man could touch his mother-in-law.

The rules of behaviour between the wife and her husband's father and " other fathers " are the same, though she calls them not *muko* but *sezalawe*, a word derived from *kuzala*, to bear, which emphasizes their relationship to her husband and possibly her status as a member of their group.

The husband and the wife's male relatives of the same generation call one another *muko·domi*. They also must treat one another with respect, but the respect is expressed by means of gifts. At least a fowl must be killed when a *muko·domi* is entertained, and, when a wife attends mortuary ceremonies in her own clan, the husband, when he comes to fetch her home, must bring a gourd of beer to the male relative in charge of the proceedings. It is to these men that the wife will appeal if she wishes to leave her husband, and it is therefore to his interest to be punctilious in respect for these obligations. In particular, he must retain the favour of the brother who handed his wife over to him (whom the natives call the *real muko·domi*), for the latter continues to act as a sort of guardian to the wife. Any question of the dissolution of the marriage goes in the first instance to him ; in the past the claim to the children was his affair, and if a child died and the father failed to notify him of the death he would hold the father responsible for it and demand compensation.

Organization of the Household

In the days when polygamy was general, the first wife occupied a definitely superior position. Only she was married with the full ceremonial, though informants differed as to which ceremonies were omitted in the case of later wives. She was called *Saba·du*, the same title given to a chief's right-hand man ; she was responsible for the performance of all magical rites which her husband's welfare required ; she settled quarrels both between the other wives and between them and the husband ; in his absence, she could have one of the other wives punished for adultery ; and, in the case of a chief, the children who were sent to be brought up in his household lived in her house. In a poor household where there were few or no slaves she could also order the other wives to fetch wood or water for her.

A chief gave titles to all his wives, whose meaning would seem to imply the allotment of special tasks to each—Cook, Brewer, Keeper of the Wardrobe, Lighter of the Pipe, and so forth—but which actually merely indicated an order of precedence. Each new wife was given her title in the presence of the others on her emergence from seclusion. A wife who behaved badly could be deprived of her title and another promoted to it. The title most highly prized was *Kabe·ja* ("Little Princess "), which designated the favourite.

The division of labour within the household, and the respective rights of husband and wife, have changed little in modern times, as far as theory goes, though the modern disregard by wives of their obligations is generally lamented. Broadly speaking, the man is responsible for the house itself, for clothing the family, and for brewing beer, and the wife for the food-supply and for making mats and baskets. Such household objects as have to be bought may be bought by either. In the past, cultivation was entirely the woman's province ; the husband did not regard it as his duty to help her with the preliminary clearing of the ground, though I think it probable that, where he could, he would have this done for her by slaves. It must be remembered that the man had duties to perform outside the household, for his chief and the king. Women took pride in this work, and in a large household cultivation was the last task to be handed over to servants or slaves. Wives of great chiefs, though they might leave the root-crops to others, still had each her own plantation of bananas which she looked after herself. For a woman to feel too ill for this work—except for a few days before the birth of a child—is even now regarded as an admission that she is at death's door.

In modern times the cultivation of crops for sale is largely done by men, and most women regard such work, if they do it, not as a duty but as a means of earning money for themselves. Often husband and wife have separate patches of cotton, and the proceeds of the wife's are entirely her own property ; while I knew a wife who actually left her husband because he told her to work on his cotton patch. It is quite untrue that the introduction of economic crops has simply meant more work for women. Primarily they are the source from which the man pays his taxes, in which his wife is under no obligation to help him ; in the second place, now that European stuffs are popular and barkcloths made for sale by not more than three or four men in each village, they are the modern source of the household's clothing, and again, for this reason, belong to the province of the man, unless he earns the necessary money in other ways.

In the ordinary partnership of daily life, the wife is by no means completely subordinate. Yokana Waswa described the position by saying that the husband was the master of the house and the wife his steward. The house is his because he built it, but it is her duty to look after everything in it. The crops which she has planted are hers, and any surplus after the family is provided for is entirely at her disposal. The one exception to this rule is the type of banana used for beer; these cannot be sold without the husband's permission.

The husband is expected to explain at the outset the household routine which he wants to have observed—times for meals, his favourite relishes, and so forth. Once laid down, this is not varied; if he attempts to make innovations later, or fails to come to meals at the agreed times, his wife is justified in leaving him. Other just grounds of offence are that he does not give her enough clothes, or that he does not provide the fowl which custom demands when her male relatives visit her. The duties to which the husband attaches most importance are that his wife should wash his feet every night, that she should never cook him a meal without any relish, and that when she goes away from home she should not stay away longer than the time fixed by him.

Matrimonial Dissensions

The husband used to express disapproval of minor offences by refusing to eat the food cooked by his wife. The quarrel was then discussed before some old women of the village, and if his offence was thought to be justified the wife had to go home and get from her brother a fowl to cook for him by way of amends; incidentally, she got a scolding from her brother for having made this necessary. But this custom is now obsolete. In the days of polygamy, it was rare for a husband to drive his wife away, as if he disliked her all he had to do was to neglect her. Chiefs sent home wives discovered in adultery as a more merciful punishment than killing or mutilating them. But divorce occurred far more often through the wife leaving her husband.

The wife is expected to be particularly long-suffering as regards what we should consider major offences. That she will be beaten from time to time is taken for granted, and is not considered to justify her in running away unless her life is actually in danger. It still happens sometimes that a man beats his wife to death, and, if he is thought to have had a good reason, he is not severely condemned by public opinion.

A girl is brought up to believe that the dignity of the mistress of a house demands decent concealment of dissension within it. (*Ofuga enyumbayo, obi kako bingi*— " You are mistress of your house and must cover up much in it ".) Above all, she must never quarrel with her husband in public. One of the commonest complaints against modern wives is that they are too ready to tell tales of their husbands. If the wife is the partner who is expected to be submissive, she is also not without the consciousness of a certain superiority which enables her to make allowances. The attitude towards an unfaithful husband may be summed up in such phrases as " We know what men are "—a literal translation— and " If you are sensible, you won't make a fuss ". If the husband's fancy lights on a friend of his wife, a reasonable woman ought to be pleased and even act as a go-between. But if the husband does not take his wife into his confidence she has a right to feel offended. In this case, his method is to bring his mistress into the house while his wife is away fetching wood or water. The wife should put up with it two or three times, but after that she can protest and leave him.

Divorce

The proper course for an injured wife is to go to the brother who gave her away. Unless the husband is willing to let her go, he goes to look for her, taking a gourd of beer, or nowadays four shillings, the price of a gourd of average size, as a mark of respect to her family. If this gift is not brought, even the native clergy uphold the wife in refusing to return. Once the beer is drunk, the wife must go back ; but she will make her brother refuse to accept it till the quarrel has been discussed. Both sides put their case before such relatives as are at hand, and even if it is agreed that the husband is in the wrong they try to persuade the wife to go back to him. She cannot be forced to do so, but the marriage is not dissolved unless the husband formally demands the bride-price back ; the wife's relatives cannot offer to refund it and so set her free. A man will sometimes wait two or three years before finally giving up his wife ; but when the actual divorce took place the custom was formerly that the bride-price was returned whoever was in the wrong, the only exception being that a man whose wife had left him because she found that he was a sorcerer would not have the face to claim the goods. The most common reason for a wife to leave her husband without justification was, of course, that she wished to go to another man. In this case she could not go straight to him, but had to go home and be formally married from her brother's house and the bride-price paid for her. Her family would naturally try to make the new husband's bride-price cover the amount that had to be refunded to the other, but there was no question of the second husband paying it direct to the first—one of the many points which demonstrate the fallacy of arguing from this payment that women are bought and sold like chattels.

When the marriage is dissolved, whatever the reason, the children remain with the father. The wife when she leaves her husband is entitled to take with her all her own property, though she often gives it away among her friends to save the trouble of carrying it. Such property includes all the household goods and clothes which her husband has given her, and anything which she may have received from her own relatives or bought with her own earnings. The only exceptions are the cooking-pot and water-pot, which in the past were surrounded by magical beliefs that are now almost forgotten. To break one of these pots was an action which had to be formally atoned, and—though it was impossible to obtain enough data to speak positively on the point—they seem to have been thought to be so closely connected with the welfare of the house and its master that it would be fatal to remove them. But now that the clay pots have been replaced by aluminium saucepans and paraffin-tins for drawing water this prohibition may have died out altogether.

Divorce and Bride-Price in Modern Conditions

The bride-price in pre-European days was a guarantee for the stability of the marriage and an inducement to the woman's relatives to use their influence to prevent its dissolution for frivolous reasons. In modern times, however, its position has considerably changed. The main reason for this is, of course, that a Christian marriage is theoretically indissoluble, while from the legal point of view natives who have contracted Christian marriages are subject to the same law as Europeans and can therefore only be granted a divorce by the High Court. Since the native courts cannot dissolve a marriage, they clearly cannot order the refund of the bride-price ; and it seems that they refuse to do so even in the case of marriages by native custom. Most natives believe that this is done by the orders of the British Government, but actually there is no British provision whatever to prevent the refund of the bride-price in a marriage by native custom. It is still often voluntarily returned, and when the question is considered from the point of the injured husband most natives would agree that this is the only decent course. But the same people, when they put themselves in the father's place, regard the bride-price as simply his legitimate return for the trouble of bringing up his daughter. Kanywamagule refused to let his daughter become a nun for this reason, and, when I told him that we had no bride-price in England, asked, " Then do they bring up girls for nothing ? " It would still be quite unfair to say that fathers regard their daughters simply as a profitable commodity, but now that the bride-price is sheer gain to them they are rather willing than otherwise to see a daughter change her husband three or four times, and the disgrace which they would formerly have felt, though it has not disappeared altogether, is considerably lightened by this consideration.

From the point of view of the young man contemplating matrimony, the money payment demanded nowadays is a much heavier burden than the gifts of the old times. He may be able to raise it by contributions from his relatives, but if he is earning wages he is often expected to raise the whole amount himself, and the possibility of its being a dead loss to him, with the many attractive alternative ways of spending money, is a strong deterrent to early marriage.[1] One of the main incentives in the past, that an unmarried man had no status in the community, " no place of his own," and could not have his own house but always lived under parental authority, has now vanished. A man is now regarded as adult not when he marries but when, at eighteen, he becomes liable for poll-tax. Family ties are still stronger than in many parts of Africa where wage-labour has revolutionized native society. But there is just the

---

[1] It may be asked why the bride-price does not fall in accordance with the law of supply and demand. The answer is that the Baganda do not make the constant calculations of profit and loss which are assumed as the basis of economic laws in modern civilization. Moreover, though they may regard the bride-price as a welcome addition to their income, no man would dream of trying to marry off a daughter because he wanted to raise money for a given purpose. It seems obvious that fathers must, in the long run, reduce their demands, but experience does not seem to teach them to ask less at the outset. They sometimes hold out for years, while a daughter leaves home and goes to her lover, or carries on an openly recognized liaison with a man whom every one speaks of as her husband.

difference that the young man now normally leaves home to earn his tax-money—and, after that is paid, the price of the bicycle and the European clothes which are every young native's ambition—in an employment which he has probably chosen for himself without consulting his father, and comes back a person who has stood on his own feet without any family background. He usually does come back and build his house near his father or some other older relative ; but, if the father then moves to another village, the son more often than not stays where he is. He is then, of course, entirely free from any control, and can enjoy the satisfaction of irregular liaisons without the responsibilities of marriage or the burden of earning the bride-price.

Polygamy and Christianity

Polygamy is dying out for the same reasons that make early marriage unpopular—the expense of marriage, the expense of bringing up children, who now have to be not only dressed in European clothing but sent to schools which do not give education free, and in the case of the wealthy man the many other satisfactions which compete for his money. Moreover, the latest estimated census figures show, instead of the former preponderance of females, a slight preponderance of males. But the Christian code of sexual morality is by no means as firmly established as the missionaries could wish. Except among the few natives in the capital who are constantly in touch with missionary thought, there is no disapproval whatever of polygamy. Most monogamous wives rather envy the woman who is free to go visiting every other week ; and though I did meet one woman who advanced the argument that two wives can never agree, I observed pairs of wives who seemed to be the best of friends and, if anything, in league against the husband.

The missions are willing so far to meet the native point of view as to say that they have no objection to a

native having two wives provided he does not call himself
a Christian ; they have even put the point to the king,
whose bad example to his people they much deplore.
But the time for such an argument is past. Christianity
is now definitely the religion of the Baganda ; it is taken
for granted in exactly the same unthinking way as it is
by many Europeans. It is also an inevitable con-
comitant of education, since all education is given through
the missions ; and every Muganda now wants education.
Lastly, the Baganda have been taught to despise such
pagans as are left, and to regard Christianity as an
integral part of the superiority in the social scale whose
material indications are a corrugated iron roof, a motor
bicycle, and a suit of European clothes. For a Muganda
of the present generation to declare that he preferred
not to be a Christian would require at least as much
moral courage as for an Englishman a century ago to
proclaim himself an atheist.

Many of them, however, have given the question of
polygamy serious consideration. Catholic natives, in
particular, very much dislike being excommunicated, and
a good many try to find arguments to convince themselves that the priests are not justified in so penalizing
them. Aluizi Zalembekiya quoted to me, with an air
of finality, the text " And God said, Be fruitful and
multiply ". The commonest argument, that advanced
by the notorious Malaki, who founded a new sect some
half-dozen years ago, is that monogamy is simply a
European custom and not in the least essential to
Christianity—an argument with which one feels much
sympathy.

The Christian women of the capital, supported by
European missionaries, took the opportunity of a recent
case of intestacy to make a public protest against
official disregard of the Christian code. The Lukiko
(the king's council) appointed as successor to a wealthy
chief his son by his second wife. The women went in
a body to the Lukiko and demanded that the king should

order that in case of intestacy only the eldest son of the first wife should inherit, and that no one might leave property to the children of any but this wife. The king acceded to the first but not to the second request, and I happened to meet with one of the first cases under the new law at Kisimula. Whether it will lead to greater respect for the marriage-tie remains to be seen.

CHAPTER V

ECONOMIC ORGANIZATION

Up to this point we have considered the family and household as the setting in which an individual grows up and is prepared for the serious business of life. With the constitution of a new household by the marriage contract, and the beginning for two persons of their life as adult members of the community, we must turn to its other aspect, as the group whose joint activities supply its members with the main necessities of life. This will lead us on to questions of other economic phenomena in Baganda society—the activities which involved co-operation with persons outside the household, the means of obtaining by exchange goods which the household itself could not supply, and the circulation of wealth by other means than of economic exchange.

The division of duties between husband and wife has been briefly mentioned, but we have now to examine the range of products with which the household had to be provided and their sources, the processes by which they were obtained, with a closer scrutiny of the system of division of labour within and outside the household, and the extent to which work falls into a routine determined by climate and seasons.

INVENTORY OF OBJECTS PRODUCED

Though the Baganda have acquired certain new tastes in food under European influence, there has been no change in this respect fundamental enough to introduce new forms of cultivation or to displace the old food-crops, and this is one of the aspects of native life in which the past is most alive.

The staple food is bananas, which are eaten fresh ; there is seldom any provision made for the storage of food, and what there is is copied from recent alien immigrants. The native beer is also brewed from bananas. The principal supplementary food is sweet potatoes ; a little taro and a few yams and vegetable marrows are also grown to provide alternatives to bananas in case of shortage. Ground-nuts, beans, simsim, and maize are eaten as relishes with the main meal or casually between meals. Other relishes are made from the fruit or leaves of various wild plants which grow either among the bananas or in the long grass, and from the enormous mushrooms which may appear anywhere. Millet is grown to ferment the beer. Every household has to have its supply of coffee-berries to offer to guests, and this used to be also the regular offering to gods and their prophets, but coffee was not grown on a large scale in pre-European days, and possibly they depended upon wild plants ; a few plants of tobacco are also grown by many households, but receive little attention.

As a food-crop, the banana occupies a unique position. The word for " food ", when used without qualification, definitely means bananas, and people begin to talk about " hunger " as soon as there is any prospect of a shortage. The root-crops just mentioned are looked upon as much inferior substitutes ; sweet potatoes supply a newly-established household whose bananas have not yet come into bearing, or are eaten when a drought has withered the bananas or a series of hailstorms blown them down. The other foods of this kind are often given to children.

The banana has also many subsidiary uses. The leaves are used when green to wrap up any kind of parcel, to wrap food in for cooking, to serve it while it is still hot, to hold liquid food, sometimes to drink from or as spoons to feed children with liquids, as stoppers for any vessel in which water or beer is carried, and sometimes to cover the head as a protection against sun or rain. I have also seen one used as a funnel for petrol. When dancing it is usual to take a leaf which has already been slit into streamers by the wind and tie it round the waist so that the streamers float out behind as the dancer moves ; and when beer is presented for any ceremonial purpose each gourd has a leaf of the same kind tied round its neck. The dried outer layers of fibre, which peel off in the same way as the skins of an onion, can be used while they are still pliable as a sort of tape, to tie up parcels or bundles of grass, lash together branches to make shelves, bind up wounds, sometimes to tie together the framework of a house, even in emergencies to tie up prisoners. The strips as they peel off are four or five inches wide and about six feet long, and by using whole strips it is possible to make large parcels which are both neat and durable. They are also tied round trees or led from gutters—where these exist—to collect rain-water in pots placed to catch it. When they are rather drier, they can be twisted into little bags which are used to store such things as coffee-berries, butter, or salt, or to carry eggs. They may be wound round forked sticks to make nests for hens, and in very wet weather are used as leggings. The withered leaves are sometimes used to thatch ordinary houses, especially cooking-houses, always for the temporary houses built for visitors who are prevented by rules of avoidance from sleeping in a house, sometimes to cover graves, and occasionally to burn. Finally the juicy inner pith forms a sponge which provides its own water.

Cattle, sheep, goats, and fowls supply the meat which is eaten on special occasions, and the prescribed gifts which we have been constantly meeting with in previous chapters. The poorest household has two or three fowls and a goat ; a better one might have six or eight goats. Nowadays, the number of cattle has decreased very much through sleeping-sickness and other epidemics, while the Baganda can no longer replenish their herds from those of their neighbours, and one sees very few except in Kyagwe. To have even one cow is rare, and very few people have large herds. The largest that I heard of numbered twenty-five, though it is true the owner said he did not consider that many. But now that the most prized possession is no longer cattle but land, which some men have acquired by selling cattle, and that there are so many alternative forms of wealth, this is no indication of the distribution in the old days. How much milk was drunk before the Baganda became addicted to tea, I do not know. It was sometimes given to children whose mothers had died. Butter is used only as a cosmetic and occasionally to smear on wounds. The meat supply is supplemented by hunting, and every man who does much hunting owns a dog. There is a little fishing in the rivers, but fish were always mainly an imported article. As far as food is concerned, the only new habit universally adopted is that of drinking tea. Dry bread is regarded as a great treat, but I have only seen it eaten once, at a wedding.

A number of trees are planted for various household uses. In the old days the *mutuba*, a species of fig, from whose bark garments and bedding were made, was so much a necessity of every household that the phrase "to plant barkcloth-trees for him" was used as a metaphor to describe the installation of a chief. With the advent of imported cotton goods, the barkcloth-tree has lost this position and one now sees relatively few. The Cape lilac supplies wood for building and furniture, the castor-oil plant for firewood. All these are often planted to form a kind of fence between cultivated land and the public path, as are one or two trees which have no other uses, but they are not regarded as boundary-marks. Gourds are also grown to serve as vessels of all kinds.

In the matter of housing, furniture, and tools, there have been so many changes that the old-fashioned household must be described by itself, as something obsolete. The house was built of a framework of elephant-grass canes supported on posts, fastened with a kind of strong creeper or with osiers, and thatched with grass, dry banana-leaves, or occasionally papyrus. The floor was strewn with grass. The furniture consisted of wooden stools, wooden bedsteads, skins and raffia mats to sit on, barkcloth hangings and blankets, and rough shelves of branches lashed together. Utensils were a hoe, a large knife for cutting branches or canes or for cutting down bananas, a smaller knife for general use, clay pots for cooking and fetching water, a large wooden trough for making beer, gourds for holding all kinds of liquids, raffia baskets of varying shapes and sizes, ropes and hunting-nets of wild sisal, mallets for beating barkcloths, and a rough needle for stitching them. Clothing consisted of barkcloths and skins— the latter mainly for children—and wooden shoes worn in muddy weather. Weapons were spears, sticks, and a shield of wood faced with wicker-work. The only form of jewellery was the bracelet ; these were made of cow-hair usually covered with brass wire, and ornamented with little iron or brass beads ; one occasionally sees ivory bracelets. Out of this list only the ornaments, metal articles, shields, and pots were the work of specialists.

THE CALENDAR OF WORK

Europeans divide the year into two wet and two dry seasons, roughly speaking of three months each. The two dry seasons are not exactly alike, that from December to February being hotter and drier, while a good many rainy days are expected during the season from June to August. Neither dry season is expected to be completely dry ; a whole month without rain is uncommon enough to be regarded as a misfortune. The difference between the two seasons is expressed in the native reckoning in the form of different names for the two rains, the rains of Dumbi (September–November) being regarded as longer than those of Togo (March–May). The dry seasons had no names but were simply called harvesting seasons. Thus the full twelve-month cycle was recognized, though it does not seem that there was any difference in the crops planted in the two seasons, and a " year " by Baganda reckoning was the period of one seed-time and one harvest.

There was no attempt to co-ordinate the activities of a whole village in any seasonal pursuit, and it is therefore impossible to draw up an agricultural calendar with anything like the precision that can be attained in dealing with communities where work is carried out at prescribed times under the orders of a leader. One can merely speak generally of the activities which characterized the different seasons. It has been mentioned already that the year now centres round the cultivation of cotton, a crop which takes nine months to ripen. This has made the difference that, of the other crops, those which need more attention, millet and simsim, are now grown in the period between the harvesting of cotton and the sowing of the new crop.

Bearing this modification in mind, it is safe to speak in the present tense of the seasonal routine of work. Roughly speaking, the rains of course are times of planting and the dry seasons of harvesting. But the preparation of the ground for planting the new crops begins during the dry season, when the grass is cut down and burnt. Other activities of the dry season are burning down the long grass, housebuilding, and making barkcloths, which is better done in dry weather because the finished cloth has to be spread in the sun to dry. For building the dry season was always preferable, because the elephant-grass which provides the cane framework of a house had reached its maximum height, and nowadays it is doubly so because a house is built in a series of separate days' work sometimes lasting over weeks, and an unfinished house runs less risk of being damaged by rain. The modern mud wall has to be built after the rain has begun.

The planting of seasonal crops begins as soon as there has been enough rain to soften the ground; three successive days are considered enough. The next six weeks or so are the busiest period of the whole cycle, partly because of the advantage of getting the seeds in in the first part of the rainy season when the rain is heavier, partly because on cool cloudy days it is possible to work right up till noon.

After the main crops are in attention is turned to supplementary work—planting out banana shoots, barkcloth and castor-oil trees, and any of the plants of which only a few are grown at a time, such as coffee where this is not grown for sale, marrows, taro, and yams.

In the next period the crops have to be thinned, and then comes a stage where all the work that has to be done is weeding; this, however, is no light matter, for in the fertile climate of Uganda weeds flourish exceedingly.

There is no fixed period for the beginning of harvest, as there is none for the beginning of sowing, but harvesting goes on all through the dry season. Most crops are not harvested all at once, but small quantities are taken in as they ripen or are required. The exceptions are simsim and millet; in their case, the whole crop is gathered at once because before it is ready for use the grain has to be dried and winnowed.

This completes the cycle from seed-time to harvest; though it must always be borne in mind that, owing to the absence of any co-ordination of work, there is no sharp break between one such cycle and the next, and some people are always beginning a new planting before their neighbours' crops are harvested. The contrast between the old calendar and the new, with the cotton crop as its pivotal point, can be best shown by the following table, which gives in parallel columns the characteristic activities of each month before and after the adoption of cotton-growing.

CALENDAR

	PRE-EUROPEAN	MODERN
March.	Clearing ground. Planting all kinds of crops. Planting banana slips.	Planting millet and simsim on old cotton patches. Planting coffee.
April.	Clearing ground. Thinning and weeding crops already planted. Sweet potatoes ripen and begin to be dug up. Fishing in floodwater.	Clearing for next season's cotton. Burning old plants. Planting sweet potatoes on patches.
May.	Weeding. Maize, beans, etc., ripen. Harvesting millet and simsim begins.	Clearing new ground for cotton. Fetching seed from ginneries. Burning old plants.
June.	Weeding. Harvesting. Working barkcloth.	Sowing cotton. Picking coffee.
July.	Grass fires. Clearing ground. Building. Working barkcloth.	Sowing cotton.
August.	Grass fires. Clearing ground. Building.	Thinning cotton on earlier patches.
September.	Planting.	Planting maize, beans, ground-nuts, etc., but not millet or simsim. Planting coffee.
October.	Thinning and weeding.	Thinning and weeding.
November.	Crops ripening.	Crops ripening.
December.	Harvesting. Working barkcloth.	Crops ripening. Cotton picking begins.
January.	Grass fires. Building. Working barkcloth.	Cotton picking. Buying begins.
February.	Clearing ground. Planting banana slips. Working barkcloth.	Picking and selling cotton. Clearing off old plants.

Rains of Togo. (brace covering March–July)

Rains of Dumbi. (brace covering August–October)

PROCESSES OF PRODUCTION

(a) Agriculture

To understand the actual work involved we must consider each of these activities in detail.

The first step in every agricultural process is the clearing of the ground. This is done by cutting the grass down with a knife or, if it is not too long, hacking

it off short with a hoe. The grass is burnt sometimes
where it lies and sometimes in a heap at the side of the
patch ; the stubble is then broken up with a hoe, the
roots thrown out, and the clods of earth loosened by
hand. The old-fashioned hoe, which is still sometimes
seen in use, consisted of a stick naturally bent at an
acute angle, to the short arm of which was tied a heart-
shaped blade. The modern form is a straight stick to
which a European-made rectangular blade is fastened
at right-angles by means of a ring. This gives much more
purchase, especially when used by men, who raise the
hoe above the head at each stroke, but even this cannot
turn over the ground as thoroughly as if it was dug with
a spade.

The banana, as the one permanent form of cultivation
and as the most important crop in the eyes of the Baganda
themselves, deserves special attention. To start a new
banana-grove a woman gets slips from a neighbour.
They are planted in rows five or six feet apart, in holes
dug to receive them. It is possible to transplant a slip
when it is so old that it will bear in about six months,
but the young shoots, which are more often used, take
eighteen months to come into bearing. In the case of
a new household, a patch would be planted in this way
in each of two or three rainy seasons, perhaps fifty slips
being put in at a time. Once well established the grove
is extended from time to time by planting out a dozen
or so slips ; sometimes a whole patch from which cotton
has been cleared will be planted with bananas, but more
commonly the cotton alternates with other seasonal
crops.

The bananas require a good deal of attention. The
grove is scrupulously weeded, and the more careful house-
wives heap up the weeds round the roots to serve as
manure. Old trees are also used in this way. The
tree is cut down and the stem divided into its separate
layers, which are spread neatly side by side with the
outer convex edge upwards. Ashes are sometimes piled

round the roots. The withered leaves have to be cut off from time to time, or their weight will weaken the tree and make it liable to be blown down in a gale. The women reach them by tying a knife to the end of a long pole, and use this apparently unwieldy instrument with great dexterity. The dry leaves, if they are not required for any other purpose, are also sometimes heaped up round the roots. Finally, trees which are heavy with fruit begin to lean over, and have to be propped up with poles ; though this precaution is apt to be neglected till a storm has actually blown some down. Although no real damage could be done by a person walking through a banana-grove, the owners very much dislike it. One often sees the gap between two trees closed by tying together a withered leaf of each. It is possible that this is due to fear of sorcery rather than of any material damage, but no one ever suggested that that was the reason.

Roscoe [1] gives names for thirty-eight types of banana and the natives are said to recognize a great many more. But only three main divisions are really important— *toke*, the type eaten every day, *mbi·de*, which is used for beer, and *gonja*. The *toke* is eaten while green and is almost tasteless. The *mbi·de* produce the tiny rather sweet bananas which Europeans like to eat ; they are cut down green but allowed to ripen before being made into beer. The *gonja* is large and rather sweet, and two or three at a time are baked or boiled to eat as a " snack " or as a relish with the main meal.

When bananas are required for eating, a whole bunch is cut down at a time. One such bunch will provide a meal for two or three persons. Occasionally they are peeled, sliced up, dried in the sun, and pounded into meal, from which a kind of porridge can be made. This used to be a favourite way of preparing food to send to persons who were away from home working in the capital, but no one would eat bananas cooked in that way for

[1] *The Baganda*, p. 431.

I

preference. They are still exported in this form to neighbouring tribes.

Beer requires a large quantity of *mbi·de*, and three or four men or boys generally put in a day's work cutting them down. They are then placed in a hole in the ground, covered with dried leaves, and left to ripen. This takes two or three days. In the later stages any one who likes may come and help, and, having done so, will turn up complete with drinking-cup when the beer is ready. The ripe bananas are taken out of the pit and peeled, then placed in a trough made of a hollow tree-trunk, and kneaded with a kind of grass used for this purpose only. Sometimes the bananas are laid in another pit well lined with layers of fresh plantain-bark with leaves over them, and the kneading is done with the feet. Grass is strewn all round the edge of the pit so that the men kneading do not get earth on their feet. When this is over, the whole mass is placed on a sloping platform of branches and stamped on once more, this time to press out the liquid, which runs down green banana-leaves into an enormous basket so closely woven that it is quite watertight. The juice is quite often drunk unfermented, but even when not fermented with millet it ferments by itself in two or three days and becomes at least as potent as the deliberately fermented drink. If it is intended to make it into beer, millet, very finely ground, is put in it and it is placed in the basket or trough, in a hole in the ground, covered over with grass and dried plantain-leaves, and left from one to five days to ferment. It is tested from time to time by sucking it through a hollow reed ; the time taken is supposed to depend on the quality of the earth.

The banana-grove once planted remains permanently in the same spot. The area of seasonal cultivation changes to a certain extent. A good deal of this cultivation is done at some distance from the houses, on any part of the village land that the cultivator fancies, and people often choose a different patch each year.

But the patches in the immediate neighbourhood of each house seem to be cultivated over and over again. Most of the seasonal crops are grown from seed ; maize, millet, ground-nuts, and beans are sown in rows, two or three seeds together, and thinned later. Tall and short plants, such as maize and ground-nuts, are often grown in alternate rows, and one sometimes sees a row of maize planted as a border to a plot of some other crop. Occasionally a rope of plantain-fibre is stretched across the plot to keep the rows straight, but usually they are planted entirely by eye. In some parts of the country a peculiar kind of yam is planted which requires special attention. The plant is a kind of prickly creeper which has to be raised above the ground if the root is to develop well. This is done by training it to a tree ; sometimes the end is fastened over a high branch and held by tying to it a stone wrapped in plantain-fibre. Little holes are sometimes dug near the root to catch any rain that may fall during the dry season.

Simsim is a crop which has its own peculiar method of cultivation, with which are associated certain magical rites. The seed is a tiny grain which is sown by one woman who scatters it broadcast while others smooth the earth over it. Though the belief is not now taken very seriously, it used to be held that these assistants should be women from other households than the owner of the plot, and their help was also necessary at all the subsequent stages of cultivation—thinning, weeding, and harvesting. The plants were then laid on a large wooden frame till they were dry enough for the grain to be easily shaken off into a barkcloth. The final stage was winnowing in large flat baskets, and this too was done co-operatively by the same group of women.

Millet, too, has to be dried and winnowed, but with it the process is simpler. The ripe heads are simply broken off the stem, which is left to wither in the ground, and piled in a heap in the yard to dry, being covered with banana-leaves if it comes on to rain. Then the grain is shaken off, winnowed, and pounded small in a mortar.

Millet and simsim are stored in the house in big baskets. The millet may be eaten in time of famine, but it is normally only used in brewing. Simsim is eaten either raw, roasted, or pounded into a sort of cake, and may be eaten either by itself or to flavour a meal.

Sweet potatoes are grown from slips and have their own method of planting. The earth in which they are grown is heaped up into a series of little hills, and into each of these two slips are thrust and covered over with earth. This is said to make them grow fat, and it probably has the effect of preventing the roots from growing too closely ; the shoots grow into such a tangle that thinning would be impossible. The whole process is done very quickly and easily by women who are used to it ; a row of heaps is made first with the hoe, then the slips are picked up, put into the heap on the opposite side from the person planting them, so that they are pulled towards her, and covered over, all in one movement. In fact to do this requires a good deal of skill. The roots are dug up with a stick, not from any ritual harking back to old times, but in order to avoid cutting through the stalks with a knife.

While millet, maize, ground-nuts, and simsim have all a certain cash value, and Government is at present doing its best to encourage the cultivation of ground-nuts for export, the crops which, *par excellence*, are grown for sale and not for consumption are cotton and coffee. As has been said, the introduction of cotton has modified the whole economic cycle.

Of the actual process of cultivation there is little to be said. The cotton is sown in rows, in holes made by hand, two or three seeds to a hole ; if all three come up, two are pulled out when it is thinned. It has then to be kept weeded, and the ripe bolls should be pulled off as soon as they burst. When all the cotton is picked, the trees are sometimes pulled up and burnt at once but more often left to wither in the ground.

I have described how the cotton crop has been fitted into the native calendar by displacing one planting of millet and simsim. Another way in which new and old crops are combined is that the September crop of beans or ground-nuts is often sown between the rows of young cotton-plants, which are by that time about nine inches high, and later protect it from birds. Since the cultivation of cotton two years running on the same patch is strictly forbidden by Government, there are now elements of a rationally planned rotation of crops, but beyond the fact that a cotton crop seemed to be usually followed by one of sweet potatoes, I was unable to make any observations on this point.

Coffee is only extensively grown for sale in the Masaka District to the south-west of Uganda, though one does see coffee-plantations elsewhere, and its extension is being encouraged. Coffee-growing implies more permanent residence in one spot than used to be favoured by the Baganda, and it is mainly done by men who have bought their land. The trees are grown from seed, and the young shoots are protected from the sun by little straw shelters. Only the *robusta* variety, which does not require much attention, is grown. The trees take about five years to come into bearing, but then bear twice a year ; the berries have simply to be picked and dried in the sun out in the yard. They are then sold to Indians who pay casual labour to shell and grind them. No attempt is made to produce a high grade or to protect the trees against disease.

(b) Barkcloth-Making

The *mutuba* tree, from which barkcloths are made, is planted simply by cutting off a branch and sticking it in the ground. It grows quickly to a great size, and the main care which it needs consists in binding the wound round with plantain-fibre where the bark has been

stripped off and cutting off the aerial roots, which grow
from the wound and if left alone make the tree useless.
A strip of bark not more than two or three feet wide is
taken off, the outside layer scraped off and the rest
beaten out with a grooved mallet against a log. The
worker uses three mallets, with grooves of different sizes.
The coarser-grooved mallet is used for the preliminary
beating, whose main object is to squeeze the sap out of
the bark, the finer ones for the later stages. They are
made from a species of hardwood-tree ; formerly every
man made his own, but they are now bought from
carpenters. They are always kept very carefully tied
up in a scrap of barkcloth.

The bark is alternately beaten out and spread in the
sun to dry. In the early stages it is beaten first in one
thickness, then folded in two, then in four, the mallet
going regularly backwards and forwards and the worker
pulling the bark towards him with his left hand. Presently
it gets so wide that the mallet has to be passed from one
hand to the other, and at the next stage two men are
needed. On a really large barkcloth four men will
work at once. In the final stages the bark is sprinkled
with water to make it supple ; old-fashioned experts do
this by squirting the water from their mouths. When it
is beaten out to its full size it is spread on the ground for
several days in the sun and turns a rich red-brown colour.
Holes in the cloth, due to knots in the bark, are patched
almost invisibly, nowadays with an imported needle
and thread ; in the old days, holes were pierced with a
piece of iron and fine strips of plantain-fibre pushed
through with the fingers.

(c) Housebuilding

The old-fashioned house was a dome-shaped building
with roof and walls in one. The cane framework was
held together by a series of concentric rings of grass
bound together with osiers, the central one being only
about eighteen inches in diameter. The inmost rings

were supported on temporary posts while canes were laid over them and fastened to them with osiers. When the framework was wide enough to reach it, the permanent outer circle of posts was placed in position, and the canes were then continued beyond it to the ground. The temporary posts were removed and replaced by four permanent posts in the centre of the house and a wider intermediate circle. Over the doorway a sort of porch was made by bringing the canes forward from the lowest ring and resting them on two outside posts. Here, too, the canes reached down to the ground. This whole framework was thatched over with bundles of grass radiating from the centre. The central bundle was firmly tied to a stick which formed the pinnacle of the whole house ; this prevented loose ends from making an untidy appearance. The others were simply laid on the roof. Bundles of grass resting on the ground were tied to the lower part of the framework all round, so that the thatch appeared to reach right down to the ground, except over the doorway, where, in the better-built houses, it was trimmed to a neat edge. The door consisted of a frame of canes fastened together with strips of coarse barkcloth, which was placed across the opening at night.

The modern house is built on an entirely different plan. It is a rectangular building with a pitched roof and mud walls supported on a framework of canes tied together at right angles. The ground-plan of the outer walls is first marked out with strips of plantain-fibre and the main posts set in the ground. Notches are cut in the top of these for horizontal logs to rest on. Two taller posts are set inside the house to carry the central log or ridge which supports the roof, and to it a number of light rafters are attached, which rest on the top of the walls and project beyond them to form eaves. Next the framework of the walls is filled in, and inner partitions are made in the same way. Windows are made simply by cutting an opening in the canes.

Thatching is done from the eaves upwards ; the grass is handed up to the thatcher in bundles just as it was fetched. The lowest row is tied to the reeds underneath, but nothing is done to secure the others except that sometimes, when the whole roof is finished, a log is laid horizontally about half-way down the slope on each side. Some people give each bundle a twist to make it lie neatly, others simply lay it on the roof, blades pointing downwards, and spread out the blades a little. A good deal of trouble is taken to make the thatch lie flat, but it is very seldom clipped off evenly at the edge. In the better houses, the projecting eaves are supported on outside posts set on a raised step of earth just wide enough for someone to sit in the shade. The walls are made by slapping wet mud on them. Carpentered doors and window-shutters may be added ; otherwise these are made in the same way as the old-fashioned doors.

(d) Hunting

Small game such as wild pigs, a kind of large wild rat, skunks, etc., are hunted in the long grass close to the villages. Nets of rope made from wild sisal are hung on the grass by the edge of a path, and as many men as like to turn out stand by with spears, while one or two with dogs try to drive the game into the nets and shout for them to be moved when necessary. For such fishing as is done, basket-traps are fastened in the river by stakes, or a sort of maze of canes planted close together is built on the river-bank to trap the fish at flood-time.

(e) Economic Magic

It is a remarkable fact that, so far as any magic was ever practised in connection with these activities, this was almost all of a purely preventive nature. In agriculture there was no belief in any possibility of promoting the fertility of crops by supernatural means.

There were means of averting disasters, for example stopping hail, excessive rain, or high winds, and in case of drought women appealed to the goddess Nagawonyi, taking with them offerings of food-plants, and believed that rain would fall before they reached home.

The cultivation of simsim was the one agricultural activity to which regular magical rites were attached, and these were entirely preventive. When the first shoots appeared, the woman who had sown it performed a mimic representation of the depredations of a kind of malignant being called Musezi, or prowler, who is believed to pull up young crops by night. When the crop ripened, the owner pulled up a bundle of plants and laid them at the cross-roads outside the village, so that any evil in the crop might be removed by the next passer-by. This may have been intended to provide against the possibility of deliberate ill-will or an " unlucky hand " among her assistants. Finally, before distributing the crop among them, she had to pound a little and roast it for her own husband so as to be sure that he should be the first to eat of it. The last rite, however, seems to have been directed to protect the general welfare of the household rather than that of the crop.[1] Again the only magic connected with crafts consisted in sexual taboos, principally in prohibitions against women handling the tools or material, or coming near while work was in progress.

A man who met a woman before starting on any important work or enterprise—forging, potting, hunting, fishing, or war—would go home and wait till next day.

Hunters had their own particular god, Dungu, whose prophet they consulted before setting out. The prophet might warn them not to go or might tell them that Dungu had given them some particular animal, but no one knew anything of his dispensing charms. There were vague memories of magical herbs which were tied

[1] See below, Chapter IX, for a fuller discussion of methods of magic.

into the nets and rubbed on spears when hunting dangerous animals, but again the only definite statement made with regard to hunting-magic referred to a precaution—that huntsmen must not abuse one another because this " spoiled the hunt ".

DIVISION OF LABOUR

We must now consider how these tasks were allotted among the various members of the household, and how far they required the assistance of non-members. Hunting, fishing, building, brewing, and barkcloth-making were men's main activities. They made their tools for these purposes—ropes, nets, beer-troughs, mallets—in so far as these did not require specialized skill. Spear-heads, for instance, had to be obtained from smiths, and it is doubtful if every man could make his own barkcloth-mallet. Unskilled woodwork was their province, as was the dressing of skins and the care of the barkcloth trees. Warfare must also be mentioned here, for it was the principal means of acquiring cattle.

Women's duties were cultivation and cooking. Each wife had her own banana-grove and her own patch for root-crops. Unfortunately I failed to discover whether each woman was free to decide what she should plant or whether this was arranged by the senior wife or by the husband. Their subsidiary occupation was weaving mats and baskets ; they went themselves to the forest for the raffia. Boys herded goats until they were old enough to help with barkcloth-making. Cattle were herded by Bahima herdsmen captured in war, who were rewarded by being allowed to drink the milk. Older boys and girls or slaves fetched wood and water.

With the decrease of polygamy and the disappearance of slavery, the household has been reduced to a much smaller group of persons. In so far as the traditional occupations are still carried on, they are mainly allotted within the household in the traditional way ; but most of the traditional occupations of men have fallen into disuse. There is no more war, no more work for the chief, no work for the king for any one who can afford to commute his service for a money payment, and very little barkcloth-making. Instead men are now not bread-winners—that is still the woman's function—but earners of money to provide the household with clothes and the new " necessities of life " which European contact has created. The majority play their new part by growing coffee or cotton ; some practise crafts like tailoring or carpentry. Not many married men leave their homes to work. A considerable number of men, both bachelors and widowers, now live alone, which means that they have to grow and cook their own food, but there is still no question of a married man doing such work. The popularity of education means that children's services are not as freely available as they used to be, and one sometimes sees an old man herding goats because his children are at school. Every one who can afford it now pays labourers from other tribes to do such rough work as clearing fresh ground.

Co-operative Activities

The activities which required the co-operation of members of more than one household were housebuilding, hunting, barkcloth-making, and the cultivation of simsim. Possibly also a poor man with a very small household would have to call on help from outside for brewing beer. Houses had to be renewed every three or four years if they were not burnt down before. The owner invited his neighbours to help, and the men fetched the materials for the framework and did the actual building while the women cut grass for the thatch. The owner rewarded them with a feast when the work was done. There was no definite obligation on any one to help, but a person who consistently refused to do so would find that he could not get much help when it came to building his own house.

Hunting is still practised according to traditional methods and with the traditional organization. The method described above requires a minimum of three or four men, but even now as many as a dozen still sometimes go out together. No permanent co-operating groups exist ; a man who has seen game simply blows a horn and any one who wishes to join in the hunt turns out.

The meat is distributed among the group in accordance with their share in the operations. The man who directs the proceedings, ordering where the nets shall be placed and driving the animal into them, receives half of the chest. The one who summoned the hunt gets one leg, the other half of the chest, the head, and the skin. The animal must be killed by the owner of the net in which it is caught ; if he is not on the spot, he has to be fetched. His reward is "one whole side", two legs and the connecting piece. The man who fetches him has the right to strike the second blow, and receives the neck. It is thought essential for the animal to be speared three times, and the third spearsman gets the last four joints of the backbone (with the corresponding ribs, presumably). The rest of the back goes to the chief on whose land the animal is killed, and one shoulder is divided among the remaining huntsmen. This account was given me by Yokana Waswa, and I never had an opportunity of checking its anatomical correctness. Nor have I information on the way in which the leader of the hunt was chosen.

Barkcloth-making may have been formerly kept within one household, the head of the household working with two or three boys. Nowadays very few men do it at all, and three or four of these will join to use the shed in which the beating is done. This possibly modern institution, and a similar arrangement sometimes made by smiths, form the only permanent groups which now exist for any form of economic co-operation. Each man brings his own bark, and the owner of the shed does not exercise any very obvious special authority, though in the rare case of a dispute as to whose work should be done first he would probably decide.

It has been mentioned that in the past the women who helped to sow simsim had to be taken from other households than that whose plot was being sown. The one who sowed the seed was not necessarily the owner of the plot, but some one especially skilled. When the grain was finally ready for eating it was distributed by the owner of the plot " in proportion to the work done ", the sower not getting a specially large portion. The owner was expected only to keep one basketful and distribute all the rest, but I was told that some knew no better than to give a small basinful to each assistant. It was not good manners to complain at the time, but a woman who was dissatisfied with her portion would probably be found too busy to help next time she was asked.

One special case of co-operation outside the household must be mentioned to make the list complete. A woman whose bananas are not yet in bearing could obtain food from a neighbour, in return for which she worked in the latter's grove.

For all the co-operative activities except hunting a chief had a claim on the labour of his subjects, as we shall see when we come to discuss the obligations of the Muganda to his chief.

It is too late now to discover what was the real mechanism through which these co-operative activities were carried on—what was the stimulus to each individual to play his part, the mere expectation of a mouthful of meat and a drink of beer, or some less obvious motive inherent in the complex of reciprocal relationships. Africa has not yet yielded an analysis of the nature of social obligation in primitive communities such as has been made by Malinowski in his *Crime and Custom in*

Savage Society, and it will have to be among some less Europeanized people that this is sought. But it seems clear that the Baganda activities, none of which involved a prolonged effort or a complex division of duties, did not give rise to permanent co-operating groups whose members were closely bound together through their share in some pursuit.

Whether in the old days such co-operation as there was was, in fact, one of the duties of kinship, I do not know. Informants always suggest that it was quite haphazard, but this is the kind of prosaic detail which is easily forgotten. In a system where it was more or less a matter of chance how many relatives a man would have in the same village, there could not have been the allocation of co-operative tasks strictly on kinship lines through which canoe - building, trading, and fishing are organized among the peoples of Oceania. Observation might, perhaps, have revealed a tendency to go first to one's own clansmen for assistance. Such everyday co-operation was definitely not one of the duties of a blood-brother ; he was rather a recourse in grave emergency.

There is altogether much less of such co-operation now than there seems to have been in the past. It is doubtful whether, in fact, cotton and coffee-growing take up more of a man's time than used to be given to fighting, expeditions to the capital, and attendance at the chief's council, but the natives like to think that they are much busier than they used to be, and this is made an excuse for refusal to help a neighbour. Housebuilding is almost always done nowadays by hired workmen, and, if either the labour or the money to pay it is not available, a house may remain half-finished for weeks. It is also possible for a man to build a house of the modern type by himself, though no one likes to do this. In the case of simsim, the declining belief in the necessity of the magical processes has meant that where it is grown one household can manage it.

A new development has arisen with regard to beer in that many men who have been induced, on becoming Christians, to give up drinking it now make it for sale. If this is their aim, they clearly cannot invite the assistance of all and sundry, or their whole profit would go in rewarding them. It is really possible for two people to do all the essential work, and these two will divide the proceeds ; or a man who has permanent hired servants will use their work. It also sometimes happens that a woman living alone will hire men to brew beer for her.

WAGE-LABOUR

As a result partly of the decline of voluntary co-operation and partly of the disappearance of slavery wage-labour has become a normal feature of Baganda life. The labourers are almost entirely drawn from other tribes. Occasionally a Muganda who is suddenly called upon to meet some liability such as his poll-tax will do this by arranging to work for a month for a friend, but no one would think of making that his regular occupation. The Baganda regard themselves as belonging to the employing class. Some do unskilled labour on European plantations, and to-day, when their own crops are so unprofitable, they would be glad to have more such opportunities. But they consider that their proper sphere is, at any rate, in the realms of skilled labour and management.

Natives of all the surrounding tribes come into Buganda to work. Some only want to earn their poll-tax and go home ; others come in as labourers and then settle permanently, building their own houses and sending for their families. One often sees a little village of some alien tribe standing by itself not far from the Baganda village where the first arrivals worked.

A man who grows an acre or two of cotton likes to employ about five labourers. When I was there not many had more than three. They build their own rather miserable hut on his land and his wife supplies them with food, which they cook themselves ; most people complain that they steal food in addition. Both man and wife give them orders ; they do all kinds of work except banana-growing, which most women would refuse to relinquish. Among the highly educated and rich natives near the capital a husband often provides his wife with a male servant with the express object of lightening her work, but, though some look to this as an ideal, I do not think there is yet any household where the wife does no cultivation at all. One or two men now grow bananas as a commercial proposition, for sale in the capital ; in their case the work is beyond what one woman could do, and is done by paid male labour. Wages vary from 7/50 to 12 shillings a month, the ruling rate being that paid by the Indians.

The relationship between the family and the labourers is generally a very amicable one. When there is a visitor, the hired man comes and sits in the doorway and listens to the conversation, which he frequently does not understand ; the children are often found talking to him in his hut while he cooks his meal ; there is no attempt to exact respect from him or keep him at a distance—an attitude towards labour which does almost as much to make European employers unpopular as serious ill-treatment. On the other hand, they frequently fail to receive the wages due to them.

It is more common to employ three or four men for a month to clear the ground for planting, or for a day or two to build a house, than to have a permanent staff of hired men. There is a fairly large floating population of casual labour, especially near the main roads from the outlying kingdoms, where travelling natives stop on the way for a night or two and do a day's work for their food or a few cents. The herdsmen are now not captives in war, but Bahima from Ankole who have lost all their own cattle and rather than stoop to agriculture prefer to herd another man's in return for the milk and the payment of their taxes—the " poor whites " of this native aristocracy.[1]

SPECIALIZATION

For all kinds of metal work the household has always had to call in the aid of the smith, who is a specialist. He now uses scrap-iron bought from Indians, but in the old days he obtained his iron from neighbouring tribes, notably the Ba-Koki to the south-west ; there was no smelting done in Buganda. The profession is confined to certain clans, where it is passed on from father to son, and it used to be thought that if a member of any other clan tried it the fire would burn him ; but smiths were never regarded as outcasts as they are in so many East African tribes.

At the present day, when there are very few left, it is customary for four or five to share a forge, but there is no co-operation in the actual work. It is easier to have an assistant to work the bellows, but not essential. Each smith brings his own iron, and there seems to be no return made to the owner of the forge beyond a general acknowledgment of his superior authority.

The specialists in pottery and woodwork seem to have been largely people of the inland tribes who are not Baganda. These tribes still export their pots, but native woodwork is now quite obsolete.

TRADE

It is now quite impossible to reconstruct a picture of Baganda trade in pre-European days which would have any real value. Such a picture would need detailed investigation of phenomena apparently too insignificant for the present generation to remember them ; it is in such everyday details that the recollections of old days are vaguest.

[1] Cf. Driberg, *The East African Problem*, p. 31.

K

There was certainly always a good deal of trade, both internal and external. One of the main functions of the institution of blood-brotherhood was to provide a man with friends on whom he could count for hospitality and help in distant trading expeditions. But though any man might occasionally go on such an expedition to raise his bride-price, for instance, or the goods required to pay a fine, it was only a regular activity in the case of the few specialized craftsmen.

The principal imports were iron from Koki, salt from near Lake Albert, and fish from the peoples of the islands. The Bavuma, the people of a large island in the northern part of the Lake, also traded clay pots. These were exchanged for bananas and barkcloths. All the neighbouring pastoral tribes exchanged cattle, sheep, and goats for dried bananas. Women did not, of course, go on trading expeditions, and it is not clear what happened when bananas were sold—whether the man who sold them, who would have to have his wife's permission to take them, was then entitled to keep the proceeds. Another commodity frequently traded was fish, both from Lake Victoria and from the smaller lakes, which produce a peculiar kind of very fat mud-fish that is still very popular. Baganda who were not themselves fishermen might buy fish from the island people and hawk them inland. The people of the lake-side villages sometimes caught otters and exchanged their skins—which were used to make wristlets and were very highly prized—for cattle and barkcloths. The most profitable present-day commodity—beer—was not an article of trade in pre-European days.

Markets had been only recently introduced by king Mutesa when Europeans entered Buganda. Their object is said to have been the sale of foodstuffs, though it is difficult to understand why this should have been necessary. The king himself " opened " the first by having his own cattle slaughtered for sale. It was called *Munaku yegulira*, " the poor man buys for himself," the poor man being a man who had cowries, but no person who could give him food. The second was opened for women to sell bananas.

Cowries were introduced to the country by the Arabs, and were at first principally a medium of foreign trade. They came to be used in all transactions, but they did not replace barter. They never became the sole medium of exchange or a standard in terms of which every other commodity could be valued ; and they differed also from money in that their use was not solely that of a means of exchange, but they were also used to decorate various valued objects.

GIFTS AND SERVICES

This completes the description of the means by which the Baganda household was supplied with its various necessities. We have now to consider the calls upon a man's labour or his wealth for purposes other than the satisfaction of his own desires. These arose from two main causes—obligations towards a superior political authority and obligations towards individuals with whom he was connected by the bonds of kinship or marriage. To be strictly complete the list should also include transfers of wealth in the form of compensation for injuries. Every transaction of this type forms a single element in a larger whole which has to be described in its own place. The gifts which passed between kindred, or between a husband and his wife's family, have been mentioned already in connection with the events of family life which occasioned them, and the whole series of obligations towards chief and king, both in the form of labour and of taxation, forms an integral part of the system of government. The payment of fines is part of the system of criminal law. But our account of economic life is not complete until we have brought together the aspects of these different phases of society which are essentially economic, and thus set side by side all the different ends for which labour is expended or wealth circulated.

(a) Services to Chiefs

Every Muganda was the subject of some chief, from whom he obtained the land where he built his house and his wives grew their crops, and his tenure of this land depended entirely on the good-will of the chief. Thus his specific obligations are not comparable to a payment of rent. It was not solely upon their performance that his tenure rested ; moreover, they were not a means by which the chief secured a share, as a modern landlord does, of the wealth produced from land over which he exercised rights.

The most convenient word to describe a subject as opposed to a chief is "peasant", it being understood that the use of the word does not imply any analogy with the status of a peasant in any particular European system. A peasant could be called on at will by his chief to build his houses and the high fence which surrounded them, or to send food to the chief when the latter was in the capital, and he was obliged to send the chief a gourd of beer from every brew (perhaps one-eighth of the total quantity). Specialists had to supply their wares free on demand, and itinerant traders—principally hawkers of fish—since during the time they stayed in the village they were subject to the chief's authority, were taken to him and gave him a portion of anything they were selling.

Peasants' services to the king, which were organized by means of the authority of the chiefs, consisted in building the houses and fencing of the royal enclosure, weeding the paths all over the country to keep communications open, hunting wild animals, and fighting. Both war and work in the capital might take the peasant from his home for months at a time. There was supposed to be a certain rotation in the assignment of building work. Neither weeding paths nor hunting took up very much time.

Taxation consisted in barkcloths at the rate of one from each man, which were collected at such times as the king ordered, and were made fresh for the purpose. A barkcloth represented two days' work. They passed through the hands of two chiefs, the peasants' immediate superior and the head chief of the district, each of whom took out his own share. As far back as any informant remembered 250 cowries could be given as an alternative. There was no mention of a deliberate levy of cowries only.

The process of distribution of the spoils of war was essentially similar to taxation. Warfare was organized by the chiefs on behalf of the king, and it was the duty of every able-bodied man to take part in it. The whole of the spoil, consisting in cattle, goats, and slaves, was theoretically the property of the king. It was all brought back to the capital, each chief bringing in the booty captured by his followers. The king took as much of it as he thought fit, and distributed the rest among the chiefs in some sort of rough proportion to the amount they had brought in. They, in their turn, distributed rewards to those of their peasants who had acquitted themselves well.

The transfer of wealth by way of compensation for injuries can conveniently be dealt with here, since the chief's prerogative appears also in this connection. Injuries such as theft, adultery, false accusation of sorcery, and very occasionally murder, were atoned for by the payment of goods by the guilty person to an amount agreed upon with the chief by the injured person and his relatives. A large proportion of these were taken by the chief himself, and the rest given to the injured man, who shared them with those relatives who had helped him to plead his cause. In the case of a very poor man, the injured party simply plundered his house and took anything they could find to the chief, who took out his share and left them to divide the rest.[1]

[1] A form of transfer of wealth in compensation which did not come within the purview of the political authority was the gift of a fowl, supplied by her brother, from a wife to an offended husband.

All these processes produced the same result—the concentration of particularly prized forms of wealth in the hands of persons in authority, so that superior wealth was not the reward of superior economic activity, of hard work or skill in bargaining. But it would be completely misinterpreting the facts simply to dismiss this process as the privilege of a class whose position enabled them to deprive the common people of the fruits of their labours. The chief's privileges were the reward of his services in carrying on the business of government, his position depended upon their effective performance, and if they were primarily services to the king, one at least of them—the administration of justice—was also recognized as a benefit by the people. Moreover his wealth enabled him to reward his followers—by killing meat for them, for instance, when they were working for him, and by specially favouring with gifts individuals who had distinguished themselves in war or in council— to be lavish in hospitality, and to a certain extent to help the needy.

(b) Customary Gifts

If the chief's superior wealth carried with it obligations of superior hospitality and generosity, for the peasant too one reason for the accumulation of certain possessions was the obligation to make gifts on specified occasions. Most of this giving did not take the form of direct exchanges, or even of exchanges in which the return gift was made after a delay, such as are described by Malinowski [1] among the Trobriand Islanders and Firth [2] among the Maori.

It will be important to consider what return, if any, was expected for the various types of gift, or what motives other than such expectation operated to ensure that the due gift should in fact be given. The best way

---

[1] Malinowski, *Argonauts of the Western Pacific*, pp. 81–2, 95–100, 352–7.

[2] Firth, *Primitive Economics of the New Zealand Maori*, pp. 407–410.

of indicating the outlay which they represented will be by making a list of the occasion and nature of all gifts which the ordinary person was called upon to make. The occasions fall into two main types—ceremonials of family life, and the distribution of food outside the household, either by way of entertainment to guests or by sending presents when food is especially plentiful— e.g., when meat is killed (or nowadays bought) or at harvest time. Under the first head, the great majority of gifts are due from certain individuals to other individuals to whom they stand in a particular relationship, though there are a few occasions on which small gifts are expected from every one present ; under the second, the obligation is vaguer and more general. The following is the list itself :—

I. Special Occasions

(a) Gifts due from specified individuals

A. Marriage

Presents by bridegroom.

Preliminary gifts to girl, including one barkcloth.
3 packets of salt to girl and her parents.
2 gourds of beer to girl's brother and father.

Beer to amount demanded by girl's father.
Cowries to amount demanded by girl's father.
Small delicacies or clothes as demanded.
} Bride-price proper (in case of first wife) supplied in part at least by other relatives of bridegroom.

1,000 cowries to girl's mother (*kasimu*).
Barkcloth to girl's mother.
Beer and goat on wedding night for feast.
Barkcloth to bride's *sengawe*.
(If unsuccessful in sham fight) cowries to bride's friends.
Cowries to bride at all stages of entry into house.
Barkcloth to bride's attendant.
Goat to bride.
Barkcloth to bride's mother ; sent back with the butter.
Cowries to bride's friends who bring her feast.
Hoe to bride.

Gifts by bride's parents to bride.

Plantains with vegetable seasoning—specifically from her mother—" to take the butter from the road ".

Materials for feast of " taking back the butter "—from both parents—including fowls and possibly goats.

Gifts by bridegroom's parents to bride.

Cowries to " stop digging ".

Cowries to " put down the water-pot "

Goat and barkcloth.

Gifts due on later specific occasions from husband to wife's family.

Redemption of children ; cow or goats, barkcloth, 1,500 cowries to wife's brother for each child.

Beer to wife's brother when fetching wife who has left him.

Beer to person in charge when fetching wife from mortuary rites of a relative.

B. *Other Occasions*

Child's first sitting up ; father gives barkcloth to his mother.

Naming of ordinary children ; father's mother gives cowries and coffee-berries to child's mother.

Ceremonial on birth of twins ; father kills two goats and two fowls for feast. Father provides food for feast and goat for gift (1) at his own parents', (2) at his wife's parents' house. Gives a goat and barkcloth each to " little *Salongo* and *Nalongo*". Gives wife a goat, a barkcloth, 2 strings of 90 cowries.

First marriage of son ; father provides beer and contributes cowries to bride-price.

A man might also be called on to contribute towards the bride-price of a brother's or blood-brother's son.[1]

(b) *Gifts which may be made by anyone*

Cowries and coffee-berries during the celebration of the birth of twins.

Cowries and coffee-berries on first visit to any new-born child.

[1] Now that the bride-price consists of money, it is possible that a greater number of relatives are appealed to than before by a man who is not earning a good wage, though some raise the money independently.

Barkcloths for a burial.

Beer " to console the bereaved " immediately after the death.

C.   *Hospitality and Food Distributions*

Every visitor must receive some form of food, either to eat or take away ; the commonest gifts in order of value are a sheep, a goat, a fowl, eggs, coffee-berries. At least a fowl must always be given to a wife's brother or sister's husband.

First fruits sent to chief and friends.

Meat when killed is distributed among friends.

The fact that on various occasions it is prohibited for parents to eat food sent by a daughter indicates that it must have been common for her to make such presents, but I have no data on this point.

It is clear from this list that the gifts which passed between relatives form by far the greater portion of the total, and of those the majority centred round marriage. It has been seen that the whole ceremonial of marriage involved numerous occasions on which gifts were made on both sides, though the greater burden of obligation was on the bridegroom, and that he had further gifts to make to his wife's brother in order to establish his full rights over his children. With the full description of the marriage ceremony and analysis of the contract before us we can say, without the risk of seeming to regard marriage as in any way analogous to a purchase, that nearly all these gifts were in one way or another a return which the man makes to the wife's relatives for giving her to him. The preliminary gifts were made to obtain their favour to his suit ; next came the gift of beer which was drunk at the public betrothal ; of the series of individual gifts to her close relatives—mother, brother, *sengawe, mperekeze*—some were returns for actual services in connection with the ceremonial, but some were explicitly recognized as expressions of thanks for having brought up an agreeable and virtuous woman whom the husband was glad to marry ; and lastly, the gifts which he made to redeem the children were again expressly described as a return to the wife's family for giving him their mother. It has been suggested earlier that the especial hospitality due to the wife's male relations was faithfully given in practice because of the decisive influence which they could exercise in case the wife wanted to leave her husband. The beer brought when the wife has actually run away is recognized as a return for her brother's persuasion on the husband's behalf, for, if he cannot make this persuasion effective, he refuses the gift. The bride-price itself, since it was returnable if the marriage was dissolved, cannot be considered as a return for services, for it resembled a pledge rather than a payment.

Other gifts which are clearly a return for services are the barkcloth which a man gives his mother for coming to make his child sit up, and to " little *Salongo* and *Nalongo* " at the twin-birth ceremonies. None of these gifts demand a return in kind. The major part of them, however, being given in connection with marriage, were gifts which every man who gave them at his own marriage also received from other sources at the marriage of his daughters or sisters.

As regards the obligation to contribute to a young man's bride-price, it may seem that he had to do nothing to deserve it. Yet, as it was his father who took the initiative in collecting it, presumably he did not do so unless he was satisfied with his son's choice. As for the father's claim on other persons for assistance, the duty of the blood-brothers to contribute was absolute and part of the unlimited obligations on both sides which the pact implied ; other relatives were free to refuse an appeal for help, but whether there were any particular services which father or son could render in order to secure their assistance I do not know.

The one case of giving in which there was economic reciprocity was the obligation of hospitality between brothers-in-law. This obligation is still taken very seriously, and I have seen a man who had no fowls going anxiously from house to house trying to buy one because a sister and her husband had arrived on a surprise visit. Again the question of return only arises if a return visit is made ; but there is a practical certainty that it will be made at some time or other.

This case links up the gifts prescribed between relatives with the general obligations of hospitality, that is of providing food to be eaten by non-members of the household. This sometimes used to form a pure economic payment, as when a man made a feast for the friends who had helped him build a house. But most hospitality is simply given in accordance with the general rule, which holds good to this day, that no guest can be allowed to depart without some gift of food, either eaten on the spot or taken home, and for this the return is simply that a generous man can expect to meet with generosity. The possible gifts in order of importance are a cow (very rare), a sheep, a goat, a fowl, eggs, or coffee-berries.

A man who kills meat for some other reason than to make a feast is expected to make presents of it to his friends. This is unconnected with the obligations of kinship, and it would be thought reprehensible to confine such gifts to relatives. It would be said of such a person, " He only knows his own clan." Whether permanent groups were formed, within which such gifts circulated, I do not know. As soon as the maize begins to ripen, children can be seen everywhere going to and fro with parcels of cobs on their heads which their mothers are sending as presents. Such presents were formerly sent to the chief of the village. Nowadays the village parson or schoolmaster receives them from his flock. They also pass between friends, but I have extremely scanty information on this type of gift exchange.

In so far as the nature and amount of a gift was fixed, and its giving obligatory between two individuals on a definite public occasion, the question of the sanction of the obligation, of the motive from within, or the social mechanism from without, which ensures its fulfilment, is not difficult. It would be inconceivable that a public ritual should be held up or spoilt because one of the performers could not give the necessary gift at the right moment—though it is easily conceivable that a lazy person might not trouble to produce the object himself, and instead might borrow it and fail to repay the debt.

But where the amount was not fixed, as in the case of the feast given by the father to his daughter, in all forms of hospitality or presents of food, and gifts which were not absolutely obligatory, the question is more complicated. As we have said, in no case was a definite return in kind due from the recipient. In some, expectation to " be done by as you did " in a general way was operative ; but where such return as was received was indirect—that is, it came to the giver from a third party —such expectation played no part as a motive for generous giving. The strongest pressure here came from the intense general interest in all gifts and, above all, in gifts of food, which has not decreased at all under modern economic conditions. Any one who returns from a visit—even to a European—is greeted with the inquiry, " What did you eat ? " and a complete enumeration of all the food eaten during two or three days is eagerly awaited. When any one distributes meat the fact, and the recipients, at once become known, as I learnt from the quite unembarrassed way in which people would come and complain to me that they had received no share when I was making presents. This interest and this publicity formed the main source of pressure on the donor not to fall below the average in generosity ; while he was positively encouraged to display this virtue by the fact that ability to do so was a sign of wealth—indeed, in the limited possibilities of a primitive economic system, one of the few ways in which superior wealth can be made conspicuous.

The necessity of making these gifts had not as much importance as an incentive to production as it would have had if a greater proportion of them consisted in agricultural produce. It did not provide a stimulus to plant a large area or to take especial pains with any particular crop. But it played a considerable part as an incentive to the acquisition of wealth by other means—of cattle by warfare and cowries by trading. The obligation to give something made it necessary to produce or accumulate a certain minimum of goods and, beyond that, social ambition—the desire to excel in display and generosity—was to all but the idlest a stimulus to further acquisition.

But if this acquisition was not principally a matter of direct economic effort, of producing or exchanging goods, what are the activities to which the Muganda was stimulated by the obligation to give and the desire to give lavishly ? This question can only be answered fully when the entire political system has been analysed. But one can answer it briefly here by repeating what has been said above, that superior wealth was the privilege of authority, and adding to this that authority was the reward of conduct pleasing to one's superiors, so that in the last resort the wealthy man became so by the exercise of political virtues—obedience to authority, wisdom in council, courage in war. Trade was not a means of increasing one's possessions in general, but rather of acquiring specific objects when they were required, and mere extra energy in producing everyday commodities was not enough to make the difference between a rich man and a poor. That difference was made by the possession of cattle—the most highly-prized form of wealth—and of slaves in numbers sufficient markedly to augment the household production ; and this was achieved by rising to a position of political authority.[1] In comparison with this, the normal goal of the Muganda's ambitions, which, it may be noticed, combined wealth, power, and social prestige, direct attempts to increase one's possessions were unimportant and the possibilities of acquiring

[1] See below, Chapter VII, for an account of the way in which such positions were attained.

wealth by inheritance or in compensation for some injury too infrequent to enter into an ordinary person's calculations.

ACCUMULATION OF WEALTH AND CREDIT

It has already been mentioned that the Baganda economy did not include provision against shortage by the storing up of the principal foodstuffs. Those foods which were preserved were millet and simsim, which had to be harvested all at once so as to be winnowed, and grasshoppers, ants, or the tiny brown flies of the Lake, which had to be captured when they swarmed. These were stored simply because they could not be used all at once, but I know of no attempt to make one supply last until the next came round.

Nor do household goods such as clothing or mats seem to have been produced in excess of requirements by the ordinary peasant. I have mentioned that the barkcloths which were collected as a tax were always made for the purpose ; there was no question of a stock of unused barkcloths to be drawn upon. Modern observations can throw no light on this point, since even those families which still use barkcloths in preference to wattle and daub partitions, blankets, and cotton garments, do not nowadays produce their own. The effect of the system of taxation, however, was that the king and chiefs did have a large reserve, and each of these had a steward, whose duty was to look after them.

It is only in connection with livestock—cattle, goats, and fowls—that we see an accumulation of consumable goods. These were not objects of ordinary consumption, but were reserved for special occasions involving a reward to labourers, a ceremonial feast or gift, or especial hospitality. Cattle and goats, with cowries also, were handed over in compensation for injuries.

The system of credit which was a well-established feature of Baganda life functioned mainly in connection with cattle and goats. Whether, and to what extent, cowries were also borrowed, I do not know. People never gave reasons why a man should be obliged to borrow, but presumably this might happen when he was called upon to make a gift, and probably also when he had to call in the services of a prophet; it is possible, too, that a man might borrow the goods required to pay a fine. No interest was charged. I have no data on the question to whom a man would turn for a loan. A blood-brother was the surest source of assistance, since he could not refuse, but there might not be one at hand in an emergency. There was no obligation on a clansman to lend goods, though evidently they sometimes did so, since it was stated that disputes over debts between clansmen were dealt with by the clan head.

The normal recourse seems to have been to go to a neighbour, for failure to pay was one of the commonest charges brought to the chief's court, and is described by a special word (*kulyazamanya*). A large cowry-shell or a wild banana-seed was usually handed over as evidence that the debt had been contracted, but it seems sometimes to have been necessary to appeal to the ordeal when a debtor denied his liability. The members of his clan were called on to redeem him, but would not be willing to do so more than once or twice. If they refused, the chief might pay the debt for him and take him into his service; or, some informants said, he could be sold out of the country. The latter alternative can, I think, only have been possible after the Baganda came in contact with the Arab slave-trade. There was no forcible seizure of property, since other goods were not taken as an equivalent for borrowed stock. Repayment was always claimed at once on the death of a debtor and was a first charge on his estate; this was an essential safeguard to the creditor, since the dead man's possessions would be dissipated and the heir was not necessarily left in possession of a sufficient proportion of them to pay the debt.

VALUES

Now that we have completed our description of the means by which wealth was produced and circulated, it is perhaps possible to draw some conclusions as to native standards of value. In making this attempt it would not be impossible to proceed by ascertaining the price-in cowries of various commodities and listing them in the order which resulted. Natives even now will volunteer statements as to the equivalent in cowries of a cow or a barkcloth, and Roscoe managed to collect quite an extensive list of prices.[1] But a scale arrived at in this way must be misleading, because what is really implicit in it is the perpetual calculation of alternative ways of utilizing a limited purchasing power that characterizes a society in which the individual's wants are supplied indirectly through the medium of money. Such questions as how many goats he would give for a cow were not relevant to the primitive Muganda, who would rarely, if ever, be in a position where he would have to make the calculation. Trade was to him a means of acquiring specific objects for which some need arose, not a perpetual process of increasing his total possessions by profitable exchanges.

Moreover, to this day no transaction between natives takes place without haggling, so that it would be dangerous to take as an exact statement of relative values even a list of prices supplied by natives. A multiplication table in which each commodity can be expressed in terms of the next lowest would give an even more incorrect result than it would in our own community, where the result

[1]

1 cow	= 2,500 shells.
1 male slave	= 1 cow.
1 female slave	= 4 or 5 cows.
5 goats	= 1 cow.
1 goat	= 500 shells.
1 fowl	= 25 shells.
1 cock	= 50 shells.
62 lb. ivory	= 1,000 shells.

See Roscoe, *The Baganda*, p. 450.

of such a calculation would at least be true at a given moment of time, even if it did not remain so long enough for any one to act upon it.

Such a table has a certain value in that it does arrange some commodities in a definite order of importance. But since the native's estimate of his goods does not depend on a reckoning of the alternatives which he has gone without in order to secure them, nor yet on their potentialities as a source of gain, it is desirable to add to such a list by inquiring whether any type of possession was particularly prized, and for what reasons.

The facts are already before us in our description of the ways in which wealth was accumulated by the king and chiefs, and of the gifts prescribed by custom. In these descriptions the commodity which emerges as unique, and definitely the hallmark of the wealthy, is cattle. As we have seen, this was not because the rich man's surplus of other goods was exchanged for cattle ; nor did his possession of cattle enable him to increase his riches in other respects, nor even add much to his material comfort. Their main use was to make feasts for his inferiors—in the case of the king for his chiefs, of a chief for his peasants—and to give away on the occasions where custom prescribed a gift, and the humbler man's gift was a goat. They were, in fact, above all a source of social prestige, and this prestige was gained very largely by parting with them. Thus we find that the fact that the most highly-prized commodity was also the most highly-priced in itself tells us hardly anything about its real significance. If a man did sell a cow, he would obtain a higher price for it than for any other single object ; but the main importance of the cow had nothing to do with buying and selling.

The next commodity which must be mentioned is barkcloths. These were within the reach of every one, and the superior quantity which he did in fact possess is never alluded to as among the enviable characteristics of the rich man. But the fact that they were taxed, and

L

were the commonest prescribed gift to a woman, shows that their possession was generally regarded as desirable. Here we are dealing with a value which is much more directly economic, for barkcloths wear out relatively fast, their production costs a certain amount of labour, and the utilitarian advantage to a large household of being well supplied with them is obvious. Goats, the other principal form of gift, again have an obvious utilitarian value. The descending scale of values of gifts given by way of hospitality has already been noted.

But it is not possible, as can be done in the case of an economic system where all commodities are priced and compared in terms of money, to estimate the Baganda scale of values by one single standard. When one compares the reason why cattle are desired with the reason why barkcloths are desired, it becomes clear that different commodities are valued from points of view so different that the values cannot be reduced to a single common denominator, and one must be content simply to mention those to which, for any reason, particular importance is attached. When these reasons are given, it is seen that there is little conscious comparing of values as between different commodities, and that such questions as the quantity of one commodity which it would be worth while to sacrifice in order to obtain another do not enter largely into economic calculations. In other words, the situation is similar to that which has been analysed by Firth among the Maori [1]; the possession of most goods is prized for its own sake rather than for the sake of other goods which might be acquired by disposing of them.

MODERN CONDITIONS

Nowadays the main incentives to production are economic need, the necessity of meeting the various

[1] *Primitive Economics of the New Zealand Maori*, p. 391.

modern money obligations which fall on every adult male, and economic acquisitiveness, the desire to obtain European goods.

Every adult Muganda has to pay annually a poll-tax of Shs. 16/50, a special tax of Shs. 10 if he wishes to commute his duty of a month's unpaid labour on public work—mainly roads—and, if he has a house, a rent of Shs. 10. Ten shillings is reckoned as the amount which he could earn in a month. These payments replace his former services to king and chief. He has also to provide clothes, pots and pans, chairs and tables, beds and blankets, for his household, and to send his sons, if not his daughters, to school. He fairly frequently wants to buy beer, which sells at 4s. a gourd. He would like to buy a bicycle, and eventually to acquire a patch of freehold land on which he will build a house with a corrugated iron roof and joinery doors and window-shutters, and attach to himself two or three hired servants. It is in such ways rather than in lavish giving that the modern Muganda displays his wealth. The ownership of land now makes the essential difference between the rich man and the poor.

The customary gifts have to a certain extent died out with the ceremonies to which they were attached. The obligation of hospitality is as strong as ever, though it will be interesting to see if it survives the efforts of Europeans to persuade the Muganda to commercialize all his possessions. The main occasions now for lavish expenditure are weddings and feasts in celebration of twins. I observed no case of the latter, but obtained from Lutaya a complete account of the contributions made by friends to his bride-price and of the cost of his wedding party. This I reproduce as showing, on the one hand, the extent to which his marriage involved persons other than himself in expenditure, and, on the other, the outlay which was necessary for the ceremonial itself.

Contributors to Bride-price.	*Shs.*	
Yosamu Ziryawulawo (father) . . .	22	
Eriya Bina (grandfather) . . .	11	(proceeds of goat given to sell)
Zedekiya Bitawera (father's brother). .	10	
Yusufu Bifulanye (father's brother) . .	7/50	(proceeds of sheep given to sell)
Yakobo Mugaga (own brother) . .	10	
Yonasani Kabogoza (father's first cousin) .	2	
Yokana Lutwoma (father's first cousin) .	14	
Lutaya and Valentina (latter's son and wife).	2	
Miriamu (sister)	1	
Yokana Walusimbi (husband of above) .	10	
Samwiri Nganda (native parson of village).	1	
Paulo Gozani (native deacon) . . .	3	
Yafesi Kibirige (headmaster of school) .	2	
L.P. Mair	8	(wages as interpreter)

Neighbours.
Eriya and Foibe Waswa	1/50	
Serwano Mayanja	4	
Kitubu	1	
Gusta Mulu	2	
Kigenyi and Kidza	2	
Kafero (schoolboy)	1	
	115	

When this sum was reached, the father-in-law agreed to waive the remainder ; the original total fixed, I think, was Shs. 160. Thus, in this case, the bridegroom raised only a very small part of the sum himself. I gather he collected it simply by going from house to house asking for it, and am not aware of any particular service which he had rendered to the donors so as to have a claim on their generosity. However, the list which he gave me as consisting of necessary wedding expenses, which were met by himself, reached an even greater total. It will be seen that it includes certain household items ; in his case, he already had a house and furniture. It is as follows :—

	Shs.
Marriage fee	10
Wedding clothes	25
Photograph	30
Drummers	14
Bride's clothes (hired for wedding) . .	5
To bride's brother and bridesmaid . .	4

		Shs.
Kasuzekatya [1] (paraffin)	. . .	8
Sugar and tea	. . . . .	3
Blanket	. . . . . .	3
Soap	. . . . . .	2
Clothes for wife	. . . . .	7
Saucepan	. . . . . .	5
Tea Port (sic)	. . . . .	3
		119

There are three main ways of earning money—by growing crops for sale, by practising some craft in the village such as tailoring or carpentering, or by working in European employment. The profitable specialized crafts nowadays are all those which have been learned from Europeans. Barkcloth-makers are specialists simply because so few men care to do this work, but neither they nor smiths or potters earn much money. The successful craftsmen are those who sew garments, usually by hand, occasionally with a sewing-machine, and those who make simple furniture—beds, tables, chairs, doors, and window-shutters—with European tools. Near main thoroughfares a few Baganda keep " hotels ", where food is sold to passing travellers and a night's lodging provided ; and a very small number keep general stores which stock the same miscellaneous goods as the Indian shops.

Most young men prefer to start life in European employment, as house-boys, office-boys, or askaris. They also drive Indian-owned lorries or motor buses. They may rise to relatively responsible positions in shops or become plantation foremen. The clerks in government offices are all Baganda ; these, if they do well, may become administrative chiefs. Some become schoolmasters or native parsons. In most of these occupations there is no difficulty about their living with their families. Even where a man leaves his family the separation, in a country every part of which can be reached in a day by motor bus from Kampala and where the majority of the population

[1] This is the name formerly given to the beer brought on the wedding night. See p. 82.

can and do write letters, is a much less serious matter than in those regions where natives have to travel weeks on foot to their place of work. Many Baganda prefer the certainty of a fixed wage to the uncertainty of crops whose fluctuating prices they do not in the least understand, and to-day, when plantations are being abandoned all over Africa, one is often asked in reproachful tones, " Why have the Europeans all gone away ? "

Even children are quite alive to the attractions of earning money. Many boys and girls have their own cotton-patches, and their parents let them have the proceeds, which they spend usually on clothes. A good many boys look after the children of the Indian shopkeepers who congregate at every cross-road. When the silk-cotton grass is in flower children gather it and sell it in bunches to stuff mattresses ; one pair I remember were trying to earn the price of school exercise books, but more often such small revenues go on ornaments for girls and sugar-cane or pea-nuts for boys.

The Baganda have become quite accustomed to the use of European currency both as a means of acquiring imported goods and as a medium of exchange among themselves. It has replaced many of the old-fashioned customary gifts, not only the bride-price itself but, for example, the beer which was brought at mortuary ceremonies or the barkcloths which friends contributed to shroud a corpse. Cents are now given to new-born children instead of cowries. Shillings have not yet replaced the goat and the barkcloth as ceremonial gifts, and some native doctors still take payment in kind, though this may be only from patients who have no cash.

But the general attitude towards money has features which are quite different from what is taken for granted in Europe. There is nothing abnormal to the average Muganda in being entirely without any for months at a time. Such a conception as that of an annual income is quite foreign to him, as is any idea of spreading out irregular earnings. It has been pointed out that in the

days of cowries he had not the habit of calculating
relative values in the way which is second nature to a
person whose entire range of needs is satisfied indirectly
through the medium of money; and, though we have
now provided him with a standard medium, he is still
as far as ever from such a habit of calculation.

To the majority of the population the proceeds of their
cotton is their sole revenue for the year. The opening
of the buying season corresponds with a period of intense
activity on the part of all creditors—private persons,
landowners, schools, and the government. Some
administrative chiefs establish a little office near the
ginnery where every native is stopped as he comes away
with his money and asked for his poll-tax; some men
evade this by sending their wives to sell the cotton.
For a week or so the schools are half empty because the
children have gone home to fetch their fees. When
existing obligations have been met, the greater part of
what is left is usually spent at once in the Indian shops,
which put up all their prices for the occasion, and the
native then settles down to do without further acquisition
till the next cotton season, or till he wants something
so much that he is prepared to get into debt for it, which
he does the more cheerfully as he can always hope that
next year's prices will equal those of the boom years.
Most natives believe that the price is fixed by the
government, and that when it is low they are being
deliberately oppressed; they also do not understand
fluctuations in the course of a single season, and any one
who gets a lower price than his neighbour is convinced
that he has somehow been cheated. A certain amount
of money remains in the villages and passes from hand
to hand in exchange for beer, till it reaches a man who
makes it for sale but does not drink himself, and is
exchanged for something else.

The high prices given for beer—a commodity which
any one can produce with very little trouble—give the
most striking possible illustration of the failure of the

Baganda to make those calculations which are assumed as inherent in the nature of " economic man ". It never seems to occur to any one that by brewing his beer himself he could save his money to buy something which he cannot make ; nor, on the other hand, does the high price tempt more producers into the market so that the price falls. If this illustrates a failure to make a very simple calculation of economic advantage, a typical instance of inability to make the opposite type of reckoning is the father who lets his daughter wait for years for a husband rather than reduce his demands for bride-price.

The idea of attempting to earn a regular money income in any other way than in the employment of Europeans or of the native government is by no means general. This is perhaps partly a question of marketing. In Kyagwe, where there are flourishing weekly markets, one finds men working pretty regularly at barkcloths and pots and women at mats, which they can generally dispose of in normally prosperous times. Occasionally such men do not even own barkcloth-trees, but buy the bark. Here, too, some women carry on regular trade as middlemen on an infinitesimal scale. I knew one who each week bought the same quantity of fish from the lakeside market and the same quantity of butter from a herdsman who came from a considerable distance, and retailed both, making a profit of perhaps fifty cents every time on the two transactions. From this, being a widow, she reckoned to keep herself in clothes. Where there is no market, craftsmen generally work to order, and some of them, regarding each order as a windfall, simply spend the whole proceeds in beer. One never finds a craftsman who keeps finished articles in stock, though smiths sometimes make a number of knives at a time and hawk them about.

The attitude towards saving may be summed up in a " proverb " which I actually saw pinned to the wall of a house—" A shilling in the house is worth a thousand at the bank." This may be accounted for partly by the fact that there has never been any attempt to popularize small local savings banks, and that no one has any really safe place to keep money. A certain amount is saved up, mostly by old women, who bury it in the earth inside the house. Young people who want to borrow often have recourse to old women. Some natives do lay by enough money to meet their annually recurring obligations, but the vast majority of expensive commodities, from bicycles to land, are bought by instalments as soon as a man finds himself with enough cash in hand for the first payment. Natives do not charge one another interest, and whether they borrow at interest from Indians I do not know ; of course they pay it when they buy goods on the instalment system. A great deal of the business of the native courts is concerned with debt ; the procedure nowadays is either to give the debtor a fixed period to raise the money, to put him in prison for a day or two, after which it is sometimes forthcoming, or, in the last resort, to distrain upon his property.[1]

Even the large landowners, whose revenues come in quite independently of any effort of their own, for the most part do not regard themselves as possessing a fixed income within whose limits they must live. They are much more prone, as soon as some expensive attraction—such as a motor car or a trip to Europe—presents itself, simply to sell as much land as will pay for it, and the inevitable diminution of future income troubles them not at all.

[1] A method which is said to be efficacious is to have the debtor approached by his father's ghost. But as this can only be done by another spirit interested in the transaction acting of its own volition, the cases in which this method is used are infrequent.

CHAPTER VI

LAND TENURE

THE basis for all the household activities that have been described is the land on which the house stood and the crops were grown, and we have now to consider how, from whom, and on what conditions, the Muganda obtained this essential—in other words, the legal system of land tenure. This we shall find to be inextricably bound up with the whole system of political authority.

It has been mentioned already that each clan claimed as its own the hill on which its original ancestor was believed to have settled, that this was the residence of the head of the clan, and that its members could claim the right of burial there. But it was not here that the young Muganda went, when his marriage was approaching, to get a site for his house, nor yet did he settle close to his father. Here the Baganda present a marked contrast with what is often thought of as the typical African tribe, where groups of kindred inhabit from generation to generation an area conceived as specifically theirs by right of the ancestors whose bodies are buried there and whose spirits protect it, and where non-members of such a group, though they may live on its land, either have a different status or have in some way to be ceremonially affiliated to the group.

RIGHTS AND DUTIES OF PEASANTS

A Muganda who wished to obtain land went to a territorial chief, who might or might not be also a clan head but would almost certainly not be the head of the young man's own clan. His first house would probably be in the village where he grew up, but even as to this there was no definite rule. The procedure of application and allotment, with the rights exercised by the occupier, remain unchanged to this day, though the introduction of individual tenure and a money rental have altered the conditions on which land is held. If the applicant has seen a site that he likes, he asks for it; if not, the chief's representative gives him one. His wife has to be consulted before the site is finally selected; if it is not new ground, the state in which it is left is taken into consideration, and in any case the distance which she will have to go for water is important. If the newcomer settles near other houses, the limits of existing allotments are indicated to him, though no formal boundary marks are set up. Usually there is a narrow path between adjoining plots. In any direction in which there are no neighbours, cultivation can be extended indefinitely.

The general appearance of the site, apart from changes in the house itself, remains what it always was. The house usually stands facing the public path, with a cleared space in front of it extending to the path. In the immediate neighbourhood of the house is the banana grove, and beyond it such land as remains is devoted to seasonal crops. There is always a portion left fallow, and here, in the days of polygamy, each new wife cleared a fresh patch.[1] In those days, too, a man with many sons might be given a large plot on which his sons could build when they married; but this was an exceptional procedure. They were then not liable to be called upon to work for the chief, though the father might send a son in his own place. Similarly, if, for any reason, a plot became too large for the original occupant and his relatives, he might allow friends to build there, and an old peasant told me that he had at one time eight such friends living around him. He could ask such

---

[1] This patch was under her control while she was cultivating it, but she retained no rights in it if she left her husband. Whether the plot was allotted by the husband or selected by the wife, I do not know.

"tenants" to work for him. If he himself left the village they were not disturbed by the chief, but merely became "his men", while the boundaries of the next occupant were indicated so as to leave them in possession of the land which they actually cultivated. This custom has lapsed mainly because under the modern system an adult man living in a separate house is liable for rent even if the house is on a site originally allotted to his father.

A peasant who has a small piece of surplus fallow land may allow friends to grow seasonal crops upon it until he is ready to take it over himself. No return is demanded for this, though custom prescribes that he should receive a present out of each crop, and he is entitled to take back the land at any time.

There are two cases in which the chief can exercise his authority over a plot once allotted. If it includes a large uncultivated area this part of it may be re-allotted, and a portion of the bananas may be temporarily marked off to supply the needs of a newcomer whose own bananas are not yet in bearing. In this case the latter's wife must keep this portion in order.

A plot when abandoned reverts at once to the chief, and to take food from it is stealing. Formerly a man who abandoned his home forfeited all claim to return. Nowadays a man may retain his rights in a plot by leaving a relative there, though even then they lapse after a time.

Fallow land not allotted is called "the chief's long grass land". Any peasant, children included, can clear and cultivate land in any part of this, without even notifying the chief. The claim of a person who first cleared a patch of this land holds good even if he abandons it for a season or two, the theory being that it is his as long as any traces of his cultivation are visible. In fact people tend to clear a different patch every year, and only lay claim to a previously cultivated plot when they see someone else beginning to work upon it. Disputes of this kind are frequent ; but the claim of the first cultivator is not upheld unless he can convince the chief's representative that he is merely leaving the land fallow with a view to further cultivation in the near future. Otherwise, as a village worthy pertinently remarked in one such case, there would be no vacant land left.

Goats can be herded in any fallow land, whether allotted or not, and need not be kept within the bounds of the owner's village. In practice they are usually taken away from the immediate neighbourhood of cultivation to prevent their straying into crops. Cattle, since they prefer short grass, are naturally herded outside the village ; but, if they wander through cultivation on their way to pasture, the owner has no claim against the herdsman if he has neglected to fence it. The law says that a landowner may fence grass land to keep cattle off, but I know of no case where this is done.

The elephant-grass which provides canes for building and for making simple beds, benches, and tables, and the short grass which is cut for thatching and for spreading on floors, may be taken from any fallow land. Clay deposits are also common to all.

An ant-hill on land which has been allotted is the property of the occupant. Taking ants involves a certain amount of trouble. A framework of canes is built over the ant-hill and, when the ants swarm, bark-cloths are laid over this so that they are forced into a hole dug to receive them. Once a man had made such a frame over an ant-hill in the long grass land it would be assumed that he was going to take the swarms unless he actually failed to do so. By the time he had taken every swarm from an ant-hill for, say, a year it would be definitely regarded as his. If this man left the village, his neighbours might indicate to his successor in the same plot that the claim existed, but I was told that they would not be likely to do so unless the ant-hill was a poor one.

Forests have always come under the authority of some chief, though in the past this authority merely meant that large wild beasts killed there were regarded as his property. Any one, whether or not he was a peasant of the chief in question, might cut wood there for any purpose. Now, however, the only right of the peasants is to cut firewood. Trees for building their own houses may be cut free with the permission of the chief ; but any which are used for commercial purposes (i.e. making doors, window-shutters, and such household furniture as is turned out by native carpenters) have to be paid for.

Fishing in the rivers is free to every one.

The obligations of the peasant to his chief in pre-European days have already been enumerated, and it has been pointed out that they were not analogous to a payment of rent. There was no conception of the land as a possession of the chief from which he derived profit by letting other people work it. His right to admit and evict peasants was part and parcel of his general position as the political authority over the area in question ; as the natives themselves put it, *Tafuga taka, afuga abantu,* " He has rights not over land but over people."

Moreover, even full performance of these duties did not guarantee the peasant in the occupation of his land. The chief could turn him out and plunder his goods for almost any reason, though the fact that it was to his interest to have as many followers as possible set a common-sense limit to the exercise of this right, and he definitely would not evict an occupant merely in order to give the site to someone else. The peasants on their side could leave whenever they liked, and this was an effective way of expressing dissatisfaction, not only because every chief desired the wealth and prestige of a populous village but because, if his followers dwindled noticeably, that would be a reason for his deposition. According to some informants, the move had to be made by stealth, since if the chief got wind of it he would send his servants to raid the house. So long, however, as he did not forfeit the chief's pleasure, the peasant's authority over land in occupation and cultivation was absolute, and the site could pass to his heir when he died.

When a chief was moved, his peasants moved with him or not as they pleased. Only persons who had been especially favoured by him were considered to be under an obligation to go with him, but if he was popular the entire village often followed him. Otherwise, they might wait to see what the newcomer was like, and then go if there was a change for the worse. Upon the death of a popular chief, many of his peasants would try their luck elsewhere.

AUTHORITY OF CHIEFS

It is now necessary to consider who were the chiefs and what was the exact nature of their authority, and this involves anticipating the description of the system of government at least so far as to state how the chiefs obtained their position. Theoretically, the whole country and all that was in it was not only subject to the king's authority but actually belonged to him ; hence his power of life and death, his right to the spoils of war, to tax his subjects, and make use of their labour. He made his will effective throughout his kingdom by the appointment of chiefs, of whom it may with equal truth be said that each controlled a certain area of land or that he controlled the whole population within that area. Formal acknowledgment of his authority and theoretical ownership was made, on the appointment of a new chief, by a payment of cattle from the chief himself, and cowries from every peasant in the village, to the king's messenger who installed him. Till that payment had been made only the royal representative could have bananas cut for beer in the chief's plantation—the chief himself could not do so—and peasants who had come with the new chief could not begin cultivation.

The country was not divided into a fixed number of chieftainships. There were ten main divisions—*masaza* —whose heads were called *bakungu* or great chiefs. These exercised a certain authority over the other chiefs in their divisions, though not in matters concerning the allocation of land to peasants. The number of these lesser chiefs, or *batongole*, was unlimited. They were appointed to office as a reward for services at court, or sometimes a peasant received this honour on the recommendation of his own chief, and to make the appointment the king might either fill a post left vacant by death or promotion, create a vacancy by deposing the holder, or make a new chieftainship. Every king created one new chieftainship soon after his accession to commemorate his reign.

All these chiefs—with the exception of two of the *bakungu* whose office was hereditary, a reward for services rendered to early kings by their mythical ancestors—held office at the king's pleasure. Failure to carry out the duties of government—to remit taxes punctually, keep the paths open, and so forth—cowardice in war, unpopularity, which was taken as a sign of bad government, or any personal offence towards the king, was punished with deposition. Lesser chiefs were even sometimes turned out simply to install a more favoured successor. Conversely, satisfactory service was rewarded by promotion to the control of larger and larger areas. This constant change was a very marked feature of Baganda life. It was every Muganda's ambition to rise in this way, and there are still old men alive who have held nine or ten different chieftainships. Thus the chiefs neither had nor desired permanent tenure of any one position. The only definite security which a chief had was that he would never revert altogether to the status of a peasant ; however deep his disgrace, he would at least be left in control of some ten or twenty men. Moreover, a chief's heir would normally succeed to his father's position, and only in case the heir to an important chief was a child would he be given a lesser area or taken into court service with a view to finding a place for him later.

Every chief, so long as he retained his position, was the sole authority, under the king, over the peasants under him, and even orders from the king were only given through him. For certain purposes, the *bakungu* acted as intermediaries between the king and the lesser chiefs, but they could not give orders to the inferior chiefs on their own behalf. Thus the *mukungu's* rights of control over land were confined to that part of his district which was expressly allocated to him—a large area in proportion to that held by lesser chiefs, but certainly not the greater part of the district. It was also his duty to know the limits of existing grants within his district and point them out to a newcomer. Areas once granted do not seem to have been divided, at least so long as they were cultivated ; it is possible that an area of waste land might be granted to a new chief within what had been the bounds of a former grant. Boundaries were not artificially marked, but " every one knew them " ; they were normally not based on actual cultivation but were natural features such as rivers. Even with the larger population of pre-European days, which is said to have numbered a million and a half, there never seems to have been any shortage of land such as would make boundaries important.

In addition to the grants to chiefs, land was assigned in each of the ten districts to the king's chief minister (*Kati·kiro*), to his mother, and to the sister who went through the accession ceremonies with him, and the king's sons had each his own village. These lands served the individuals in question as a source of revenue, and were administered by chiefs appointed for the purpose and having the same status as other chiefs. Land was allotted for the temples of the two war-gods—Kibuka and Nende—and possibly also for other gods.

M

CLAN LANDS

This description has left out of account altogether the hereditary clan lands (*butaka*). Their position is the subject of a controversy which has assumed considerable prominence recently owing to an appeal brought by certain clan heads against the land settlement of 1900, in which their rights were overruled. The point at issue is whether the clan heads or *bataka* too held their position at the king's pleasure or whether their ancestral rights took precedence of his authority. The number of persons in question must have been considerable, since not only the heads of clans themselves but the heads of each *·siga* and *mutuba* had their own *butaka*.[1] Only a minority of the *bataka* took an active interest in fighting the case.

The two parties, the *bataka* and the administrative chiefs, who, as members of the Council set up in 1900, were responsible for the allocation of freehold lands, appeal to different versions of the mythical history of the Baganda kingdom. According to that told by the *bataka*, the first inhabitants of the country came there under the leadership of one Buganda, and each clan settled on the hill which it now claims as its senior *butaka*, the residence of the clan head. At that time they had no king but they chose one of their number to rule over them, giving him the title of *Sabataka* (senior landowner). They promised to obey him, and he in turn promised to leave them and their heirs undisturbed in possession of their land.

The alternative version knows nothing of *Sabataka*, but states that the first king of Buganda was Kintu, who conquered the country from the snake Bemba. The *bataka* say that Kintu was the great-grandson of *Sabataka*, that his father was king of Bunyoro, and that he conquered the country at the invitation of the people, who were outraged by the cruelties of his uncle Bemba.

[1] See Chapter III, pp. 33–4.

Both sides agree to the next chapter of mythical history. Kintu did not die but mysteriously disappeared. He was succeeded by his son Cwa, and *his* son Kalimera was so anxious lest his father should meet the same fate that he would never let him out of his sight. This annoyed Cwa so much that he banished his son to Bunyoro, where his brother was king. There Kalimera committed adultery with the king's wife, was discovered, and had to make his escape, but his son was preserved by a ruse of Mugema, one of the chiefs who had gone with him. Kalimera died before reaching home. Meantime, Cwa *had* disappeared, and as the heir to the throne, Kimera, was still an infant the country had to be ruled by a regent. This interregnum lasted for twenty-five years, during which the country went to rack and ruin. Then Kimera came back to claim his kingdom, set everything in order, and re-allotted the land among the clans—according to the *bataka* by restoring the position in the days of *Sabataka*, while their opponents hold that the first allotment was made at this time and that all claims thus go back to a grant from the king, who was entitled to make similar re-arrangements when he thought fit.

On these *butaka* the descendants of the original founders had the right to be buried ; they could also live there if they wished to do so, but they had to perform the same duties for the clan head as for any other chief, and there does not seem to have been any preference for living on the *butaka*. The majority of their inhabitants were always non-members of the clan who attached themselves to its head as they might to any other chief.

The respect in which the *bataka* claim that their position differed from that of other chiefs was that they were not removable at the king's pleasure. They appeal for support of their claim to the myth of *Sabataka* as showing that their rights are immemorial and take precedence of the kingship itself. They admit that it did sometimes happen that the king expelled a *mutaka* from his land, but maintain that the person so expelled would go to the king and explain his position, naming the ancestors whose graves were on his land, and would invariably be reinstated.

The graves are always referred to in this connection simply as evidence. Chiefs other than clan heads could also establish a right of undisturbed occupation in virtue of long residence, and they too would resist an attempt to evict them by pointing to their graves, but just as with the *bataka* the claim itself rested on their original occupation of their land, so with these other chiefs the claim went back to the first grant from the king ; there is no idea that the graves could establish a right independent of such a grant.[1] Even peasants were usually left undisturbed in land which they had occupied for several generations. The position would be explained to a new chief, who would normally respect it. But this security did not alter the status of a peasant as regards his obligations towards his chief.

Roscoe, in discussing the position of the *bataka*, states that the king respected their rights because " he dreaded the anger of the ghosts ".[2] Such a belief in the spiritual guardianship exercised over land by the spirits of the ancestors buried in it is very common among African peoples, and it is possible that it may have been formerly held by the Baganda and died out with the spread of Christianity. But there is no trace of it in the accounts given now of the relation between ancestral graves and security of tenure.

CHANGES UNDER EUROPEAN INFLUENCE

The normal functioning of the land tenure system in Buganda was first put out of gear by the religious wars,

---

[1] Thus Roscoe's rather surprising statement that " Chiefs had to be on the alert to prevent people from burying their dead in good gardens, because the gardens would thereby become freehold land," and that " if people were discovered burying their dead in a garden they were ordered to take the body away to the family estate " (*The Baganda*, p. 134) rests on a misconception.   [2] *The Baganda*, p. 134.

which, as the natives frankly assert, were engaged in by many chiefs largely in the hope of extending their lands. At the end of these wars, Captain (now Lord) Lugard divided the country among the three religions— a measure which meant a good many wholesale moves. But once the actual moving was over, the land tenure system remained the same as before. A more vital change was brought about by the Uganda Agreement concluded by Sir Harry Johnston in 1900.

The object of this agreement, which in many ways has been the salvation of Uganda, was to provide a perpetual safeguard for existing native rights. This it has done, but as far as land is concerned it has also created rights which were unknown before. For it not only allotted large estates in freehold tenure to the king and his relatives and to the three chiefs who were appointed to act as regents during the king's minority, but assigned " the estates of which they are already in possession and which are computed at an average of 8 square miles per individual " to " one thousand chiefs and private landowners ". The allotment was made by the native council of chiefs, Lukiko, which the agreement set up. In a good many cases this council disregarded the rights of the *bataka*, who were not represented there. The famous Sir Apolo Kagwa, K.C.M.G., with whom, as regent, the agreement was concluded, profited largely from this disregard. The Lukiko justify this action by the argument that they were exercising the king's overruling authority on his behalf. The *bataka* took their claims into court, and a law was passed in 1925 establishing their right to settle on their *butaka* with immunity from eviction but making them subject to the ordinary obligations of peasants towards the landowners.

Their case has received a prominence out of proportion to its importance among the consequences of the land settlement. It is true that they have suffered an injustice which is strongly resented ; the indignity for the head of a clan of becoming a peasant on his own *butaka* is felt as galling by the whole clan. But in two or three generations the resentment will have faded to something more like the attitude of the modern Scotsman towards the execution of Mary Queen of Scots than that of the modern Irishman towards the plantation of Ulster.

The fundamental change brought about by the Uganda Agreement is independent of individual rights and wrongs and much more far-reaching. It consists in the introduction into Buganda of an entirely new conception with regard to land tenure—the conception of land as a private possession at the complete disposal of an individual owner. The concurrent adoption of a money economy brought with it the idea of land as a source of profit through leasing or sale, while the assignment of land to individuals and their heirs in perpetuity resulted in the almost complete dissociation of rights over land from governmental functions.[1]

These innovations have meant more to the *bataka* than to any one else, for it is only they who have experienced what elsewhere in Africa is their most important result—the substitution of a single owner with full rights of disposal for a group each of whose members had certain definite rights in the land. Even such *butaka* as have remained in the hands of their original owners are registered in the name of one man only, and he has full legal rights to dispose of the land without consulting the rest of the group. I know of no case where this has been done, but its possibility has caused apprehension, and some people have thought it a safe precaution to buy from the head of the clan the piece of land in which their direct ancestors are buried. So far neither the registered owners of *butaka* nor other landowners have attempted to exact rent from their relatives, though they are, of course, entitled to do so.

[1] Cf. the official report of the *Inquiry into Land Tenure and the Kiban·ja System in Bunyoro*, 1931, for an illuminating analysis of the results which these new conceptions have produced in a neighbouring kingdom.

To the Baganda at large the new order has meant different changes, and so far it has not been accompanied by all the disadvantages that the introduction of freehold tenure has brought with it elsewhere. The main reasons for this are that land is so plentiful that speculation is not worth while, and that the disposal of land to non-natives is strictly controlled.

In law the security of the peasant is greater than it was before, since he is protected against arbitrary eviction ; the chief can no longer plunder his possessions, and his obligations are defined by a law which fixes the landlord's share of economic crops at a much smaller amount than that which some chiefs had previously demanded. At present some landlords go to the limits of their legal rights, but many of the older chiefs do not exact their full dues. Peasants who complain of oppression usually say that it would be no use moving because all landlords are alike ; but others will tell one that they have left a landlord who " treated them badly ", and on inquiry the ill-treatment will prove to have been a pressing demand for rent. One hears the advantages of living on Government land, where the annual rent is the only obligation, weighed against the fact that there a man who fails to pay his rent is evicted at once.

The legal obligations of peasants are defined in a law passed by the native government in 1927. The annual rent is 10s. no matter what is the area of the land cultivated. The " economic rent ", obtained by taxing commercial crops, is 4s. for every acre under cotton and for every coffee-plantation containing more than ten trees in full bearing. This amount is fixed whatever the price of cotton ; in a good year it is not onerous, but with prices at the 1931-2 level it some-times represented half the earnings of one family's patch. The landlord is entitled to the barkcloths made from one tree in every five, if his land borders on the Lake to 10 per cent of the fish caught provided he observes sleeping-sickness regulations, and to one gourd of beer in every brew. The last obligation may be commuted for a payment of 2s., which represents the price of a very small gourd ; but it may bring in as much as 10s. in a year from a single tenant.

The older landlords are not yet alive to the commercial possibilities of their position, or have not been educated to the adoption of a scale of values which allots to such possibilities the first importance. The others are largely profiting at present by the fact that many peasants are still further from the full acceptance of the gospel of production for profit.

At present "old school" and up-to-date methods can be observed side by side. Their new rights did not at first affect the quasi-paternal attitude of the old chiefs. They expected to spend a good deal of their time on their estates and to know their peasants personally, and usually were lenient in hard cases ; and to the peasants the character of the chief was an important consideration in the choice of a village. I was shown an almost deserted site which had once been a village of 300 men, with the comment that a landowner who did not live on his land need not expect to find tenants.

To the peasant the position of a great chief living among his people still represents the highest flight of human ambition. A discourse made me on the subject by one of them sums up both the qualities desired in a chief and the rewards which those qualities might expect to earn.

"A kind man deserves to rule others. A peasant will say, ' So-and-so speaks fairly,' and he takes him a present. A kind man gets followers, because he does not insist on his rights. He does not make a fuss. No one else could have founded a village like this. . . . If you have two men, where will you get [wealth] ? Two men will bring you—what ? It [the village] sinks to the ground, it does not rise. But he who has many people will eat sweet potatoes, bananas, fowls, and goats."

The trouble is that the modern landowner is acquiring tastes beyond what the offerings of his faithful followers can satisfy. He has learnt to appreciate life in the capital and to think the country dull; he generally manages to find some work under the native government, thanks to the education which his father's rents have made possible; he has been taught to be business-like and applies his knowledge to the exaction of his dues, merely visiting his land from time to time to see that the shillings are coming in satisfactorily.

However, the new era is not yet definitely established. Rents are still collected by the chief's officers, a shilling here and a shilling there, and peasants are rarely evicted for non-payment, since, if they were, Bugeza's steward told me, there would soon be none left. Many chiefs waive their cotton dues in a bad year; some do not take them from a peasant in the first two years of his occupation, and Bugeza even remitted rent during these first two years. Peasants are also allowed to work for the landowner in lieu of paying rent; the law prescribes a period of one month's work, for which 10s. would be a reasonable wage, but the landlord sometimes assigns to them instead a certain area on which to grow cotton.

Eviction requires an order from the local court, but it can still be incurred for other reasons than failure to carry out obligations towards the landlord. This is one of the few traces which still remain of the former union of political authority and control over land. While I was at Kisimula a man was threatened with eviction for failure to pay poll-tax, and at Ngogwe the man who administered the land on behalf of the Native Anglican Church told me that as it was church land people could be turned out for unchristian conduct; he instanced drunkenness and adultery. A man who is generally unpopular is almost always suspected of sorcery, and I was told of two cases in different districts where people had been recently evicted for this reason. There is no question, when a man is evicted, of allowing him to harvest standing crops, unless he had a crop from the proceeds of which he might be expected to pay his rent, in which case a threatened eviction would be postponed until he had sold it.

A peasant, on giving up his land, may claim compensation for improvements, such as coffee-trees or a good house with corrugated iron roof and joinery windows. I witnessed a case in which a man claimed compensation for a patch which he had had cleared by hired labour, but had not planted because he had unexpectedly had to leave the village.

The best possible safeguard against the future exploitation of the peasants consists in the acquisition of small holdings. A great quantity of land has already changed hands in this way, for the less intelligent of those landlords who regard their estates simply as a source of revenue find the method of sale the simplest way of raising funds. Moreover, on none of the estates originally allotted was all the land taken up by peasants, and the only way of turning the surplus to account was to sell it. A certain amount of subdivision also takes place on the death of a landlord. Normally, the greater part of the land is left to one son, but other sons, and sometimes also daughters, receive a share. Peasants and chiefs alike disapprove in theory of the sale of land merely in order to raise money, and one of the qualifications of a suitable heir is always " that he is not likely to eat up his father's miles " ; but the process is nevertheless a salutary one.

The number of registered landowners is now about 16,000,[1] as compared with 3,700 original allottees ; and these new holdings are beginning to be called *butaka*. Almost every native who has been in European employment for any length of time has managed to acquire a small piece of land, while in more prosperous times people bought land with the proceeds of economic crops. The holding may be of any size from ten to forty acres,

[1] Figures supplied by Mr. H. B. Thomas of the Land Office, Entebbe.

sometimes more. At present much of it is left uncultivated. Even with the assistance of hired labour a single household rarely cultivates more than five acres, but one often sees a holding of twenty acres with only one house. One reason for this is that the land is often chosen without much discrimination so as to include a large proportion that is too steep or rocky to be any use ; but every one who buys land buys as much as he can in the hope of finding tenants.

Though land has not yet come to be generally regarded as a trading commodity and most people consider it wrong to buy land merely to sell again, Buganda can show one interesting phenomenon in the shape of a man who calls himself a " trader in miles ". He deals chiefly in " shortage certificates "—certificates issued, when the definitive survey of native lands began in 1913, to landowners whose actual holdings proved to be less than the areas allotted to them. Such a certificate entitles the holder to choose the additional area due to him in any part of the country where land is available, and from the beginning there has been a good deal of buying and selling of paper claims. So far, however, only one Muganda has taken to it as a profession, and his activities have in the main served a useful purpose, though he appears recently to have fallen foul of the law.

Two types of obligation are imposed on landlords. There is a tax of Shs. 1/50 on every ten shillings of rent, which is regarded by the simpler-minded among them as the modern acknowledgment of the king's over-ruling authority. A prudent government taps this source of revenue at the spring by collecting it from the peasants, so that it is paid whether or not they pay anything to the landlord. Thus the amount which each peasant actually pays to him is only Shs. 8/50. There is also a tax which since 1928 has amounted to 5s. for any landlord with less than five tenants, and for those with more to 15s. or 25s., according to the district.

As happens inevitably with the introduction of a money economy and the immensely increased possibilities of material acquisition which it brings, the difference in material conditions between rich and poor in Buganda has enormously increased in recent years, and the establishment of freehold land tenure has been the most important single cause contributing to this result. But this is not in itself a source at present of discontent or social unrest, since the peasants are still in that happy state where inequality is assumed as part of the established order of things. Moreover, the motor-car owning class who send their sons abroad to be educated are still so few that the average peasant is hardly aware of their existence. When one considers the cost of government, the question certainly does arise whether more of it could not be borne by the wealthy class, but that question is not relevant to the present subject, nor has it begun to be asked by the Baganda themselves.

CHAPTER VII

POLITICAL ORGANIZATION

To the Muganda the political system of his tribe was not only the machine which dispensed justice and organized the execution of the king's commands, but a social ladder which every man of ambition might hope to climb.

The foot of the ladder could be attained in various ways. The commonest first step was for a child to be sent to be brought up in the household of a relative who was a chief. If he pleased the chief, he might when he grew up be set over a small part of the village, which would then, with the sanction of the king, become an independent chieftainship, or he might be presented to the king, if the chief he served was sufficiently influential at court, with a view to an appointment by the king himself. This latter way of advancement. was perhaps more commonly open to a man who was already a petty chief. The recommendation was backed up by presents from the candidate himself, which were brought to court at intervals for some time before the request was made. Such gifts were thought to indicate the applicant's affection for the king and his consequent suitability for office.

The surest road to success was through service in the royal household. From time to time the king made levies of children, both boys and girls, for court service. The *bataka* claim that it was their privilege to supply these children, each clan being called upon to contribute a number. The heads of the clans were responsible for their good behaviour, and any offence which they might commit was liable, in theory at least, to be visited on the whole clan ; in fact what seems to have happened was that the leading members would be punished by the plunder of their goods, or would have to offer the king lavish compensation, which they would collect as they could from the rest of the clan. Individuals were also sometimes taken into the royal household through the influence of a relative already there.

The girls were destined to become the king's wives. The boys began as attendants on the king, and were later appointed to some post in the hierarchy of cooks, brewers, slaughterers, suppliers of wood, tenders of the fire, and so forth, which the size and dignity of the royal establishment required. Their numbers were swelled by the fact that each post was filled by a number of different persons, who went on duty in rotation. Every such position carried with it the control of a small village where the holder retired when his services were not required at court, and whose revenues formed the reward of his labours. It was these chiefs who were the " *batongole* of the king " *par excellence*, though, as we have seen, the name covers persons who attained their position by other means, including inheritance ; and they, having been personally known to the king from childhood, stood the best chance of frequent promotion.

The Political Hierarchy

There was a definite hierarchy of rank among the chiefs, not, certainly, forming a symmetrical administrative pyramid like the modern system, but recognized and understood. The chieftainships fell roughly into three grades, and each chief was said to " enter into " his superior. The lowest rank comprised the *batongole*, and the *bataka* unless these were appointed by the king, as fairly often happened, to adminster larger areas in addition to their ancestral land. In each *saza* there were a number of *bakungu* or great chiefs, whose authority extended over these inferior chiefs ; there were also some " great *batongole* ", who were too important to come under the authority of another *mukungu* but did not, like the *bakungu*, exercise authority over inferior chiefs. At the head of all these came the chief of the *·saza*. The whole hierarchy culminated with the *Kati·kiro*, the king's chief minister, whose authority and dignities were almost equal to those of the king himself.

The three grades of the hierarchy played a significant part in the administration of justice, since cases which a lesser chief failed to settle were referred by him to the *mukungu* under whose authority he came, and thence, if necessary, to the *·saza* chief and even to the royal council, where they were decided either by the king or the *Kati·kiro*. Otherwise the order of seniority functioned almost entirely as a means of communication between the lesser chiefs and the king. No chief could give orders on his personal behalf to any other chief, nor to the subjects of any other chief. Even a messenger from the king—though such messengers were treated, as the king's representatives, with the deference due to the king himself—had no right himself to issue orders within the domain of the lowest chief. He had to explain his errand to the *·saza* chief, who appointed his own messenger to introduce him to the *bakungu* under him. Each of these again sent a messenger of his own to pass on the royal command to the *batongole* who came within his sphere. Any attempt to short-circuit this procedure would have been regarded as an unthinkable insult to the dignity of a chief.

The *bataka* differed from other chiefs in the type of service which was due from them to the king. It was their privilege to supply individuals who performed personal duties for him, certain offices belonging to particular clans ; in fact such persons did not perform menial work themselves, but organized it by calling upon their peasants.

Every chief's position carried with it an individual title, and there was also a series of titles denoting precedence. These titles were *Saba·du, Sabagabo, Sabawali,* and *Musale* ; after them every chief was called *Mutuba* and the precedence distinguished by numbers. Thus the leading ·*saza* chief was *Saba·du* to the king or *Saba·du* of all Buganda, the next *Sabagabo*, and so forth ; the same titles were given to the *bakungu* in each ·*saza* ; and every chief conferred them on chosen followers who exercised his authority over different parts of his land. It was the duty of the last-mentioned to allot sites to peasants who asked the chief for land, to organize and oversee the building work done for him, and to take the leading part in his council ; and their reward was the right to a fixed portion of the meat whenever he slaughtered a cow.

The order of precedence was followed on state occasions such as attendance at the king's council or when the whole country was called up for war and the chiefs gathered together, each leading his own people. Otherwise, except in the case of *Saba·du* and *Musale*, each of whom had definite duties, the titles implied no distinction of functions or of privilege ; nevertheless a superior title is eagerly coveted for its own sake to this day, when the only possible occasion that the holder can have of enjoying his rank is that of a visit of a distinguished stranger to a chief's council, when the members are introduced in order.

Saba·du's main duty was the performance of all magical rites affecting his chief, that of *Musale* to lead the vanguard in war. The *Saba·du* and *Musale* of Buganda carried out these duties for the king ; for the chiefs they were done not by chiefs of inferior rank but by their personal *Saba·du* and *Musale*. The relation of *Saba·du* with his chief was a particularly close one, whose intimacy is expressed in the statement that they were " like brothers ", so that their children could not intermarry. *Saba·du's* position carried with it the privilege not only of advising but of criticizing his chief.[1] He would be consulted when the chief contemplated any

---

[1] One informant said, "*Amufuga*," "He rules him."

drastic measure such as expelling a peasant, and peasants who felt that they were unfairly treated complained to him in order that he might remonst ate with the chief.

It has been explained how the whole series of chiefs, with the exception of the *bataka*, held their positions at the king's pleasure. They depended on him, in fact, in very much the same way that their peasants depended on them. Personal offences and failure in the performance of duties were alike liable to be visited with deposition. As far as such duties consisted in services to the king he would see for himself whether they were properly done ; as far as a chief's government of his peasants was concerned there were always plenty of people anxious to take his place who would tell tales on a chief who was losing his men through unpopularity. Failure to appear at court and take part in the king's council was a most serious offence, since a chief who absented himself was suspected of plotting treachery. Such an offender was dealt with by a sudden descent upon him of the king's bodyguard, who plundered all his possessions and those of his peasants. But the normal procedure was a trial in the royal council, under the presidency of the *Kati·kiro*, who did not necessarily decide every case in favour of the king ; his position in this respect is analogous to that of *Saba·du* in relation to a chief.

In a sense all chiefs may be described as personal servants of the king, since their duties consisted in administering in accordance with his pleasure a realm which according to the native theory was his absolute property. Actual personal contact was maintained through the chiefs' attendance at the king's council. Each one had his own house in the capital, and spent a considerable amount of time there, leaving his land in charge of a steward who exercised his full authority. This attendance on the king was very similar to the frequent attendance of a peasant at his own chief's council, which as we have seen was one of the best ways of winning favour. Mere appearance of the subject

N

was a compliment to the superior and a demonstration of loyalty, of which the superior showed his appreciation by entering the assembly and receiving the greetings of its members. In both councils any business which might be done was incidental to the main reason for the gathering. Indeed the king's council assembled as often as not to enjoy performances of music and dancing. In both, disputes were dealt with as they happened to arise by such persons as happened to be present, the chief counting only on the assistance of his *Saba du*, the king on that of the *Kati kiro*. The royal council was not a deliberative or legislative body. Decisions reached by the king and *Kati kiro* to levy taxes or make war were announced to it, but it took no part in making them.

THE KINGSHIP

If the country and everything in it were sometimes conceived as possessions of the king, the existence and welfare of the king were also thought to be not only advantageous but essential to the people. Not that magical powers were ascribed to him or that natural calamities were attributed to his ill-health or anger. There was no ritual action which could only be performed by him ; he did not in fact lead the army, and when he felt so disposed he left the administration of justice to his *Kati kiro*. The whole political organization could have functioned satisfactorily without him for a considerable period of time. But his final authority, the ultimate source of law and order and of leadership, was regarded as indispensable. " To be without a king " was in itself disastrous ; an army without a general— the king's representative—could not fight, and in a nation without a king every man's hand was against his neighbour. This was the theoretical state of affairs on the death of a king ; in practice it was averted by keeping the death secret till the new king was appointed.

Alongside this remarkably rationalistic conception

there seems to have been also a general idea that the welfare of the king was of supreme importance to the people, which was expressed in practice in his right to order ritual murders. Beliefs with regard to the efficacy of such murders were probably more explicitly formulated in the days when they were still practised. It is almost impossible now to obtain any clear information on the subject ; but dangerous as it is to ascribe to natives theories which are not explicitly stated, it seems that one may infer some such idea here from the explanations of such murders as being done " to protect (*kukuza*) the king " and " to set the land in order ".

An accession involved the taking of human life on a large scale at various stages during the ceremonial. Some of these murders were certainly regarded as magically benefiting the king, but others, particularly the indiscriminate killing of persons met by chance, were explained by Yokana Waswa as a mere assertion that the new king had entered on his reign and acquired the power of life and death over his subjects. Any illness of the king was thought to call for ritual murders to promote his recovery.[1] From time to time he was also advised by the prophets to carry out such a slaughter in order to " set the land in order " ; in this connection the action was thought to be directly in the interest of the people as a whole. Judging from the records of early missionaries such events took place perhaps once in ten years.

The murders contained no religious element, and if the term " human sacrifices ", commonly used of them, is taken to imply a belief in deities who required human lives of their worshippers, it is quite inaccurate. It is also inaccurate to confuse murders which were believed to have a beneficial effect on king and people with those which were carried out for political reasons or from sheer caprice. On the death of a member of the royal household Mutesa and Mwanga frequently had large numbers of

[1] See Chapter VIII, p. 233.

people executed who they thought had not expressed sufficient grief ; and Mwanga had a pet crocodile to whom he offered human victims, but without regarding it as a divinity. Actions of the former kind seem to have been generally considered justifiable, while the latter were disapproved and resented, though accepted as legitimate in view of the royal power of life and death.

The kingship went in direct descent from father to son. The eldest son was debarred from succeeding, but any one of the others could be selected by agreement between the *Kati·kiro* and the leading ·*saza* chiefs. There was no royal clan, every son of the king taking the totem of his mother.[1] Though not himself a member of any clan, the king as *Sabataka* was head of all the clans, and to this day questions involving a person's status in his clan— in particular, matters relating to wills and inheritance— are referred direct to his council without passing through the lower courts.

Both the general relation between the king and the whole people, and the personal relationship between him and each of the chiefs, were publicly formulated and, as it were, confirmed afresh for each new king at his accession. The proceeding corresponds essentially to what was done in the case of an ordinary heir, who at his installation was reminded of his duties to his relatives by the head of the clan and formally introduced to all of them who were present.

The new king was led to the throne by his father's *Kati·kiro* and proclaimed to the assembled people in these words : " This is your king, hear him, honour him, obey him, fight for him ! "

Next he was clothed in a new barkcloth—as was every heir by the head of his clan—by Mugema, the chief whose ancestor was supposed to have saved the life of Kimera and brought him back to Buganda. To the barkcloth was added a calf-skin. Mugema said :

---

[1] This does not mean that succession was matrilineal. If it had been, a king would have been succeeded not by his own son but a sister's son. Nor is the custom a " relic of matriarchy ".

" I am your father, you are my child. Through all the ages, from your ancestor Kimera, I am your father. This skin with which I clothe you was worn by your ancestor Kimera when he took possession of Buganda. My child, look with kindness upon all your people, from the highest to the lowest ; be 'mindful of your land, deal justice among your people. You are *Sabataka*, treat your *bataka* with honour (for you [plur : all kings] come from among the *bataka* to take possession of Buganda) ; all your men, the chiefs of the nation, treat them with honour ".

The king was then given spears and a shield with the words : " With these spears you will fight those who scorn you, who trouble you, your enemies. The king is not despised, he is not thwarted nor contradicted. You are to overcome rebels with these spears and this shield."

Lastly the *Kati·kiro* gave him a rod with the words : " With this rod you shall judge Buganda ; it shall be given to your *Kati·kiro* to judge Buganda ; you shall both judge Buganda."

Next day the rod was returned to the *Kati·kiro*, or, if he was dismissed, given to his successor ; the latter went straight from the king's presence without thanking him, as a sign that he was his equal in authority.

During these two days all the chiefs were formally introduced to the king, and those who performed personal services for him brought him gifts symbolical of these services. Immediately after their introduction each set his men to work upon the building of whatever part of the new royal enclosure fell to his share.

From this ceremonial emerges the idea of a monarch having not only rights but obligations. His subjects' duties were given in the expectation of a return from him ; their obedience was the counterpart of his leadership, both being necessary to make the people victorious over its enemies. Absolute as was his power he was expected to respect established rights, to uphold justice, and to behave with "kindness" or generosity in rewarding the deserving. This reciprocal relationship was explicitly affirmed before the active obligations of chiefs and people, in abeyance since the death of the late king, were resumed. It is noteworthy, too, that the confirmation in office of the *Kati·kiro* is done in such a way as to emphasize his position as one of equality with the king. It seems probable that his influence and that of Mugema, who was irremovable and treated with the respect due to an actual father, provided a stabilizing factor in a situation where a young king might be tempted to abuse his newly-acquired power ; for the dismissal by a new king of his father's *Kati·kiro*, though admittedly within his rights, seems to have been regarded as the prelude to a reign of violence.

It is not my aim to represent the old political organization as a system ideally constituted to secure justice and good government, to suggest that it was not capable of improvement, or to deny that it permitted and even approved forms of cruelty that shock the sentiments of a civilization to which physical violence is more abhorrent than it is to the Buganda. There is no doubt that one source of the king's power was his right to punish any offence which savoured of disrespect with death or mutilation. There seems to be also little doubt that some kings amused themselves by the infliction of physical suffering on their subjects.

All this has to be admitted, and the question precisely how the cruelties which are known to have been perpetrated by the last independent kings were reconciled with the conception of the "good king" as expressed at the accession is one which cannot be answered. But it is only fair to remember that this conception did exist and must have had some influence, particularly before the advent of the Arabs with their guns weighted the scales on the side of authority. It is worth while, too, to point out that at worst the arbitrary cruelties of the king only affected persons in or near the capital.

CHIEFS AND THEIR SUBJECTS

In the relations between chiefs and people we see again a conflict between a theoretical absolutism and an equally clearly conceived theoretical standard of fair dealing. In the case of the chiefs there was one very effective check on the arbitrary exercise of authority in the right of a dissatisfied peasant to change his master. We have mentioned already the position of *Saba·du*, whose right of remonstrance constituted a further check ; and in the case of all but the most powerful chiefs, with large retinues of personal retainers, armed resistance seems to have been not uncommon.

The general behaviour expected by the peasants of their chief, though it was enjoined only by these relatively vague sanctions and by the fear of unpopularity, nevertheless followed quite definitely recognized lines. An agreeable manner seems to have been valued at least as highly as material liberality, and an ill-tempered or arrogant chief is said to have rapidly lost his followers.

But the liberality was also essential. The essential qualities of a good chief were once defined to me as " beer, meat, and politeness." Peasants who worked for him expected cattle to be killed for them. " The chief would kill cattle when he saw that they were tired ; they ate their fill and then worked with all their might." But he was also expected to distribute meat whenever he killed, if not to kill for the express purpose of making a distribution. Any one who called on him would be given food when the midday meal was served. I cannot tell how much truth there was in the argument used by people who begged from me that they came to me " because they had no longer a chief to help them " (after Bugeza's death) ; but I should think there was a certain element.

A liberal chief might start a newly-arrived peasant in life by giving him cattle and wives, and he might similarly assist a slave. He could take under his protection a debtor, or a man who could not pay compensation for some injury;

and though the man entered his household as a slave he
would gradually rehabilitate him—possibly even privately
making him presents of the goods he required to pay the
amount due. Some chiefs would bring hoe-blades back
from the capital, where they were sold, and distribute
them among the people; and from a popular chief
occasional presents to favoured peasants seem to have
been frequent. The rights of a chief to his share of
taxation and other perquisites were defended by Waswa
on the ground that without them " he could not make
the peasants rich "; and this phrase does effectively
describe his function in the circulation of wealth.

No doubt the chiefs did enrich themselves at their
subjects' expense to a greater extent than was strictly
necessary for the fulfilment of this function; no doubt
they often behaved in a tyrannical way; no doubt the
justice they dispensed was not always strictly in accord
with those principles which we like to call British. But
it is nevertheless quite unfair to regard them as mere
self-seeking tyrants out to make the most of their position.
On the contrary, they represent a quite remarkable
degree of political organization, whose working we must
now consider in detail.

Judicial Functions

Sometimes the administration of justice is spoken of
as the great benefit conferred by chiefs on their subjects.
Litigation is extremely popular with the Baganda; they
like to argue out every petty quarrel before some third
party, and are sometimes in such a hurry to bring an
adversary before the chief that they do so before they
have made up their mind what the quarrel is. In the
old days a case was discussed in the presence of all the
peasants who happened to have come to pay their respects
to the chief, and any one might ask questions and express
an opinion. Thus this was the aspect of the chief's authority
which touched the peasants most closely and continuously.

It is rather remarkable, however, that the chief's authority did not preclude the possibility of private revenge for admitted injuries, though informants differ in their view of the extent to which such action was independent of his approval. There seems to have been a good deal of difference in the extent of effective authority over their own subjects as between greater and smaller chiefs. In any case no chief's authority was developed to the point where he was himself responsible for bringing criminals to justice. That responsibility rested always upon the injured person or his relatives.

All informants agree as to the persistence, in some form or other, of the institution of blood-revenge for murder. The more ferocious accounts state that it amounted to a petty war between two clans, which had to be continued till the deaths in the murderer's clan equalled those in that of the murdered man. The guilty man's relatives would assemble at the home of the senior clansman in the immediate locality, and prepare to defend themselves. Although the feud did not go on indefinitely, but was supposed to be forgotten as soon as the murder was avenged, a pitched battle would obviously be likely to lead to more deaths and thus to prolong the hostilities. Usually, however, the murdered man's relatives avoided this by selecting their victim from a place where the members of the murderer's clan were not numerous, or even by capturing an infant.

It is assumed that the murderer himself would never be caught unless his clan gave him up as a chronic offender —that he would either have run away or be well concealed by a relative or a blood-brother—and no necessity seems to have been felt to direct vengeance primarily against a close relative. The most blood-thirsty informants admit that it was sometimes possible to make restitution by handing over two women to the injured clan " to bear children in place of the dead man ", but they consider that only a very pusillanimous clan would accept this substitute.

Until vengeance was taken relations were broken off between members of the two sides who were connected by marriage (though not between husbands and wives), but as soon as it was over normal intercourse was resumed without the need of any formal reconciliation. The whole process, according to this version, was not the concern of any chief, since the persons involved would be subjects of many different masters.

Another version is that the murderer must first be taken to the chief, who, if he decided that the man was guilty, handed him over to the murdered man's relatives, but might try to induce them to accept compensation. The adherents of this version, two of whom had been chiefs of some importance, said that people who took the law into their own hands without first going to the chief would be punished by him if he was powerful enough. This version of course presupposes that the murderer is caught. Yokana Waswa stated that if the murderer considered his action justifiable he would go himself to the chief, explaining the circumstance, and offer a goat as amends for having done what it should have been left to the chief to do. But no other informant would confirm this.

The usual position seems, broadly speaking, to have been that in the case of a flagrant offence it was for the injured party, with the assistance of his relatives, to retort by violence. This applied to a murderer, an adulterer caught in the act, or a thief found with stolen goods in his possession. Those informants who stressed the authority of the chief stated that the correct procedure was for the injured persons to go first to the chief, who would indicate his sanction of their proceedings by sending a messenger with them. Some even said that the guilty person should be taken to the chief, and there, if compensation could not be agreed upon, put to death by him ; and that otherwise even a murderer's death would have to be avenged. But not many held this view. Others said that the injured person was justified in killing the offender on the spot and would suffer no consequence.

The chief's authority functioned essentially in cases where a crime was denied, where responsibility was disputed, or where there was a question of fixing compensation ; this last seems to have been done always under the auspices of the chief, who received a large share of the amount handed over. It is also worth noting that the cases which came before him were matters arising between persons not bound by close ties. Quarrels between members of one clan were settled by the senior clansman ; matrimonial quarrels by the senior wife, or, if they became serious enough for the wife to run away, by her near relatives. A man's relatives were expected to appear and stand by him when he was involved in a case (there is a technical term for this, *kusemba*) and this assistance could clearly be of more than moral value. Its importance is expressed in a proverb : " *Omusango ogirimu abemijunga kizibu okugusinga* "—" It is hard [*kizibu* really almost means ' impossible '] to win a case if the tassels are against you " ; the tassel standing for the fez, which used to be affected by chiefs. But the opposite view also has its proverb : " *Olulimi bwerukusoba omusango negukusinga ; owoza bulungi, abemijunga nobasinga* "—" If your tongue betrays you you will lose your case ; plead your case well and you will overcome the tassels."

According to Yokana Waswa the case would never be decided on the same day that it was brought. He gave two reasons : for the chief to see if both parties held to their story at a second hearing, and to give either side the opportunity of offering a bribe. If one only did so, he was certain of success. If both did, the chief would allow the decision to be made by the council without himself intervening. It is very doubtful if to the Baganda such a transaction appears as a perversion of justice. The phrase which describes it—*omwami alobola obuza*, " the chief picks his share "—is the same that is used of his taking his share of the goods brought in compensation or of taxes ; and the word *nsonyi*, used by Waswa of the feelings of a chief who had accepted a present from both sides, can just as often mean mere embarrassment as " shame " in the stronger sense.

There seems to be no particular value in attempting to assess the amount of compensation demanded for different types of injury. Estimates which are given are so vague that it seems most likely that there was no fixed amount, but that the injured side demanded as much as they thought they were likely to get from a man with rich relatives, while in the case of a poor man they simply plundered his house and brought the proceeds to the chief, who took out his own share and left them to divide the rest. In case of murder, where the compensation was settled amicably, the plaintiffs were represented by the senior clansman in the locality, and he received the goods and distributed them as he thought fit. In other cases the injured person himself did so. On the other side the collection was organized by the senior clansman. Some informants state that this refers to the head of the whole clan, and that he organized a levy on all members through the ·siga and *mutuba* heads, but I think that can only have occurred in really large-scale cases such as that of a person who offended a ·saza chief or the king.

Imprisonment was not known as a punishment, though persons under trial were confined in a rough form of stocks. In the case of a debtor, a system of bail existed. A trustworthy person—normally a relative—would deposit a cowry-shell as evidence of his undertaking to stand surety, and the guilty person would be set free to go and beg the goods required or raise them by trade.

It will be convenient here to summarize the extent to which the principles of collective responsibility and mutual aid, which have been mentioned as obligations of clansmen, were actually operative. The principle of collective responsibility, in the sense that all members of the clan were liable to suffer for the misdeeds of one, applied only in the case of the blood-feud and even there was not unlimited, since distant relatives might refuse to shelter a murderer. In the case of crimes which could be atoned by the payment of a fine it was rather the duty of mutual aid that came into play, for it rested with the guilty persons' relatives to redeem him or not as they thought fit ; the injured party had no *right* to recoup himself from their possessions. It was, I think, this principle, too, rather than any mystical conception of an injury to one member as an injury to the whole body, which dictated the co-operation of clansmen in helping an injured person to secure his rights ; whether the goods received in compensation were shared only with those who had given active assistance I did not discover. Nor can one now say definitely how far this duty extended ; certainly it was felt to be incumbent on all relatives living in the same village, but, except in the case of important persons, I doubt if it would have been thought necessary to go to the assistance of a distant clansman.

Corporal punishment seems to have been reserved for offences against the chief himself, in particular for adultery with his wives. It could also be inflicted by any man on his wives or slaves, but this was a private affair. It might consist in cutting off a person's lips, ears, or one hand, or gouging out an eye. It is quite impossible to estimate the extent to which such punishments really were inflicted. The Baganda, who invariably look on physical deformity as something amusing, dwell on the recollection with considerable enjoyment, and my own cook told me that his father did such things " every day ". They certainly seem to have been an every-day occurrence in the royal household, but elsewhere I should imagine that only the most important chiefs could afford to indulge constantly in such inflictions. It was only they who had regular places of execution (*matambiro*, wrongly translated by Roscoe and the dictionary " sacrificial places ").

The ordeal was kept almost entirely for cases of

sorcery, though it seems to have been sometimes employed when other charges were denied. An accusation of sorcery was only brought if the supposed victim had actually died. The most common way of detecting it was by the appearance of the corpse. But if any one was suspected earlier he would be summoned to wash the sick person and formally pronounce the words, " Siku·ta " (I am not killing you). This served the double purpose of clearing the suspected person of unjust suspicion and of removing the spell if in fact he was responsible for it. Any one who refused to do it virtually admitted his guilt. Thus the dreadful fate meted out to sorcerers was reserved for the successful perpetrator of a particularly heinous crime.

The ordeal was undergone both by accuser and accused. It consisted of a drink made from a shrub called *madudu*, which was highly intoxicating but not poisonous. The drink was administered not in the chief's enclosure but at a place outside the village where two roads met. This suggests some magical belief in the danger of bringing the *madudu* into the village, such as is found among other East African tribes, but such informants as could give a reason said that it was done simply for publicity. Whoever resisted the stupefying effect of the drink was supposed to be in the right. Both parties sat on the ground inside a ring made of dried plantain-leaves supported on sticks, and the drink was placed between them. Both drank at once. They were then invited to identify spectators and asked other questions, or they might have some object put on their heads and be told to jerk it off backwards. There does not seem to have been any attempt to make the accused person confess under the influence of the drink. The final test was a summons to step over the rope of plantain-leaves and thank the chief, who was sitting beyond it, in the usual manner of a person who has received a favourable decision.

The one who failed was said to have been " burnt "

by the ordeal, but there was no question of any actual
ordeal by fire. It is always assumed that the ordeal
generally resulted in a decision. It is also believed
that medicines could be obtained to counteract its effect,
and of course a clever sorcerer would be of all people most
likely to know such medicines ; but the Baganda did
not take the further step to the argument that success
in the ordeal in itself proved a person to be guilty, and
a man who passed through it satisfactorily was acquitted
whatever the reason might be. If both were successful
the chief was said to have been " burnt " and nothing
further was done. If neither was, both had to bring
cows to the chief. If the accuser failed to pass the test
he had to compensate the accused on a lavish scale.

A convicted sorcerer was burnt outside the village.
The reason given for this is *Batya e·vumbe* (they dislike
the smell), but that there is more than mere physical
distaste involved is apparent from Waswa's statement
that the executioners on their return kept away from the
chief's place for two or three days until the *e·vumbe*
had, as it were, evaporated from their persons. I think
there was certainly some non-material pollution involved,
probably arising from the contact with the sorcerer,
since no special awe surrounded the execution of other
criminals.

ORGANIZATION OF TRIBAL ACTIVITIES—WARFARE

The other duties of the chief consisted in organizing
the execution of the king's commands in the matter of
war, the collection of taxes, building in the royal
enclosure, and clearing roads. Of these activities warfare
stands in a place by itself, for it was regarded by the
people not as a burdensome duty but as a profitable
occupation entered upon with eager interest. It has
been mentioned that success in war was one of the main
ways of attaining wealth and position. One old man
said to me when discussing the weather, " The rain

did not matter in the old days, when we got what we wanted by plunder." Though Roscoe mentions various ways in which a man who had killed many enemies was honoured,[1] it is definitely on the plunder and not on the killing that old men now dwell with satisfaction.

The object of an expedition was always supposed to be the reduction of a tribe who threatened to become dangerous. The enemy were usually the Banyoro in the north-west, less commonly the Basoga in the east, beyond the Nile. Other neighbouring kingdoms received attention from time to time, but the predominant importance of these two may be gauged from the fact that the two war-gods, Kibuka and Nende, are distinguished as presiding over wars with the Banyoro and Basoga respectively. Invasions in force by other tribes are never mentioned. The most that is admitted is that in frontier regions they might make isolated raids by night.

The summons to war was given by beating the alarm on the king's special drum *Mujaguzo*, which was only used otherwise to announce the death of a king or his son, or the new king's accession.[2] Those who were within hearing assembled at *Wankaki*, the gatehouse of the royal enclosure, and to them the king announced the destination of the war and the name of the general, who was selected for each occasion after consultation with the appropriate spirits. He also selected the people of certain ·*sazas* " to guard the king ", which they did not by assembling at the capital but simply by staying at home. As all the important chiefs spent a large part of their time at the capital, and when not there left a

[1] *The Baganda*, p. 362.
[2] The alarm-beat is always and everywhere the same. Its rhythm may be indicated thus ♩ ♩ ♫▭ ♩ , repeated with a slight pause at the end of the phrase, and occasionally punctuated with a single heavy beat followed by a long pause. The words—every Baganda drum-beat has its appropriate words—are " ·*Gwanga*, ·*gwanga*, *mu·je* " (" People, people come ". ·*Gwanga* means the nation as a whole). Whatever may be the case elsewhere in Africa, Baganda drumming is not a primitive telegraphic code by which any message may be sent.

PLATE VI

AN IMPROMPTU COUNCIL

Kyuma—the landlord—seated in the porch; Kaiso, his dispossessed brother,
in the foreground. Plaintiff and defendant standing in the centre. The *muruka*
chief on the right with his back to the camera; next him the village "askari",
distinguished by his puttees.

PLATE VIII

PLATE VII

FUNERAL RITES

All the women set to work to weed the banana grove.

The graves are strewn with *bombo* for the woman just buried was a mother of twins.

substitute behind, there was no delay in making the
king's orders known to them. No formal message
appears to have been sent to the outlying parts of the
country, but the drum-beat was kept up and passed on
so that in one day the alarm had gone through the whole
of Buganda. Every chief sent a messenger to his own
people telling them where the army was to meet, and the
earlier arrivals waited there for the more distant
contingents. The whole force is said to have assembled
within five days. Every able-bodied man was expected
to turn out, but though the penalty for cowardice in
the field was instant death by burning, people who
simply stayed at home were merely fined on their chief's
return.

Before setting out, all the chiefs who were in the
capital paraded before the king in full array, those from
each ·*saza* under the leadership of the ·*saza* chief. The
warrior's dress consisted of skins, tied round the waist
or over the shoulders, and a fancy head-dress, while his
face and chest were smeared with patterns in ashes, soot,
and red ochre, and he might fasten round his waist a
banana-leaf slit into streamers. The general's head-
dress consisted of a crown of beads and was given him
by the king, but others adorned themselves as they
pleased, fastening flowers, long grasses, or feathers to
their heads by strips of dry plantain bark. Each chief
completed his adornment by smearing on his face some
ashes from the fire in *Wankaki*. This "war-paint"
was said to "increase the ferocity" of the warrior and to
"show that now he is really fierce", but the idea seems
to have been merely that it produced an alarming
appearance and not that it had any magical effect on
his spirits. The weapons carried were two spears, a
stick, and a wicker-work shield. Each chief as he
passed before the king brandished his spear with a
quivering motion, not used in the actual fighting but
believed to strike terror into the beholder, and announced
that he would fight bravely. Those who went straight

o

from their own lands to join the army performed this ceremony before the general along with their subordinate chiefs.

In every contingent there was a vanguard and rear-guard. The vanguard leader, *Musale*, carried the chief's *mayembe*—magical objects filled with herbs selected by specialists, and supposed to produce general good fortune rather than any one defined object. The rear-guard, and with it the duty of looking after the wounded, were the responsibility of *Saba·du*. Each of these duties was performed for the country as a whole by the appropriate ·*saza* chief.

Few leaders of military expeditions can have had less to do than a Muganda general. The main object of the expedition was plunder ; fighting was merely an incidental which became necessary if the enemy defended their property ; the organization of the army did not involve even the elementary division between fighters and raiders ; and he was accompanied by the prophet of the appropriate war-god and expected to obey his advice as to whether the day was propitious for fighting. Nevertheless the general was important as a moral rallying-point. It is assumed as axiomatic that the army would lose heart if he was killed, and regain its courage as soon as his successor was appointed, as he would be by the leading chiefs. Though he did not himself take part in all the fighting he was expected to encourage the army by his presence at every important engagement, and especially if they were in danger of being driven back. His principal positive duty was to apportion to each chief on the return to the capital the share of his own and his followers' spoil that they were to be allowed to retain, the greater part being brought back to the king.

The war lasted until the enemy were considered to have been reduced to submission—generally some six or eight weeks. Although the army moved on every day, at each halt four or five houses were built for every chief in the rough semblance of his enclosure at home. Here not only did the wives sleep whom he had brought with him to cook his food, and the slaves who carried his weapons and baggage and mounted guard over the spoil, but he even had his " audience-hall ", where his subjects came to pay their respects and bring disputes before him, just as in peace-time.

The returning army announced its arrival by sending a messenger in advance, and the king sent out a man to meet them and receive the spoil. The latter assigned his share to the general, and himself was given a share by the king.

The king received the chiefs standing in *Wankaki*, with a large pot full of beer in front of him. Only those who had acquitted themselves well were allowed to drink ; as each one came forward he was acclaimed or jeered at according to the general opinion of his deserts. The cowards were dressed up to look like pregnant women with a plantain-root tucked into their clothes, and had to wait on the others at a festive meal where, in their character of women, they were not allowed to share the fowls which were the special delicacy of the feast. Those who had distinguished themselves were rewarded with promotion and a further share of the spoil, while a peasant who had done particularly well might be presented to the king and given a chieftainship.

TAXATION

The nature of taxation has already been discussed. The organization of its collection was entrusted to a separate person on each occasion, or rather to two persons, for the *mugabe* (" leader," used of a general or the person set in command of any enterprise) had attached to him a man called *Kalabalaba* (" he who sees everything "), whose duty was to keep a check on his conduct and report on him to the king. Neither of these two did any actual work, but each appointed a representative to each ·*saza*, as did also the king's mother and sister. The group did not form, as Roscoe suggests, a sort of committee who jointly assessed the amount of taxation and subsequently apportioned it ; the sole purpose of their setting out together was to tax the whole country at the same time.

Since the rate of taxation was fixed there was no question of allotting the share of different districts. Each chief was supposed to know the number of people on his land, and report it to the messenger, so that the amount due in each case was also known. When the loads were brought in each *mukungu* took out a portion for himself and another portion which he distributed among the inferior chiefs. The royal messengers seem to have had no say in this distribution, but it was of course carried out in their presence. They then conveyed the rest to the senior *mugabe* and *Kalabalaba*, who allotted their perquisite, took their own, and passed on the remainder to the king.

PUBLIC WORKS

(a) Building

Of building and the clearing of roads there is little to say. The various houses of the royal enclosure were allotted among the *bakungu*, each of which had one of his quota kept up by the labour of his own men and assigned the rest among the *batongole* under his authority. The actual work was done under the supervision of a leader appointed by the chief. It is impossible to estimate the number of men who would be called upon from one village at any one time. There was supposed to be a reasonable rotation in the assignment of tasks, and a *mutongole* who was called on out of his turn had a just ground of complaint against his superior, though he had first to demonstrate his loyalty by getting the work done ; the proverb which expresses this principle— *Mutongole awoza akola*, " The *mutongole* does his work and then pleads his case "—is still often heard in native courts. Individual peasants could sometimes pay a substitute, and if they were selected for work unduly often would seek another master.

As regards the time which each party would spend in the capital it is easier to get evidence. Nobody puts it at less than two months. One old man said that you might have to be away from home a whole year (i.e. six months by Baganda reckoning) after which, he expressively added, you would come home and sleep. From outlying districts such as Bu·du I was told that the journey to the capital might take a month—though a month for 150 miles seems long even in primitive conditions.

While in the capital peasants lived on the site allotted for their master's house, in the little huts of grass or dry banana-leaves such as one can see to this day round a house where people are collected for mortuary ceremonies, and if they were not lucky enough to have food sent to them by their relatives obtained it by begging. From time to time the king would slaughter cattle and make distributions of meat, which reached the men in command of working parties and, through them, the more favoured peasants, but there was no question of a systematic distribution to each party.[1]

(b) Roads

Although early travellers unanimously record their admiration of the road-system of Buganda, it must be remembered that this was by contrast with regions where there were no communications at all. In the capital itself broad roads were kept open, but in the rest of the country road-making meant no more than clearing paths by which the people could be easily collected for purposes

---

[1] The materials for work—posts, grass, canes, and osiers to bind the canes together—were all found close at hand, and I found no corroboration of Roscoe's statement (*The Baganda*, p. 372) that the workmen sent their wives and children to fetch them. Indeed, this would be impossible, since they were *ex hypothesi* many days' journey from home.

of war. The labour on roads consisted merely of hoeing them clear of weeds, and of making rough bridges over swamps ; these seem to have been rare, for one is given graphic descriptions of travellers swimming the swampy rivers. A very short spell of hoeing can convert a track hardly visible in the grass to what in England would be a respectable lane. The principle on which the work was organized was very simple—that each *saza* chief was responsible for keeping open a road from his own enclosure to the capital, and the lesser chiefs for roads connecting their enclosures with his. From time to time the king would send a messenger to inspect these roads—" to see whether they shine," is the invariable expression.

THE MODERN SYSTEM

The most striking change in the modern system is the disappearance of the link between the ownership of land and the performance of political duties. Even now the two are not completely dissociated, but the intrinsic connection, and with it the whole *raison d'être* of the peasant's duties towards his chief, has vanished. Land is now acquired by inheritance or purchase ; political authority by merit coupled with education. Chieftainships are not now hereditary even in the limited sense in which they formerly were. The path to office is a different one. It leads now usually through some employment under the British or native government ; but so is the requisite experience different.

There is no sign that the people at large are dissatisfied with the new system, as they might be if they had been accustomed to government by chiefs who held office primarily in virtue of inheritance. As has been explained, there is nothing abnormal in the frequent transference and promotion of chiefs : though certainly now that the natives can no longer express their approval by moving with a chief or their disapproval by leaving him, the element of popular support in maintaining and increasing their authority has disappeared. The educated youth of the country is beginning to demand " more democratic " methods of appointment. The demand seems rather unreasonable on their part, since there are not so many Baganda with suitable qualifications to prevent any man anxious to have a say in politics from obtaining an appointment as a chief ; there is certainly no unsatisfied desire to exercise the rights of man rankling in the heart of the ordinary peasant. More serious, if it were true, would be the allegation that the native government has no freedom of choice in the selection of chiefs. Buell [1] prints an anonymous complaint to this effect, and I have heard the same opinion from Europeans. On the other hand, a responsible British official assured me that the native government's choice would not be interfered with unless it lighted on a notoriously unfit person, and I did not hear directly of any such complaint from a native.

Certainly the qualities expected of modern chiefs are of a less heroic stamp than those by which their predecessors rose to greatness. Punctuality in the remission of taxes is accounted a great merit, as is enthusiasm in encouraging cultivation of crops for sale and pushing innovations recommended by Government. The diversion of labour to European employment has never been regarded as one of their duties. They are in fact administrative officials, and their work calls for the unromantic but necessary virtues of the civil servant. No doubt the number of forceful personalities among them is decreasing, but so, with the development of modern centralized government, is the need for them.

To the peasants the most significant change has been in the nature of their obligations. Those to the landlord have already been described. The direct services to the king have disappeared, and their place is taken by the poll-tax, paid to the British Government, which returns

[1] *The Native Problem in Africa*, vol. i, p. 577.

a share to the native government, and the duty of thirty days' unpaid labour—mainly on roads—which can be commuted for a payment of ten shillings.

Under the modern system there are three grades of chiefs—*saza* chiefs, of whom there are now twenty, *gombolola* chiefs, about a dozen in each *saza*, and *muruka* chiefs, who number perhaps twenty in each *gombolola*. Each chief has a council consisting of the chiefs in the next inferior grade or their representatives ; in practice the *saza* chief's court is attended by one or two *gombolola* chiefs at a time, in rotation, the others nominating a *muruka* chief to represent them. Their functions are now confined to the collection of taxes, the transmission of orders, and the administration of justice, in which their powers are limited and their decisions subject to revision by British authority.

The *muruka* chiefs, who receive a very small salary, are usually landowners. The landlord with the largest number of tenants in that division of the *gombolola*, provided he lives on his land, can read and write, and is not too old to attend a court which may be some distance away, is thought to have the best claim to this position, though there are exceptions in practice ; his council consists of all the landowners in his district.

Here then we have a trace of the old union of landlord and political authority ; and a yet more striking trace is in the authority which native custom still allows to a landlord in virtue of his position. It is still so strongly felt that the only person who is entitled to give orders to a peasant is his landlord that the performance of all obligations to the government—the collection of taxes, turning out persons who do not commute the service for their annual duty of thirty days public labour, the notification of births and deaths, keeping village paths clear, and hunting rats and locusts—is organized by making every landlord responsible for his own tenants. It is also the landlord's duty to bring to justice any criminal who is his tenant. Moreover, though a land-lord has now no legal competence whatever, a case between two of his tenants is always taken first to him, and sent on by him to the *muruka*, one of his personal chiefs going with the parties to " introduce " the case. To omit this preliminary would be an unthinkable insult to his dignity ; and it serves a useful purpose, for quarrels which prove to be entirely without substance are often smoothed down here. (See Plate VI.)

The *muruka* also, though he has no authority to inflict penalties, often effects an amicable settlement in cases of brawling or petty theft by persuading the guilty party to compensate his victim with a fowl, beer, or a few shillings " to tie up his head ", and questions of debt can be settled here if the debtor does not refuse to pay up. Indeed these courts transact a surprising amount of petty business. I remember one case which turned on a nice point—whether a contract to make a pair of trousers at an agreed price implies an obligation to provide buttons? The question was not entirely fantastic, since the Muganda buys his own material and takes it to the tailor to be made up. I think the case was settled by a compromise on the price of the buttons.

The administration of justice is the aspect of native government which comes in for most European criticism. A proposal has recently been announced to abolish the appeal in native cases to the High Court, substituting for it an appeal to the Governor. In Nigeria and Tanganyika this is the procedure ; but in these territories the appeal to the High Court has never existed. The proposal has caused indignation among the educated natives, and among some Europeans, who hold that this step will deprive the native of an important safeguard. Serious miscarriages of justice are said to occur in native courts ; though in the *cause célèbre* which is most frequently quoted, of the sentence of a wealthy native to a period of imprisonment on a charge of rape which most Europeans believe to have been entirely false, the sentence was upheld by the British court, and I have come across no native who thinks it was unjust. The expense of an appeal to the High Court is beyond the means of most natives, and a protest which comes entirely from the wealthy class is quite likely to be due to injured vanity as to a real fear of injustice. It is also of course encouraged by the Indian pleaders who see themselves losing a source of revenue. The humbler classes have already their safeguard in the District Commissioner's powers of revision.

The native recognition of the superiority of British justice is by no means as universal as is sometimes assumed ; I have heard natives, quite without rancour, explain unexpected decisions by assuming that the British official was bribed. It is alleged that natives are much too ready to look on a case as a gamble, and therefore to acquiesce in unfair decisions ; but in my experience of the *gombolola* courts I was surprised at the number of people—frequently women—who appealed in cases where they could have no chance of success.

Even if native justice is unsatisfactory, it does not follow that the best remedy is an appeal to the High Court. Certainly in Buganda that has not the disadvantage that it has in regions where native law is still fundamentally different from British law, as it is in other parts of the Protectorate ; for almost every sphere of native life is now legally regulated in accordance with British institutions. The opposition here is between a court in which the parties do the best they can for themselves by simple commonsense arguments—and undoubtedly sometimes by lying—and one in which success depends upon " buying a pleader ", as the Baganda call it with guileless cynicism. I see no real benefit to the native in allowing him the opportunity of getting a sentence reversed through the introduction into the case of some legal technicality of which probably neither the native court nor the parties were aware. If litigation in native courts is a gamble, the appeal to the High Court is merely a more expensive gamble on a rather different issue.

If the chiefs have lost many of their former powers, they have acquired one new function through the institution of the king's council as a deliberative and legislative body. This council, the Lukiko, as constituted by the Uganda Agreement, consists of the *Kati·kiro*, Chief Justice and Treasurer (the two latter offices created by the British Government), the *·saza* chiefs, and three " notables " from each *·saza*, plus six from the whole country, selected by the king with due regard for the fair representation of all three religions. The *·saza* chiefs do not normally attend the Lukiko except for its annual legislative session, but are represented by *gombolola* chiefs, while the three " notables " are *muruka* chiefs. All these are selected by the *·saza* chiefs and changed monthly. The full Lukiko deliberates administrative matters and forms a link between the British Government and the people. It also deals, as has been mentioned, with all matters affecting clans, which, in accordance with the provisions of an agreement made in 1924, are dealt with directly by the king and are thus entirely removed from European control. No statutory provision has been made for the way in which the Lukiko is to make its decisions. The reverence for the king is still so strong that his word probably carries a good deal of weight ; but the present king only takes a spasmodic interest in its proceedings, and the moving spirit is probably Serwano Nkulubya, the Treasurer, who made such an impression on the British public when he appeared before the Select Committee on Closer Union. Seven members of the Lukiko form a court of appeal from the decisions of the *·saza* courts. There is an appeal from them to the king, and from him to the British High Court.

Unfortunately I was not able to stay long enough in Buganda to witness a legislative session of the Lukiko. It would have been very interesting to form one's own opinion as to how much spontaneous initiative really comes from within the council. A good many of its measures have certainly been passed at the instance of the British Government—a statement which is made in no spirit of criticism, since it is precisely in such matters as the development of legislation, which implies the adaption of existing institutions to changed conditions, that European advice is most necessary. The Lukiko has never been used as a means of obtaining assent to measures which the British Government desired to impose against the interests of the people as a whole. Some of its laws bear the stamp of missionary influence. The movements which are described as spontaneous native demands are often the outcome of a vaguely expressed desire that " something should be done ", put into the form of a concrete proposal by European advisers. But the proportion of suggestions coming directly from within the Lukiko itself is always increasing, and that body is certainly capable of development into a genuine native legislature.

CHAPTER VIII

DEATH AND SUCCESSION

Our account of the Baganda household, the relations of its members to one another and to the outside world, the occupations of its daily life, the possible vicissitudes of its fortunes, and the wider system into which it was integrated, is now complete. It remains to consider what happened when the household was broken up by the death of a member.

This event gave rise to three distinct necessities. The dead man's loss had to be mourned, and his body disposed of, in a manner that would be satisfactory to his spirit. His place had to be filled by someone who would take over his responsibilities towards his relatives and, if he was a chief, his authority over his village; and his property had to be disposed of.

Causes of Death

Neglect of a person during his last illness was almost certain to be resented by his spirit; and since the Baganda are quite unable to judge whether an illness is really serious, visits of condolence and gifts of food are lavished on all sick persons. So much is this an obligation that a man at Matale, whose wife was ill, told me that he could not afford to employ hired labour because he had to buy so much for her. It would not be true to say that the Baganda do not understand the idea of death from natural causes; they recognize plague, smallpox, malaria, and septic sores as causes of death, and they do not usually feel that the death of old people needs accounting for. If you ask what an old person died of, the usual answer is

Lumbe (death). But they are very prone to ascribe any death to sorcery, even if it is due to one of the causes mentioned.

Though it is often asserted that there is no cure for the effects of sorcery, attempts were in fact made to avert them. A more powerful wizard was sometimes called in, or the suspected person was summoned to remove the spell, as was described in the last chapter. Bugeza was believed to have been bewitched by one of his brothers-in-law. He refused to listen to accusations against the man until he was at the point of death, when a " doctor " who was consulted stated positively that he was guilty, and he was ordered to leave the village ; but I did not gather definitely whether it was thought that Bugeza's life might have been saved by banishing him earlier.

In the old days the practice was to expose the body in front of the house for a day or two after the death, so that any one interested could examine it for traces of foul play. In addition to poisoning, which is always regarded as sorcery, there were two types of black magic which produced different signs. In one case, the dead person's nose bled and marks appeared on his throat ; in the other, his skin presented a burnt appearance and came out in pimples. One was called ·*talo* and the other *busu·ko*, but nobody seems now to know which was which. *Busu·ko* is now believed to be a kind of magic which is laid in roads and causes pains in the feet.

There was no general presumption of guilt against the wives or any other member of the household. Only one woman, a favourite wife or a sister, was allowed to give the sick man food, and doubtless he selected one whom he could trust. Often no attempt was made to trace the sorcerer, since it is believed that they can work at any distance ; but, if someone was suspected and the signs appeared on the body, he would be taken before the chief and made to undergo the ordeal.

DEATH AND BURIAL

The nearest relatives—children, brothers and sisters, parents if alive—would be summoned before the death and assemble in the house. The woman who was nursing the sick man announced the death when she had ascertained by feeling with her hand that the breath, or the heart, had stopped. Wailing started at once—not before, for that it was thought would hasten the death. The corpse was washed and shaved by the widows— nowadays the widow and sisters—and after the two days' exposure was wrapped in barkcloths, all but the head. Every relative or friend who came to condole with the bereaved—and, in the case of a chief, each of his followers—brought a barkcloth. Nowadays they sometimes instead bring white butter muslin, or money with which this can be bought. To the survivors it was a matter of great concern that their dead should be " buried well " in a great many barkcloths, the concrete sign that he had many friends to mourn him. Before the head was wrapped up, each of the children formally took leave of the dead man by smearing a little butter across his face from forehead to chin.

The burial took place in the morning, for at night the corpse was in danger of being stolen by the *Basezi*.[1] The local senior clansman and, in the case of a peasant, also the chief were notified of the death, and each attended the burial himself or sent a representative. The senior clansman directed the proceedings. The grave was dug in the banana-grove about six feet deep and the corpse lowered in by strips of barkcloth. The earth was then thrown back by hand and piled up high above the grave ; later it was made firm by stamping on it and beating it down with poles, and, in parts of the country where large stones abound, these were heaped on it. Beer was brewed for those who had helped with the burial to drink, and if the dead man was

---

[1] See below, Chapter IX.

wealthy a cow would be killed for them. The brewing took several days, since the bananas were not cut till after the death, and after it was drunk all the mourners who had work to do at home—in particular married women—went home to wait until they were summoned for the installation of the heir, which concluded the period of mourning.

A chief was buried in one of his own houses, which was henceforth not used as a dwelling. Before the grave was dug, one of his sisters' sons cut down and burnt the post under which the fireplace was made. Two beds were placed on either side of the house, and in these slept by turns the widows who undertook the duty of tending the grave. This last custom is now obsolete ; nowadays a chief is often honoured with a cement tombstone, sometimes with a little shelter built over it. The exposure of the body is no longer practised, since burial must now take place, by Government orders, within twenty-four hours, and the custom of smearing the face with butter has been dropped. Otherwise the method of burial is the same, with the addition that Christian prayers are sometimes said over the grave.

The spirit was believed to take a great interest in the due performance of all the mortuary rites, in the survivors' grief and affection as evidenced by the wailing and the gifts of barkcloths, and in the maintenance of the grave. Indeed one reason why the right of burial in the *butaka* has little value to people whose land has passed out of the control of their own clan is that there is not likely to be any one there who will weed the grave. Graves do get overgrown when every one interested in them has gone to live a long way off ; but the knowledge of their position seems to be preserved, and occasionally a complete stranger will turn up and weed a patch of ground on which no trace of a grave is visible. Another respect in which a spirit's feelings have to be considered is that no one will voluntarily mention his name.

PLATE IX

READING THE WILL

Each object is taken from the chest as it is mentioned.

Plate X

Plate XI

RELICS OF THE OLD RELIGION

The birth-place of the river Sezibwa. In front of the sacred rock is a framework of branches on which passers-by cast handfuls of grass.

A shrine to the God of Plague (reconstructed). The split stick with a piece of dry banana-fibre thrust through it is called a "shield of Kaumpuli".

THE PERIOD OF MOURNING

The customs of mourning have hardly changed from their traditional form. The mourning lasts till the installation of the heir. During it there is no cultivation in the dead man's household, the grass strewn on the floors of the houses is not changed, and the brothers and sisters, own children, and widows, do not shave their heads. In the old days they did not wash their chests, and the widows and children were expected to observe sexual abstinence. In the case of a chief, the whole village ceases cultivation for a time, but whether they ever did so for the whole period I do not know. The close relatives who have been mentioned used to stay in the dead man's home until the mourning was concluded, being maintained by his household. Friends, more distant relatives, and relatives by marriage, pay visits of condolence. Every relative brings some little present of tobacco or salt—or nowadays money—and every relative-in-law a gourd of beer. The visitors sit down in the house, leaning against the wall or holding to a post, and wail.

Nowadays large gatherings are discouraged by administrative chiefs as leading to idleness and drunkenness, but even now the own children of a dead person would sleep in the house during this time unless they were prevented by absence at work. In that case, they would ask for leave for the burial and the ceremony of termination of the mourning. Missionaries object to the wailing as being insincere, but their influence is not effective outside their immediate neighbourhood. The visits of condolence still gather together considerable numbers of people. The final ceremony is held when the heir has been selected and a sufficient number of people assembled. In the old days it seems to have been delayed for months after the death, but nowadays the interval is not usually more than two or three weeks. In Bugeza's case it was not held till some eight months after his death, but this was exceptional, and due to the difficulties about his will. An heir is chosen for a woman as well as for a man.

THE CONCLUSION OF MOURNING

There is no Baganda ceremony in which native custom is more tenaciously preserved than this. Its character is that of a formal rejoicing to mark the close of the period of grief, and the resumption of normal life with the filling of the dead man's place. Its name, *kwabya olumbe*, means " to get rid of death ". But though after any death, even that of an infant, there is a period of two or three days' mourning, during which the women do no cultivation and their friends come to console them, the ceremonial termination of the mourning is reserved for persons who " have a place of their own "—a status in the community involving duties and responsibilities which must be taken over by a successor. In the past, only a married person was in this position—for such property as an unmarried person possessed simply reverted to his parents. The situation has changed since it became possible for an unmarried man to have " his own place " by setting up house independently, and it seems to be felt that even such an incomplete household ought not to lapse into oblivion on his death ; at least, a gathering at Kisimula agreed after some discussion that a bachelor living alone would have to be succeeded by an heir, and if he happened to own land this would certainly be necessary. But it would be interesting to see in such a case what would become of a ceremonial which presupposes entirely different circumstances.

The ritual is carried out under the presidency of a representative, appointed for a peasant by the head of his ·*siga*, and by the head of the whole clan for a chief. When the dead person is a woman, both her own senior clansman and her husband's are represented. Practical directions are actually given by the dead person's eldest

brother or eldest son, who is really responsible for the
proceedings, and is described as *mukulu wolugya* (senior
person in the household). In the case of a peasant, the
village chief or his representative should be there to
witness the installation of the heir, who must be
introduced also to the chief in person as soon as possible.
In that of a chief, the will goes before the Lukiko
for confirmation, and the heir is later formally introduced
to the king.

Many more people assemble for this ceremony than
for the burial. The husbands of the female relatives
come with their wives, and build little huts of dry banana-
leaves to sleep in, since their relationship debars them
from sleeping in the house. The proceedings begin in
the afternoon, with beer drinking, singing, and dancing,
which go on all night. Early in the morning the whole
company gathers outside the house, the men on one
side and the women on the other, and the presiding
authority announces loudly, *Olumbe lwa Gundi ndwabi·za
ne nyimbe zange ne zabana bange zo·na nzima·ze.* The
phrase cannot be translated literally ; a free rendering
might be " I have finished the mourning for So-and-so,
and all the songs, my own and my children's, I have
accomplished them ".

Then begins the ceremonial shaving and washing of
the mourners, which may last till midday, but must be
completed before the heir is installed. This should be
done by the mother of the dead person ; of course his
actual mother is very likely to be dead, but the duty
devolves upon the woman who has succeeded her. When
it is done, the mourners put on clean clothes, and in the
old days she served them a meal with mushrooms ; this
seems no longer to be done.

RULES OF SUCCESSION

Every person was expected to name his own heir, and
it was only in case of sudden death—or, possibly, where

the heir selected was a notoriously bad character—that there arose any need for a decision by the relatives. I obtained no specific information as to the persons who would take the decision, beyond the fact that the dead man's own children would feel injured if it was made in their absence. I think it would rest with them and his brothers ; it had to be confirmed by the senior clansman. Until the reign of Mutesa it was thought better that the succession should go to a brother's son rather than from father to son. This was said to " hold the clan together ", while a man who selected a son of his own was accused of " disowning " his relatives. A suitable person would probably be found among the children of brothers who had grown up in the household. It was also common for a grandchild to be selected ; nowadays the first grandson is often named as the heir at his birth, and this may have always been so. Nowadays succession goes normally from father to son or from father to grandson.

In a few cases succession could go outside the clan. One is that of a man who has no male relatives—a case which would seem impossible under the clan system, but is spoken of as common. In this case he would select a sister's child. I knew a man who had succeeded his maternal uncle in this way. I can hardly believe that a man could be unacquainted with a single other member of his clan, and think it more probable that the relationship would not be considered significant if it was too distant to be traced. Again, if a series of heirs die, the reason is thought to be the dead man's jealousy of his successors, and this is avoided by selecting as heir a sister's son, who is safe because the spirit cannot attack a member of another clan.

The Installation of the Heir

At the actual installation the heir is always accompanied by a woman called *lubuga* ; this is done even in the case of a woman heir, and the reason for it is difficult to understand. Native comments on the custom are various. Some amount to no more than a statement that it exists, like " A man cannot inherit alone, he cannot stand alone on the barkcloth " (the barkcloth on which the heir stands to be proclaimed to the company). The most rational explanation was Waswa's, that man and wife inherit together ; this reminds one of the custom when making blood-brotherhood, where each partner was provided with a fictitious wife if he was not yet married or his own wife was not present. The idea may be perhaps that in each case the relationships which the ceremony creates will affect not the man only, but his whole household. But this does not explain the practice where the heir is a woman. In this case, it was suggested that the *lubuga's* position is analogous to that of the girl attendant on a bride.

In the case of a man the interesting point is that, since succession and inheritance are purely clan affairs, his own wife cannot go through the ceremony with him and a woman of the clan has to be selected. This is not done by the dying man, but by the relatives who organize the proceedings, and seems to be left till the last minute. In one of the ceremonies I saw, the *lubuga* had not even known that she would be wanted, and when everything was nearly ready for the installation someone had to be sent on a bicycle to fetch her from the next village.

When everything is ready, the couple stand side by by side on a new barkcloth (or nowadays a piece of white cotton), all those present gather round, and the clan drum-beat is played by a man related to the clan through a woman—a task which falls to him as a non-member of the clan in his position of " slave ". The clan head gives spears to the heir and a knife to the *lubuga*, and a gourd of beer with two cups for both to drink ; if a woman is inheritor, she herself receives the knife. Nowadays a knife often does duty for the spears. The clan head then proclaims " This is the heir of So-and-so, child

of So-and-so, grandchild of So-and-so", mentioning the
actual father and grandfather and one or two more
distant ancestors, and finally the original ·siga and
clan heads. The proclamation is followed by an
injunction to fill the dead person's place worthily and
carry out his duties towards his relatives. There is no
set formula for this exhortation. I noted these extracts
from that made over the woman who succeeded Beza
at Kisimula : " They have set you in this place, a very
great place. Go, take your place, where your children
may seek you ! If you have no place, where will your
children seek you ? Look on them with kindness and
may every one love you. Hold to the things of religion ! "
The injunctions to a man are in such terms as : " Be
generous, as the dead man was, be brave, do not grudge
others food, let everyone who comes to your house be
treated as your child, do not disown a clansman."

When this injunction is finished, the heir and *lubuga*
go into the house and sit on the barkcloth and the
various relatives come in and introduce themselves, not
by name, but by explaining the relationship. Each one
casts a few cents on the barkcloth, and they may drink
from the heir's gourd. The dead man's immediate family
—his own brothers, sisters, and children—do not take
part in this series of introductions, for it is assumed that
they are known to the heir.

When I saw this done at Ngogwe, I did not know the
language well enough to follow what was being said, so
cannot describe the sort of phrases used to a man.
At Kisimula, the woman was urged by each successive
person who presented himself to be generous with food
and hospitable to all who came to her house. Two men
introduced themselves as "husbands", then came a
succession of "children", each of whom made some
reference to suckling, and finally an old man, who said,
" I am the grandfather of your children."

The next proceeding was omitted at Kisimula, I think
because in the case of a woman the relationship through

women—that between a man and his sisters' children—
is not significant. At Ngogwe the female " slaves "—
daughters of women of the clan—cleared out the old
grass from the floor of the house, while the " princesses "
—women of the clan—went off to the bush to cut fresh
grass and came back in procession escorted by the
drummer, each carrying a handful—as much as could
be cut with one stroke—on her head. When they
arrived, they found the " slaves " in the doorway barring
their entrance. A mock fight ensued in which the
" slaves " demanded cents to let the " princesses " in.
The " princesses " threw their bundles of grass into the
house over their opponents' heads, and two or three
forced their way in and began to spread it over the
floor. At length the *mukulu wolugya* flung five cents
down among the old grass, and the " slaves " then carried
it outside and fell to searching among it for the coins.
If this had not been done, they were theoretically entitled
to take anything they liked from the house by way of
asserting their relationship.

The general celebrations conclude with a meal at
which one of the dead person's goats is eaten. Tradition
allotted a certain part of the animal to the dead man's
children, another to the grandchildren, and so on through
each group of relatives, but the division has evidently
ceased to be observed, for I was given two accounts
of it which did not by any means correspond. Here,
again, the " princesses " and " slaves " are distinguished
by their positions. It was believed that those persons
on whom sexual abstinence was enjoined during the
time of mourning would die after eating the meat if
they had broken this rule of respect for the dead, and
any one who had done so had to refuse it, thus publicly
confessing his guilt.

This meal is eaten in the afternoon, and at dusk the
heir and *lubuga* go into the inner room of the house and
perform the *kukuza* rite. Where the heir is a woman,
the rite is done with the widower or, if he is dead, his

heir, not in the house but in a leaf hut built for the purpose.

Then there is another night of singing, and next day the grave is put in order—if the burial is recent it is only now that the earth is trodden down, if the mourning has lasted a long time it is weeded—the property is distributed, and most of the men go home. Women who have come a long distance go with their husbands; those who live near stay on for some days and help the household to cope with the weeds which have flourished since the death. When this is done, their husbands come for them, bringing beer or the price of a gourd " to congratulate the heir ", and take them home.

This completes the rendering of honour to the spirit and the installation of his personal substitute—an act which in itself is an honour to the spirit, for this is thought to be the chief way, apart from calling children by his name, of keeping his memory alive. It is this personal succession, and not the acquisition of the dead man's property, which used in the old days to be the most significant feature of the heir's position, and even in this respect he did not simply " step into the dead man's shoes "; the extent to which the latter's status was inherited was definitely limited.

STATUS OF THE HEIR

Unless the dead man was a clan or *siga* head, the heir did not take his name. He was not, as it were, translated into an older generation, since, as the Baganda say, " you cannot climb the ladder." The dead man's children would not call him " father " except when formally introducing him; he was usually referred to as " my father's heir ". He still treated his elders with the same respect as before, and observed the same avoidances; for example, if he " became " his father's brother by succession, he still could not sleep in his father's house. On the other hand, his sisters observed the avoidances of daughters towards him. He did not marry the dead man's widows, for, if he was of a later generation, they "called him child". He did not succeed to full paternal authority over the dead man's children but only to the necessity of providing for their wants. He was not obliged to live on the dead man's land, unless it was a *butaka*.[1]

The essential characteristic of his position was that he played his predecessor's part on occasions which required the presence of a parent, such as betrothal, marriage, and the twin-birth ceremonies ; and it was by performing some such rite that his position was finally confirmed. Thus the son of Bugeza who would have been by far the most suitable heir, Petero Mu·du, had succeeded his grandfather and in that capacity had twice had a twin-birth announced to him by his own father. Otherwise, when it became obvious that neither of his other grown sons would make a very satisfactory successor, Bugeza might, with the consent of his clan head, have "taken him from the barkcloth" of his grandfather and had someone else appointed in his place ; but his having taken part in these ceremonies made this impossible.

In connection with the guardianship of the children and the execution of the dead man's wishes, two other persons exercised a check upon the heir. Immediately after the death a clansman of the dead man (not necessarily a near relative) was appointed *mukuza wolugya* (guardian of the home) ; or he might be selected by the dying man himself. If the latter was very wealthy, three or four persons might be chosen. Their duty was to see that the dead man's wishes were carried out, to look after the property if the heir was a child, and if he was a grown man to see that he dealt fairly by the dead man's children. If he did not provide them with clothing—and nowadays if he does not send them to school—one of these men was expected to intervene, and, if necessary, to arraign the heir before the clan council, who could remove him from his position.

[1] See Chapter VI, p. 162.

Also, the dead man's eldest son was regarded as having the real authority over his younger brothers and sisters, and after it became customary for succession to go in the direct line he was never chosen to succeed his father. His business seems to have been mainly to settle quarrels between them ; the bar on his inheriting may have resulted from the incompatibility of this position with the other relationships in which the heir was involved, or it may have been held that it was part of his duty to protect their rights.[1]   It has died out under the influence of the European belief in primogeniture. As we have seen, it was he who directed the practical side of the proceedings at a funeral, and when all the older generation were dead it was he who was called " father " by his younger brothers and sisters.

In the case of a woman, the ritual aspect of her new position was the most important.   She was not expected to marry the dead woman's husband ; indeed she might often be already married.   Nowadays an unmarried woman is expected to stay in her predecessor's house and look after her children, but opinions differ as to whether she ought to stay until she is married.   The woman who succeeded Beza left after a month, amid great indignation, but some, at least, of the relatives said that she could have gone home with perfect propriety if she had waited a year.   Whether this was required at all in the old days, when the children could easily be taken over by a co-wife, I do not know.

DISSOLUTION OF THE HOUSEHOLD

In the arrangements necessitated by the dissolution of the household—the provision for the widow and

---

[1] His position is analogous to that of the one son specially appointed among the Zulu to judge disputes between his father's heirs (cf. Richards, *Hunger and Work in a Savage Tribe*, p. 135).   Whether the quarrels referred to among the Baganda were quarrels over the distribution of the property I do not know.

children, and the disposal of the dead person's property—
considerable changes have taken place in modern times.
One obvious reason for this is the virtual disappearance
of polygamy, which has so greatly altered the composition
of the household. To the changes in dealing with
property a number of causes have contributed. One is
the fact that land, and not cattle, is now the most prized
form of property, and that land cannot be distributed
or carried off piecemeal as livestock can. Another
cause is the general loosening of kinship ties outside the
immediate family, which very much reduces the claims
on the property. Finally, the modern custom of making
wills enables the owner himself to make a more precise
disposition of his possessions.

The household whose members had to be provided
for consisted of widows, young children, and female
slaves; for the grown children and men slaves had
households of their own whose position was unaltered
by the father's death, even if they had been set up on
his land.

The older widows, who had no chance of marrying
again, were expected to stay in their own houses and
look after the grave. Some informants held that any
woman who had borne a child should stay with them,
since if she went home to her own people she had to
leave her child behind. But it seems to have been
more common than not for a widow who could hope to
find another husband to go back to her own relatives
with that end in view, for such a young widow, if she
intended to go on living near the tomb, expressed her
intention in a formal manner, kneeling by the corpse
and saying aloud, " I shall not marry again." Even
then she seems to have been free to change her mind
later, simply announce that she was tired of tending the
grave, and go home. A widow who had no children
could marry the heir if she wished.

The position of slave-women was different, since they
had no relatives to go to, and they seem to have been

obliged to marry any member of the clan who wished to take them. One of them might be claimed by the chief. The eldest son and the eldest son of a sister had each a definite claim to a slave who was still a virgin, which was ceremonially asserted at the time of the burial. The corpse was wrapped up with the right hand free, and in this was placed some seeds of a wild vine called *kiryo* ; the dead man's eldest son bent down and took these up in his mouth, and then blew them over the woman whom he selected. The senior sister's son cut a piece from the strip of barkcloth with which the corpse was lowered into the grave and cast this at the woman of his choice. The fate of the rest was decided at the time of the distribution of the property.

If a peasant's heir decided not to live on the dead man's land, the guardianship of the widows who remained with the graves was provided for in another way. They came under the general protection of the chief of the village and were described as his wives, though he was not even obliged to give them clothes. Indeed all that such a woman gained from his protection was that if she wanted to bring a case into court she could go to his representative for assistance. Nowadays, when old women are constantly lending money to young men which they can only get back by prosecuting, this assistance is quite valuable ; nowadays, too, good-natured landlords do not expect widows to pay rent. They were liable for a number of services on request ; to fetch grass to strew the chief's house, to help his wives sow simsim, and nowadays, when the chief's household is relatively small, they may be asked to help cook when he has guests, or even to house a visitor. This status was definitely valued, since it was essential for every reputable woman to have a recognized protector.

As regards property, the heir's position was that of the residuary legatee. Only household implements and tools—defined once as " water-pots, baskets, spears and shields, and the big knife for working for the chief "—

were his by right. The relatives who attended the mortuary ceremonies selected what they fancied from the dead man's other possessions—livestock, barkcloths, and strings of cowries ; the " distribution " by the senior clansman seems to have been confined to arbitrating conflicting claims. Both the senior clansman and the relative who directed the proceedings were entitled to a large share, and a present was sent to the chief at a peasant's death and to the king at a chief's. None of the property was given to the widows, since inheritance was strictly confined to the clan and they were not members of the clan. But their own property—livestock or other objects expressly given to them—was exempt from the distribution. Adult children doubtless upheld their own claims, while young children were better provided for by the obligations of the heir towards them than they could have been by the assignment to them as their own property of specific objects. All creditors were expected to appear and state their claims against the dead man before the heir was appointed. What was left when all these demands were met was his material inheritance.

Thus the position of an heir involved more honour than material gain. Its responsibilities were certain, the risk of supernatural punishment for not carrying them out effectively considerable, its advantages much less definite. Yokana Waswa said that such was the reluctance to succeed that the heir sometimes had to be seized by force.

But nowadays the advantages of succession, in the case of a landowner, are very much greater. The relatives who attend a funeral cannot help themselves to pieces of land, though it is true that, if the owner of a large estate has not allotted land to any of his children other than the heir, a share is assigned to them by the Lukiko on the proposal of the clan head. But the greater part of the area goes to the heir himself, and its rents come in to him whether or not he decides to live there. A

remarkable feature of modern times is that land is sometimes left to daughters, but there is still a strong feeling
that this should not be done because it will pass to their
children and so go out of the clan. The actual
distribution of property nowadays is made on an entirely
different basis. The heir expects the greater part of
it to fall to him, and the relatives present merely receive
small objects which are hardly more than keepsakes—
a hoe, a garment, a knife. If a will is made stating
definitely what is to be given to the relatives, they may
get even less.

On the only occasion on which I was present at the
reading of a will, the dead person was a woman who did not
leave much property altogether. (See Pl. IX.)   But what
there was was expressly left to the heir with the exception
of one dress for her children (this was sold on the spot, and
brought in Shs. 2/50 to be shared among six people),
a fowl for the senior clansman, and one for the other
relatives.   In the case of a man who is relatively well off,
the chief still expects his present, but the only other
definite claims are those of the senior clansman, the
senior near relative, and the *lubuga*, who receives the
cloth on which she sits with the heir for the formal
installation and half of the cents which are thrown on it.
The heir's management of the property is still subject
to the check of the *mukuza wolugya* in the interests of
the other children.

Of the dissolution of the household as it affects the
life of the individual members, little need be said except
that the numbers concerned are fewer than before.   There
are now seldom more than two widows and no slaves,
and consequently no women to be apportioned among
the relatives.   The old rule still holds good that widows
can go home to their people, remain under the protection
of the heir, or live independently under that of the chief.

CHAPTER IX

RELIGION AND MAGIC

IN no aspect of Baganda culture does the attempt to reconstruct the days before European penetration meet with so many difficulties as in the region of religious beliefs and practices. The pagan religion is now nowhere openly practised, and survives only in the naming of children after one or two of the most important deities, in the activities of certain persons who profess to exercise supernatural powers under the influence of spirit possession, and in the fragmentary and often contradictory memories of a few old people. It is almost impossible to make of such memories a coherent whole in which the real meaning and value of the old religious system to the Baganda would appear.

I shall begin by describing the general beliefs as to the relation between the living and the dead, and the attitude of the Baganda to their immediate ancestors. These beliefs provide a basis for the understanding of the cult of the generally recognized divinities, who appear to be conceived as having formerly had a human existence. Magical practices are intimately bound up with religious beliefs ; for the main occasions of religious ceremonial were the public pronouncement of oracles, and distribution of magical prescriptions, by the prophets to persons who came to consult them, and it is to revelation by the divinities that the prophets were believed to owe their knowledge. The nature and uses of magic, both beneficial and harmful, will be discussed, and the ways in which sorcery may be employed as an instrument of law and order. Finally we shall have to mention certain types of supernatural punishment which do not appear to be connected in any way with the activities of divinities, ancestor-spirits, or sorcerers, but which have their own part to play in upholding specific rules of conduct.

ANCESTOR-SPIRITS (*Mizimu*)

Baganda religion, though it was in a sense a cult of ancestors, was something very different from what is usually meant by "ancestor-worship". It was not to the spirits of his immediate ancestors that the Muganda looked for protection or assistance in time of trouble, not around them that ritual observances centred. But only when the general beliefs as to the relation between the dead and the living have been described can we place in their proper context the beliefs with regard to those exceptional dead persons who were treated as divinities or *lubale*.[1]

The traditional idea of the life after death has remained unshaken by Christianity. The Baganda have no difficulty in reconciling it with the new conceptions. They make the same adjustment as the uneducated European who believes equally in heaven and in ghosts. The *muzimu*, or spirit, is believed to remain for most of the time in or near the grave, though it can travel any distance. It is invisible, "like wind," and the sudden gusts which sometimes blow up the dust at midday in the dry season are believed to be passing spirits, who may seize upon and choke any person whom they meet ; for this reason some mothers, I was told, do not like their children to play out of doors at midday.

But these chance manifestations of unknown spirits are of interest merely as showing what the nature of the *muzimu* is supposed to be. The belief which formed the basis of the whole religious system was that the spirits of the dead remained in close contact with their own descendants, could be placated by means of offerings, and when they wished to communicate with the living

[1] I use the singular, despite the grammatical inaccuracy, because the word, in this form, is commonly used among Europeans in Uganda.

could do so by taking possession of a person through whose mouth they spoke.

There is little evidence that the spirits were looked on as a source of blessings. It is occasionally said that a piece of good luck might be attributed to them, but I never came across an actual instance, while cases of their malevolence are constantly quoted. The cult which formerly existed seems to have been mainly directed to placate this malevolence ; indeed it is doubtful whether any regular rites were performed until some spirit had demanded them by a visitation. There are vague memories of spirit huts at which offerings of beer were made, and statements that a man might " dedicate " a fowl to his ancestors ; this does not imply a sacrificial meal, but means simply that it was kept on the premises, not given away, and replaced when it died. Thus the ancestors do not seem to have been clearly conceived, as we find them in Bantu society, as exercising after death the same authority and protection over their children as they did during their lifetime. There were apparently no benefits which it was thought to be specifically within their province to confer, nor any recognized formulae of prayer. No accounts of family ceremonies give any indication that the ancestors were believed to be present at them, with the exception of a single statement that the spirits gather to join in the wailing over a dead man. On the contrary, it was once expressly stated to me that the formal appointment of an heir to take the name and status of the dead person was all the remembrance necessary. This statement illustrates a very significant aspect of the Baganda view of the relation between the living and the dead.

This is not regarded as a prolongation beyond the grave of the ties of mutual obligation by which living relatives are bound, because, on the death of every adult person, his place is filled by someone who is made responsible for the performance of his duties to his relatives. If the heir fails in these duties, the spirit will punish him ; but the spirit itself does not remain in continuous contact with those it has left behind. Its active intervention is practically confined to visitations in which it expresses anger at some injury. This is done by "possessing" one of its descendants. The spirit is supposed to enter the stomach by the mouth and cause a type of indigestion known as *kigalanga*, whose first symptom is said to be a very cold feeling. This is regarded as the manifestation *par excellence* of spirit possession, but many other illnesses may be ascribed to this cause.

The first thing to do on such an occasion is to "make the spirit speak". This can be done by the administration of medicines which appear to be generally known, and does not always require a specialist, but it sometimes takes several days. Once the spirit has declared itself, usually by speaking through the mouth of the victim, and its requests have been attended to, the patient recovers. If the spirit's anger is implacable, the victim dies, and it is believed that, in such a case, it may seize its victim by the throat and kill it instantly. But no one has ever known anybody who died in this way.

Usually the spirit was placated by an offering. The commonest course for a woman was to dedicate a part of the banana-grove to the spirit. This meant that, when working there, she used a special knife and wore a special barkcloth, which, when not in use, were kept apart in the house. The barkcloth and knife were procured by her husband, or the father of an unmarried girl, and the barkcloth was placed over her while she was still ill. If the victim was a man, the offering consisted of a barkcloth, a goat, and a large knife for cutting firewood. In his case, he honoured the spirit by wearing the barkcloth only when out visiting and not at work.

Such public acts of propitiation are no longer performed, but there are very few people who do not believe as strongly as ever in the visitations of the spirits. The

injuries which are thought to be thus punished are
wrongs done to the dead person in lifetime or to his
memory, wrongs done to the heir, through which the
spirit feels itself injured, or unsatisfactory conduct of
the heir to his relatives. In the first group, the
type of grievance ascribed to the angry *muzimu* is neglect
during its last illness, failure to carry out the mortuary
rites properly, or neglect of the grave. Such injuries
may be visited either on the person responsible or on the
heir—the latter if the spirit refuses to be placated ;
in this case, it will attack every heir until one is appointed
who is related through a woman, and is therefore immune
from attack as being of another clan. The spirit whose
anger is most feared is the *sengawe*, whose claims to
especial respect during lifetime are made effective largely
by the fear of her vengeance after death.

While I was at Kisimula three cases occurred of illness
supposed to be caused by spirits. One was that of a
little girl who was afflicted with a bad headache by the
spirit of her grandmother. She recovered very quickly,
and I heard no details. Another was the case mentioned
in an earlier chapter of a young woman who nearly had
a miscarriage through the use of native medicines. In
her case, there was not at first any general agreement as
to the cause of her illness, and she was taken to the local
maternity centre by her father and her mother's brother.
Here she was examined by the visiting European
supervisor, who wanted her moved to a hospital where
she could have European attention. This necessitated
consulting her husband, who would have had to pay for
the treatment, and he flatly refused to allow it, holding
that the disease was supernaturally caused. Shortly
afterwards, she recovered sufficiently to walk home.

By this time the general opinion of the village had come
round to her husband's view, but for some days the spirit
refused to speak. Every day numbers of people
assembled at her father's house and sat talking for
hours ; she sat among them, alternately talking and

laughing and grimacing with pain, for it is thought dangerous to leave an invalid alone, lest, by going to sleep in the daytime, he should aggravate the disease. After some days, I heard that the spirit had spoken at last. It was one of those—I failed to discover which— whose graves were near the house of the girl's grand- parents, and it was angry because she had broken a pipe and a bowl. She was told to go at dawn to the house of another relative—actually her *sengawe*—which was also near the grave, because the spirit had taken up its abode in the thatch over the door. (This is a favourite haunt of spirits, but they can be kept off by hanging up a wild gourd under the eaves.) The spirit would then go back to its grave ; the girl was to wait a little to give it time, then go to the grave, lay her hand on the head and go away without looking back. Unfortunately, I did not observe the actual relation between the revelation of the spirit and the girl's recovery.

The same girl was said to have been possessed on an earlier occasion by fifteen spirits at once. Two of these had grievances of their own, but the others had simply been called in by them to reinforce their attack ; it seems that sometimes a spirit which does not quickly get what it wants will return to its grave and fetch the inmates of any neighbouring graves, or it may even enlist the support of relatives whom it meets on the way. In this case, the spirits directly concerned were a grand- mother, whose grave was not kept clean, and a sister of the girl's mother, whose heir had not received her share of the beer brought for her betrothal. This was felt as an injury by the spirit because " If my heir had drunk it, I should have drunk it ".

The other case which actually occurred when I was there was that of the child of one of Bugeza's widows, Sefoloza. I first heard that she would not be able to leave the place with the other widows because she had a sick child who was being treated by a local native doctor. Several of her children had died already, and in the case of this one, I learnt later, the doctor had revealed that the deaths were caused by the mother's *sengawe*. The latter during her last illness had been sent away by her brother, Sefoloza's father, to die on his freehold land where he wanted her to be buried, because he was afraid that if she died at Kisimula he would not be able to have her body taken there. This she had very much resented, and her spirit was determined not to accept as her heir a daughter of the man who had treated her so badly.

Other cases cited of behaviour which was liable to anger a spirit were failure to pay a debt or to make some gift, particularly in connection with marriage ceremonies. Thus the general belief in the life after death provides a sanction not for morality in general but rather for the satisfactory performance of specific kinship obligations.

It is also worth mentioning that the spirits of persons who have died a violent death are sometimes believed to revenge themselves on any person who approached the scene of the event. For instance, there are certain fords in the river Mayanja where the spirit of a drowned person attacks any one who tries to cross in similar circumstances to those in which it was itself drowned. The human sacrifices which Roscoe[1] says were offered at wells were explained by my informants as being occasionally necessary to placate the spirit of a drowned child and not as dictated by the cult of any *lubale*.

DIVINITIES (*Lubale*)

It is in this context of general beliefs that we must examine the ideas of the Baganda concerning the peculiarly powerful and important spirits who formerly, as *lubale*, were the object of a public cult. The *lubale* are the spirits of persons who gave evidence of super-natural powers during their lifetime, and who

[1] *The Baganda*, p. 458.

manifested themselves after death not only, like other spirits, for their personal ends but also in order to help the living by foretelling the future and by revealing to them magical means of obtaining wealth, fertility, and success in enterprises of all kinds. This they did through the mouths of prophets who, once possessed, were formally dedicated to their service. Two of them were honoured by human sacrifice—one, Kibuka, the war-god, for the specific reason that he met his death by violence and treachery.[1]

Theoretically, each clan had its own *lubale*, but the cult of each divinity was not confined to the members of the clan. This explains the fact that only a few *lubale* are now universally remembered—Kibuka and Nende, the war-gods, Mukasa, the giver of children and especially of twins, all of whom were particularly honoured by the king, and Kaumpuli, the god of plague. Kings on their death acquired a position analogous to that of *lubale*. That is to say, their spirits could possess the attendant on their tombs and cause him to prophesy. But they did so only for the personal benefit of the reigning king.

The connection between the *lubale* and the members of its own clan was a close but not an exclusive one. Each *lubale* seems to have had a single temple, and this, unless it had been deliberately transferred by the king to a place near the capital, stood in the clan lands and was under the authority of a priest (*Kabona*) appointed

---

[1] The sacrifices to Kibuka—whose death-roll has been swelled in popular European belief by adding to it all kinds of murders which were not sacrifices at all—have made such a profound impression on the minds of European observers that they see in them the whole content of Baganda religion, and are convinced that the destruction of that religion has, in itself, rescued the people from untold horrors. A pamphlet issued on the jubilee of missionary activity in Uganda refers to the "impression left of dark mysterious power by the *lubale* . . . the one power before which even an irresponsible despot quails in fear ". This power was illustrated at a historical pageant by a representation of a court execution ! Such a statement would not be accepted as a complete description of any religious system by a sociological student. But since the present study aims at describing the changes which European contact has affected in a primitive culture, it seems desirable expressly to controvert a view of the previous state of affairs which is widely held.

by the clan head. A portion of the land was allotted to the god, and the *Kabona* had the same rights over the peasants who lived on it as an ordinary chief. The temple was the scene of the public cult of the *lubale*, and in it were preserved the relics of the god, or some object which was supposed to be his material manifestation (e.g. Kibuka's navel-cord and spear, or the large stone which was sacred to Mukasa). But the cult was open to any one who wished to join in it.

Private prayers, however, were offered only to the *lubale* of the suppliant's clan. He would build a small shrine in his banana-grove and offer beer and cowries there. Two typical prayers were quoted to me by different persons, both short enough to reproduce. One ran, *Lubale wa·tu, tukume enyumba, tutule bulungi* (" Dear *lubale*, may we keep our house safe, may we dwell in peace "), and the other, *Lubale wa·tu, ompe obulamu, ompe obuga·ga, nzale mwana* (" Dear *lubale*, give me health, give me wealth, may I beget a child "). The appellation *wa·tu*, which in ordinary life could often be translated " old chap ", throws on the relations between divinity and worshipper a rather less lurid light than that in which they are commonly depicted.

The central point in the *lubale* cult was the belief in spirit possession. The *lubale* selected as their mouth-pieces certain individuals through whom they spoke, both in answer to inquiries and spontaneously. The connection here between *lubale* and clan was that a prophet was always possessed first by the *lubale* of his own clan, though once his formal initiation as a prophet was completed he might become the vehicle of any divinity. The prophet who was actually attached to the temple was expressly selected by the god ; on the death of one a successor could not be appointed till the *lubale* had indicated his wishes by possessing the person he had chosen. Probably the prophet attached to the temple spoke only in the name of his own *lubale*, but there were numerous others who practised in their own homes and were not regarded as being consecrated to the service of any particular god. These private practitioners might claim to speak in other names than those of the generally recognized *lubale*, and in particular of wild animals, lions, leopards, or crocodiles which belonged to the neighbourhood. These were living animals, not spirits.[1] It was believed that a lion or leopard would enter the house of its prophet and sit among the people, and that it would not attack the village unless driven to do so by the dictates of hospitality to a visitor !

Such prophets might come to be known as associated with some particular *lubale*, and, in so far as the *lubale* had specialized provinces, it would of course be necessary for a person in need of a particular form of assistance, if he could not go to the temple, to find a prophet who was known to speak for the *lubale* concerned. But the private prophets tended to form an undifferentiated class rather than a series of orders.

Nor was there any sharp differentiation between the provinces of the various *lubale*. Each individual appealed for the same general benefits to his own clan *lubale*, and, at any rate in the case of the private practitioners, a prophet when consulted did not know which *lubale* would first respond to the invocation. In the two present-day cases of which I have records, this invocation took the form of a general appeal to all the *lubale* of Buganda and the neighbouring countries. A consultant in search of a cure for illness, of magic to recover stolen goods, of a charm for child-bearing or the acquisition of wealth, would look for a prophet with a reputation for " speaking well ", rather than the servant of some particular *lubale*. Any *lubale* could answer such requests. Thus the king when ill would consult Kibuka, the war-god, and I have seen child-bearing charms distributed by a prophet of Kaumpuli, the god of plague, while a chief before he set out for

[1] Cf. Roscoe, *The Baganda*, p. 288.

war would consult the local *lubale*, whoever he might be.

SPECIAL PROVINCES OF *Lubale*

At the same time, there were certain matters— national safety, national as distinct from personal success in war, dangerous activities such as hunting and fishing, and calamities of various kinds—which were exclusively within the control of individual *lubale*. Kibuka's presidency over warfare has been repeatedly mentioned. The appeal to him when the king was ill may possibly have been due not merely to the fact that he was the *lubale* whom the king especially honoured, but to the idea that such an illness was a national danger caused by the presence of evil influences in the country, against whom Kibuka's prophet from time to time uttered warnings when the king's messengers consulted him. The remedy for such dangers consisted usually in the murder of persons met near the capital who had some arbitrary distinguishing mark specified by the prophets. This is recognized by native commentators as a form of purification required in order " to set the land right ", and is clearly distinguished both from the purely political murders, which are described as intended " to show the power of the king ", and from rites performed simply with a view to pleasing the *lubale*.

I have mentioned already that Kibuka is in fact one of the two gods—or, according to some versions, the only one—to whom human sacrifices were made. The other is the *lubale* of the river Mayanja, whom the king consulted during the accession ceremonies. It was universally agreed that their position in this respect was peculiar ; in the case of Kibuka, it was explained by the fact that he met his death by treachery when fighting for the Baganda against the Banyoro, so that his spirit required to be appeased in just the same way as the spirits of ordinary persons mentioned above. According to Sir Apolo Kagwa, the sacrifices were of prisoners of war and were demanded by Kibuka when he prophesied and when his temple was rebuilt, nine or eighteen at a time [1]; I obtained no details myself on this point.

Of the *lubale* who presided over calamities, and were appealed to when they occurred, the principal were Kaumpuli, the god of plague, Kawali or Ndawula, of smallpox, Kiwanuka, of lightning, Musisi, of earthquakes, and Nagawonyi, the goddess of drought.

Mukasa was the *lubale* appealed to by fishermen. The hunters' god was Dungu, who, as supernatural owner of all wild animals, would announce to the hunter who approached him before setting out : " I give you such and such a beast ; go and kill it ! " or might warn him to put off his expedition.

Another way in which some *lubale* were distinguished was that certain types of magic were practised exclusively by their prophets. The purification of a village from plague could be done only by a prophet of Kaumpuli ; those of another deity, Mwanga, had a method of divining with small strips of leather which was peculiar to themselves ; those of a female *lubale*, Nabuzana, who were themselves women, had a special method of exorcising sickness.

OBJECTS ASSOCIATED WITH *Lubale*

Certain natural objects, such as wells, large rocks, and trees, were also believed to be associated with *lubale*, and treated with respect. The trees could not be cut down, the water of the wells was used with especial care, and not for all purposes, and beer and sometimes hoe-blades were placed by them and by the rocks as offerings. Stories were told of their miraculous behaviour, and occasionally they were believed to confer benefits such as wealth on those who treated them properly. In some cases a particular *lubale* is said to have been

[1] *Empisa za Baganda*, p. 219.

seen near the spot ; the rock which marks the birth-
place of the river Sezibwa is an example. (See
Plate X.) Usually, however, the connection with personified spirits is so vague that the phrase "to have
a *lubale*" seems to mean nothing more than to be
endowed with supernatural qualities. This type of cult
seems to be essentially different both from that of the
mizimu, which rests upon the persistence after death
of personal relationships, or from that of the *lubale*
as such, which is based on reliance on their aid in securing
success in matters beyond human control. It arises
rather from that interest in objects of the natural
environment in which some writers have found the
explanation of totemism.

CEREMONIAL

Except in the case of the *lubale* specially honoured by
the king, information regarding public ceremonial is
scanty, and it is even doubtful how far there were fixed
occasions for it. I was more than once assured that there
were no periodic ceremonies associated with the seasons.
Roscoe's statement that the king made annual offerings
to Mukasa for the fertility of the crops [1] is not confirmed
by Sir Apolo Kagwa, is inconsistent with the complete
absence of belief in magic for such purposes, and is
inherently improbable since the Baganda agriculture
cycle would require such an offering to be made, if at all,
not every year but every six months. The new moon
was the occasion for a ritual cessation of work, but no
two informants agree as to how long this lasted, whom
it affected, or whether it was accompanied by the
rendering of any special honour to the *lubale*.

The ceremonial centred always round the "appearance" of the *lubale*—the utterance by his prophet in
a hypnotic condition of oracles and answers to inquiries,
and, where the temple contained relics of the god, their

[1] *The Baganda*, p. 298.

display before the assembled people. Sir Apolo Kagwa
states that Kibuka " appeared " once every month, and
Nende every two and a half years.[1] Whether or not
there were fixed occasions for consulting the other *lubale*,
any individual inquirer had always to arrange in advance
the day on which he would approach the god and the
gifts he would bring, so that it was generally known when
the *lubale* proposed to speak, and those who wished to
be present could gather at the temple. Any one who had
a request to make had to approach the *Kabona*; the
latter made the necessary business arrangements and
presented the inquirer to the prophet, indicating the
gifts which he had brought. The proceedings began with
an invocation to the *lubale* uttered either by the *Kabona*
or by the prophet himself. The audience then sang the
songs especially appropriate to the *lubale* concerned,
to the accompaniment not of the usual music but of
rattles made of gourds with dry seeds inside or of a double
layer of canes with seeds between. The descent of the
lubale upon the prophet's head was indicated when the
latter began to make violent jerky movements and sometimes got up and danced. When these preliminaries
were over, he attended to the requests of the persons
who had come to consult him, which he was supposed to
be able to interpret without their offering any explanation.
The ceremony ended with more dancing and singing and the
consumption of the beer which the inquirers had brought.[2]

These were the essential features of every consultation
of a *lubale*. The degree of dignity and elaboration which
characterized them varied from the magnificence of the
" national " temples of Kibuka, Nende, and Mukasa,
the gods on whose advice the king depended, to the comparative informality of the séances of a private prophet,
held for the benefit of local peasants. The temples of
the less important deities held an intermediate place.

[1] *Empisa za Baganda*, pp. 220–4.
[2] Accounts of the two contemporary séances of which I have record
are appended to this chapter.

Such a ceremony was always held after the rebuilding of a temple, as a formal invitation to the *lubale* to take up its residence in its new home ; and a private prophet, if he moved to a new village, would hold a similar feast to " settle in " his *lubale*. It was probably also held when thank-offerings on a large scale were made by the king or an important chief.

In the case of the " national " *lubale*, the king was directly interested in the upkeep of their temples, and rebuilding was done upon a summons from him to the chiefs concerned, and sometimes allotted among the *batongole* in the same way as building in the royal enclosure. Mutesa had temples built for these gods at his capital, to which they were believed to come from their own homes, " rushing over the Lake with a sound like hail " or, as modern simile has it, " like an aeroplane," when he called upon them ; whether this was an innovation is uncertain.

Both Roscoe and Sir Apolo Kagwa [1] describe the hierarchy of officials, each with his own title, precedence, distinctive dress, and duties, attached to the " national " temples, and, in the case of Kibuka and Nende, of the daughters of the king and other women who were appointed " wives of the *lubale* " and attended upon him when he prophesied. The prestige of these " national " *lubale* rested at least as much upon the elaborate and lavish nature of their cult as upon confidence in the efficacy of their oracles. What struck the popular imagination and is remembered now is the extent of the temple household, the numbers of the gods' servants, his flocks and herds, and, above all, the celebrations which attended a consultation by the king. On such occasions the king sent presents of all kinds, the number of objects of each kind being always a multiple of nine, which were conveyed by some of the leading chiefs.

The less important temples similarly drew their revenues from the offerings of persons who came to consult the

[1] *The Baganda*, pp. 290–323, and *Empisa za Baganda*, pp. 209–226.

prophet, and acquired their servants in many cases from the children of persons to whom they had given fertility. The private prophet accumulated in the same way his herd of goats and store of barkcloths and cowries from the preliminary gifts which he demanded of consultants and the presents brought him if his advice or medicine was effective. These do not seem to have been stipulated for in advance, but brought as a recognized obligation towards the *lubale*, failure in which would incur his anger.

INITIATION OF PROPHETS

The prophet was first marked out for his career by the choice of the *lubale*, manifested in his possession by the spirit, but he could not begin to prophesy till he had been ceremonially initiated by an older practitioner. The usual signs of possession by a *lubale* were different from those of possession by a *muzimu*. The person concerned " went mad ", wandered about in a distraught manner, and slept out of doors. It was also possible, especially in the case of a child, for an illness of any kind, which ordinary means failed to cure, to be interpreted as due to this cause. The theory seems to be that the *lubale*, having selected a person as its mouthpiece, becomes angry when he does not prophesy and tries to kill him, and that the illness is the result.

The avowed purpose of the ceremony of initiation (*kutendeka*) is to make the *lubale* speak, but it represents also the formal reception of a new member into the body of practitioners and his public dedication to the service of the god, and it was probably accompanied by some esoteric instruction, particularly as to the efficacy of different herbs and charms. It was presided over by the leading prophet of the neighbourhood—that is the one whose general repute was highest, for there was no fixed order of seniority. The arrangements were made by the father of the person possessed, even if the latter was a grown man, not only because from the nature of his condition he was not responsible for himself but because the ceremony involved the creation of a quasi-filial relationship of the initiate to the initiating prophet.

The initiation took place at the latter's house at night, in the presence of all the local prophets and as many of the general public as cared to be there. Usually a number of persons were initiated at the same time. The proceedings began in the manner of the usual invocation to the *lubale*, with shaking of rattles and singing of hymns. As the hymn belonging to the *lubale* which had seized each person was reached, that person rose to his feet and then fell to the ground as if dead. The senior prophet then covered him with a new barkcloth, and also, according to one account, put round his neck the string of wild banana-seeds, interspersed with cowries (*lutembe*), which is normally worn by a prophet when exercising his art. He invited the *lubale* to accept the barkcloth— which the initiate would in future wear when prophesying—and let the patient recover. (*Lubale nga gwe o'ta omuntu oyo, muleke. Alame, kwata lubugo luno.* " *Lubale*, you who are killing this man, leave him ; may he recover, take this barkcloth ! ")

The initiate then rose up, and the senior prophet took him on his knees and " called him his child ". I was given no typical formula for this part of the proceeding, but the phrase occurred in nearly every account, and one informant elaborated the relationship thus : " The man who initiates him becomes his father ; he cannot disobey him." The new prophet was henceforward bound to give his initiator the same help in sickness or trouble, and general respect, that he would give to his own father, and could expect from him the same generosity ; his claim to anything he asked for when visiting the senior prophet's house was also compared to that of a blood-brother.

Next he was taken to the inner part of the house, where some informants hold that he was simply left to sleep, while others say that secret instruction was given him by those already initiated. In Bu·du district there was a definite period of instruction when the novice was taken out into the bush by the whole company, brandishing bundles of leaves and twigs made up of all the plants which he would use for magical or medicinal purposes. Many people firmly believe that the prophets required no human instruction whatever, but simply prescribed for each occasion as commanded by the *lubale*, the continuity of their methods, if there was any, being due to the identity of the *lubale* and not to the existence of a body of tradition. Whether or not the prophet's instruction began on the day of his initiation, he must obviously have received it at some time, and it was almost certainly the duty of his initiator to give it him.

On his emergence from the inner room, or in Bu·du on the return from the expedition to the bush, the prophet was formally handed the insignia of office—a spear and stick, a pair of rattles, a pair of baskets for receiving small offerings, and a cow-hair fly-whisk, which he apparently used to fan himself with when in the frenzy of possession. Prophets of Kaumpali carry instead a little stick decorated with cowry-shells, with which they beat themselves on the head when possessed. The *lutembe*, according to most versions, was given him not by the senior prophet but by his own father, who might also provide him with good barkcloths, decorated with cowries, to wear when prophesying.

The ceremony concluded apparently with the killing by the father of each initiate of a goat, whose meat was shared by the whole company. The blood was made to run past the door of the house, so that everyone stepped over it as they came out. One or two versions stated that the initiates were given the blood to drink as a final test of the genuineness of their possession by the *lubale*, and that any one who could not keep it down was thereby proved to be spurious.

The new prophet had then to introduce his *lubale* into his own house. He prepared a place in the house to keep his insignia, built a hut for the *lubale* in the banana-grove, and then invited his friends and relatives to a beer-drink provided by his father, at which he spoke for the first time in the name of his *lubale*.

PECULIAR CHARACTERISTICS OF BAGANDA RELIGION

These two types of ceremonial comprise the whole of the organized religious ritual of Buganda. The peculiarities which distinguish it from the religious ceremonies of Bantu Africa are clearly related to the peculiar features of the whole social organization of the people. Just as in economic and political matters, the control of land, and the government of its inhabitants, this organization rested not on kinship ties but on a system of territorial authorities responsible to the tribal head, so in religious observances the unit which acted in co-operation, in so far as it is definable at all, rested on a territorial basis. It was the question of locality, not of kinship, that decided to which of the prophets an inquirer should go ; in the cases in which the cult of the *lubale* had a more than individual import—in appeals to them in time of war, of plague, or of drought—it was always the local group which approached the local prophet. The cult of the main temple of each *lubale* on the clan lands had the same tenuous connection with the daily life of the ordinary clansman as did his theoretical right to live on those lands.

Another peculiarity of Baganda religion is that there was no ceremonial in which it was obligatory for any one, outside the servants of the temple, to participate, no occasion for a national gathering such as are recorded almost everywhere among the Bantu, and certainly no gathering of kinsmen at the temple of the clan *lubale*. The cult of the *lubale* by the king himself was certainly regarded as performed on behalf of the nation, but the active participants in it were only the chiefs whom he designated as his messengers. The one tribal gathering

R

took place in connection with the king's accession, and did not include a religious element. The only public manifestation of tribal unity is thus not an affirmation of common dependence upon human head and tribal deity together, but simply of common political allegiance to the king. Religious beliefs do not here serve, as among so many primitive peoples, as a mainstay of the political system ; the king's supreme authority, upon which the whole system rests, is not derived from any supposed supernatural powers or upon religious functions which only he could perform, but upon a tradition going back to the conquest of the country by his remote ancestor, in which the *lubale* have no part. The duty of the king to honour and consult the gods arises from the recognition of his responsibility, as their acknowledged head, for the general welfare of his people, not from any peculiar personal relationship with them, and is on a par with his duty of administering justice. This rather loose association between the religious and the political system is perhaps the product of the foreign invasion, in which the conquerors made their power effective by force alone, which is the historical origin of the Baganda kingdom.

THE PROPHET AS MAGICIAN

The prophet's position rested originally on his personal relationship with the *lubale*, made manifest by his possession and recognized as genuine in his initiation. But his subsequent activities were not confined to acting as the *lubale's* mouthpiece, and while the truth of his utterances is mentioned as the criterion of a prophet's success, his prestige rested at least as much upon the use which he made of the magical knowledge which the *lubale* was supposed to reveal to him. This included harmful as well as beneficent magic, and to judge by the stories of present-day magicians, which are a favourite topic of conversation, the real test of greatness was the use which he made of such knowledge to further his personal ends.

The most prized item of it, and one which was not vouchsafed to all prophets, was the recipe for making a kind of magical object called a ·jembe (pl. : mayembe). The word means "horn", but though some mayembe were cows' or buffaloes' horns they might also be made from a wooden tube or a leather bag. Their magical quality lay in their contents, which were known only to the maker, but which seem to have included mica from deposits on the hillsides. Some types are thought to have contained snakes introduced into them by miraculous means.

I never met any one who expressed disbelief in the magical properties of mayembe. The existence of persons who make use of them is still generally believed in, and one is regaled with endless stories of their achievements. The ·jembe is itself credited with personality ; it can speak to the owner on its own behalf ; it can travel long distances to do his behests—to kill an enemy, for instance—apparently in an immaterial form, for the object itself remains in his house, and on these journeys it may enter a strange house to sleep, and manifest its presence by giving the owner a very uncomfortable night. The owner can make replicas of the original for sale, which bring the purchaser general good luck or occasionally more specific advantages like the power to cure sickness or (in old days) the capture of much loot in war, but these copies never rival the potency of the original.

Thus the prophet of the established religion appears as one and the same with the sorcerer whose activities are universally dreaded, and among the Baganda, as elsewhere, black and white magic are seen to be linked. It is true that the natives do not clearly recognize this identity. They distinguish between basamizi or prophets and basawo or doctors, holding that the latter owe their skill to knowledge acquired empirically or learnt from their fathers and not to divine inspiration. But though there probably are persons who deal in native medicines without setting up to be prophets, it is certain that healing by means of herbs and charms was and is an important part of the business of the latter. It is true, too, that sorcerers or *balogo* are invariably referred to as a class apart, who learn their evil secrets heaven knows how—probably from their fathers, as a respectable person learns his craft—and whose identity rarely becomes known, so cunning are they at casting their spells over long distances. But it is quite certain that the activities of prophets to this day include the provision of injurious magic for ends which are regarded as justifiable. We shall have to return to this point in its place in the discussion of the methods and ends of magic.

PLACE OF MAGIC IN BAGANDA LIFE

It has already been made clear that the prophets were not looked to for that assistance in economic activities which is so commonly the function of the magician. Though there was a recourse in case of drought, the Baganda had no rain-maker whose magic was regularly called upon, nor any rites associated with the various stages of the agricultural year. In connection with the more hazardous pursuit of fishing from canoes in the Lake, magic, and the prophets as its source, seem to have played a wider part ; but such fishing as goes on to-day is left to the peoples of the islands, and it is rare to meet a Muganda who knows anything about it.

The one activity in which magic exercised a positive organizing force was warfare. As has been mentioned already, in the conduct of the war itself the prophet played a more influential part than the general. But it was not only over the course of the actual fighting that they predominated. The time and place of the war, the selection of the general, and probably also the districts whose inhabitants were to stay at home " to guard the king ", were decided by them in answer to inquiries. One of the prophets went in person with the army, and the general was guided by his daily pronouncements throughout the campaign ; he seems also to have ordered the observance of different magical precautions on different occasions, but what their nature was I did not discover.

Magic to produce courage was mentioned by one or two informants. This, they said, consisted of a brew of all kinds of herbs with pieces of lions' and leopards' flesh which were fed to the warriors by the *musawo* on the point of a spear. This magic was distributed to all the chiefs who were present in the capital before an expedition set out. It might also be dispensed on behalf of a chief to his people if he happened to have under his authority a *musawo* who knew the magic. Such experts are said to have been very rare, and apparently unconnected with the prophets of Kibuka.

In other departments of life recourse to magic was a purely individual affair, and seldom sought in connection with any particular practical activity. Hunting magic is the main exception to this rule, and of this no one knew much except vaguely that medicine could be obtained to tie into the nets, and when hunting a lion to smear in its footprints and cause it to return. Another case in which magic was used for some specific occasion is litigation ; a man would acquire a charm for success before pleading a case. The *jembe* of loot in war has also been mentioned. Charms for the acquisition of wealth were not apparently connected with any particular occasion such as a trading expedition.

But the main objects of magic seem to have been of a remedial or, less commonly, of a preventive nature.[1] The *lubale* of plague, of earthquakes, lightning, and

---

[1] The situation is comparable to that described by Evans-Pritchard among the Azande, of whom he writes : " Nature is not thought of as controlled directly by magic but is looked upon as neutral unless manipulated against man's endeavours by witches." (" The Zande Corporation of Witch-Doctors ", *J.R.A.I.*, 1932.) The Baganda do not ascribe all natural calamity to human malignity, but they do look on magic rather as a recourse in difficulty than as indispensable to the success of any activity.

drought have been mentioned. The provision of cures for barrenness and for illness of all kinds seems to have represented the greater part of the activity of prophets in general. The war-magic which private individuals could obtain, consisting in medicine to smear on the body in order to turn away the enemy's spears, is of the preventive type, as is the magical precaution taken by a retreating army of stopping the pursuit by placing in the path a cow's hide containing leaves and—according to one version—the body of an infant.

Then there are various types of purificatory rite which a prophet might recommend to have performed in order to avert a threatened calamity, as often as to put an end to one which had already occurred. The extreme case of such measures is represented by the executions which were ordered by the prophets of Kibuka on behalf of the whole country.[1] To purify a village, a chief might be ordered to kill a man, and would choose a friendless person from among his subjects. A lesser person would make up a bundle of various plants specified by the prophet and have it laid on an ant-hill, or at a cross-road; where the evil would attach itself to the next passer-by.[2] (Despite this explanation, it seems to be held that this person would in some way remove the evil without having himself to suffer.) A rite which does not contain this representation in concrete form of a ridding of the evil is the planting of an *mpongo*—a plot of land cleared and sown in one day by joint work of the whole village. In this plot, a quantity of every kind of food-crop was planted, as well as a barkcloth-tree garlanded with banana-leaves. When the millet from this plot ripened, the chief had beer brewed with it and summoned the prophet to drink, and the latter would declare : " The evil has gone to such-and-such a village." [3]

[1] See above, p. 233.

[2] The owner of a plot of simsim had always to do this with a bunch of the plants as soon as they were ripe, to remove any evil that might be attached to the crop.

[3] Evans-Pritchard describes a rite similar to the first of these as being regarded by the Azande without pronounced moral approval or

Similarly the magical rites which private individuals performed on their own behalf were all of a precautionary nature. Many of these have already been described in their context—the precautions observed during pregnancy, the methods employed to avert heavy rain or hailstones, and the *kukuza* rite, symbolizing sexual intercourse, which accompanies so many occasions in Baganda life. The essential nature of this rite, which appears to be still generally practised, will become clear from a comparison of the various events to which it is attached. It is performed by a husband and wife after the birth of a child, on its attainment of maturity—which is evidenced in the case of a boy by the production of his first independent piece of work, of a girl by menstruation—on the night of a daughter's marriage, and after the first formal visit to them which marks her entry upon her duties as a wife ; if the woman is suckling a child, it is done before and after she goes on any journey, and Roscoe mentions its performance on the return of a husband from war[1] ; it is performed by a girl with her lover, as well as by the girl's parents, after the ceremony of atonement for seduction ; by husband and wife when the door-post of a new house is set in the ground, and— according to one account—before the thatching begins, and when first eating grasshoppers, simsim, and a small bean called *mpindi*, of which both leaves and fruit are eaten. It is also performed by an heir with his *lubuga*, and by a female heir with her predecessor's husband as the final rite of the installation.

It is thus always a rite of inauguration. It marks the beginning of a new phase or activity—a period in an

---

disapproval. ("Sorcery and Native Opinion," *Africa*, 1929.) My impression of the Baganda comments was that they were mainly concerned with the undoubted benefit to the community of the removal of evil, but that when actually called on to consider the ethics of its transference to an innocent person they resolved the problem by the argument that he could remove it without himself suffering from it. I heard no comments on the morality of the second type, which was not widely known.

[1] *The Baganda*, p. 363.

individual's life, the separation of husband from wife and their reunion, the reconciliation of a daughter with her parents, the entry of an heir upon a new kinship status, the first consumption of certain seasonal kinds of food. In each case it appears to be believed to exercise a general protective effect over the period which it inaugurates. No positive result is ever said to come from it, but it is held to be of such importance that, if the rite were omitted, one of the persons who ought to have performed it would die.

Another type of protective magic is used against a particular type of sorcerer, the *Basezi*, or prowlers. These are human beings who roam by night, clad only in dry banana-leaves, or naked, and can be heard hoarsely whispering " Wa-wa-wa !" Their main object is to procure human flesh on which to feed ; this they do by raising the dead from their graves, by capturing living persons whom they may meet, or even by entering houses and taking people out. In their spare time they amuse themselves by playing malicious tricks ; they pull up crops, eat the seeds, and leave the stalks lying on the ground, knock down banana-trees, enter houses and throw things about, or simply kick the door in. Unlike other sorcerers, who are actuated by motives of self-interest or revenge, the *Musezi's* attentions are quite indiscriminate.

The only safeguard against the attacks of the *Basezi* appears to be to perform a sort of inoculation of their practices on the ground which it is wished to protect. Thus the owner of the plot of simsim runs across and across it in imitation of a *Musezi*, while her friends throw clods of earth at her and shout, " There is the *Musezi* ! " and then they all pull up a few seeds and eat them. In the same way, on the first night when the king slept in a new royal enclosure, the chief *Kasuju* had to prowl around the enclosure clad only in a skin tied round his waist in the likeness of a *Musezi*. This procedure, like that of the women with the simsim, is described by the verb *kusera*, from which the *Basezi* derive their name.

Similar in the manner of its acting is the rite which follows the *kukuza* rite when the door-post of a house is set in place ; husband and wife must urinate in the house to protect themselves from the possibility that someone else might " spoil the house " (in a magical sense) by doing so. In the same order of ideas the owner of a plot of simsim safeguards the household against injury that might be caused by outsiders eating the seed which has been distributed by taking care to be the first to eat the crop. For this reason a small quantity is cooked and eaten on the very day the winnowing is done, before the distribution has been made.

SORCERY

If the Baganda are lacking, by comparison with other primitive tribes, in the apparatus of magic directed to specific constructive ends, they yield to none in the belief in magic as a means of inflicting injury on one's neighbours, or sorcery. Such magic, as has been pointed out, is generally said to be known only to the sinister class of *balogo*, though the stories told of famous prophets ascribe the same powers to them, and a significant comment on the activities of one of the leading practitioners of the present day was : " He could not cure people of such evils if he did not know how to cause them." The *balogo*, it is believed, can be induced to practise for hire as the prophets do. But, though their general methods are well known even to children, nobody can give any details as to their procedure. The essential feature of this type of magic is the material object used ; I have heard the operation of a curse distinguished from sorcery by the criterion, *Tewali ·dagala* (" There is no medicine "). The primary meaning of the word *·dagala* is " leaf ", and its use in this sense indicates that the sorcerer's material consists mainly in decoctions of plants. The general opinion is that the *balogo* find their materials among the wild plants in the long grass.

All the types of sorcery universally believed in operate through the contact or close proximity of the victim himself with the magical object. The belief that parts of the victim's person can be used as the material for sorcery directed against him plays little part in Baganda ideas. There are four main methods of setting the magic to work. One is simple poisoning, which may be done by mixing poison with the victim's food or secretly inserting it in his drinking gourd. The next is the transmission of disease by medicines smeared in the palm of the sorcerer's hand so that the victim touches it when they greet. I was told that the prevalence of cataract which I noticed at Kisimula was due to the unusually large number of sorcerers in the neighbourhood who spread it in this way.

A third method is to bury some object where people will step over it—in the doorway of a house, if a single victim is aimed at ; in a public footpath if the intention is to destroy a whole village. The marrow from an elephant's tusk and a hyæna's head can be used for this purpose, and it was formerly a duty of *Saba·du*, when either animal was killed, to carry the dangerous part into the long grass and bury it out of harm's way. At the present time Moslems are said to favour this method of sorcery, for which they use a piece of paper inscribed with texts from the Koran. The last method is that of sending the magical object to do its work at a distance. This is done most commonly by smoking the medicines in a pipe and blowing the ashes towards the victim. Sometimes they land on a path where he is likely to pass, and by stepping on them his feet are poisoned ; whether people are believed to be actually killed by this means I am not certain.

Sorcery by means of *mayembe* may resemble the third or fourth class. This method is not universally known, and my household believed that the man who gave me most of my information about it—a stranger who turned up one day while a group of people were discussing the question—must have been himself a practitioner. The *jembe* is either buried in the victim's house or yard, or simply ordered by the owner to go and kill him. In the latter case the material object does not leave its master; apparently it is always supposed to return when its work is done. The *jembe* can speak in a language which the owner understands and is thus able to announce the completion of its task. The owner then kills a red-feathered cock and sprinkles the blood over the *jembe* " as its reward ".

The power, which the most famous sorcerers have, of " sending messengers " to any one who displeases them, is similar in nature, though no one indulges in theories as to the method used. The " messengers " are natural phenomena which the sorcerer is able to direct against his enemy. Thus it was believed of a very well-known sorcerer, one Andereya, who lived near me, that a man who refused to sell him some land was visited with an earthquake which shook him out of bed while leaving all the surrounding houses untouched. On another occasion Andereya undertook to kill somebody for 60s., and the customer refused to pay. Andereya threatened to " send a messenger ". But the customer, who was himself a sorcerer and had simply wanted to test his rival's power, retorted : " My messenger will arrive first," and, to symbolize the plunder of the house, took a handful of ashes from the fire, of grass from the floor, and of thatch from over the porch. That night a plague of ants made the house uninhabitable and Andereya capitulated.

The information which I was given contained no mention of spells beyond the statement that where magic is performed over a distance the name of the victim must be mentioned. Nor have I any knowledge of taboos which must be observed by the performer in order that he may be in a suitable bodily condition for the execution of the rite. Although I do believe that spoken formulae are, in general, less important here than in the cultures of the Pacific, the absence of such data may be the result of my having been unable to question any one who admitted the possession of magical powers. It is worth noting that at the séance with Andereya, which I describe in the note attached to this chapter, he did utter words over his patients, or order them to do so when performing the action which he prescribed.

Sorcery is believed to be practised from two motives— *tima*, envy or spite, and *busungu*, anger. In the first case it is rather like the "motiveless malignity" of Iago; the Man of Envy is conceived as going about burning houses and destroying crops for the pure fun of the thing. Arson is also a favourite method of revenge, but any accidental fire is invariably ascribed to *tima*. The sorcerers who cause illness at a distance in people who are not aware of having any enemies probably belong also to this class. They are not generally supposed to concentrate their malice upon especially fortunate people.

The Man of Anger, on the other hand, is the one who settles his personal scores by the use of supernatural powers, and with him we come to the region where recourse to sorcery may, in certain cases, be regarded as justified. The sorcerer himself is generally believed to be quite unscrupulous in the use of his art, and other persons may make use of him in quarrels in which they are admittedly not in the right.

Sorcery as a Legal Redress

On the other hand, it is taken for granted that a person with a legitimate grievance for which he can get no other redress will resort to sorcery. The magic in such a case would be procured from a reputable magician, and the aggrieved person would make no secret of the transaction. An old man announced in my house at Kisimula that he was "going to the doctors" (he used the word *basawo*, not *balogo*) for medicine against a youth whom we all knew quite well, who had stolen a hammer from him and would not admit it. The company generally approved

the course, and agreed that the youth was " shameless "
(*wa kye·jo*). At Matale a boy who heard us discussing
fishing technicalities suggested that it would save a good
deal of trouble to take the fish from someone else's trap.
His elders rebuked him : " If you do that, the owner
will bewitch you and kill you." It is widely believed still
that an outbreak of plague may be the result of medicine
against an unknown thief, whose effect is to cause everyone
who eats stolen meat to die of the disease. A speciality
of my neighbour, Andereya, was the recovery of stolen
goods.

Sorcery has its uses, too, in circumstances created by
modern conditions. It is generally believed to be used
against a father-in-law who refuses to return the bride-
price in circumstances where native custom formerly
compelled him to do so. This is regarded as quite
justifiable. It is also generally thought that a person who
loses a case in the High Court will resort to sorcery.

The dreadful fate meted out in the old days to convicted
sorcerers seems at first sight inconsistent with the
existence of this wide field of legitimate exercise for their
powers. But it must be remembered that in native theory
the practitioners of sorcery for legal and illegal purposes
form two distinct classes. Probably the recognized
prophets dispensed injurious magic for legitimate ends
with full public approval as part of their regular business.

The belief in sorcery, then, had its socially valuable
side among the Baganda as elsewhere, as a deterrent
to crime and perhaps also an incitement to restitution.
Even now, when the belief is condemned by the Church
and its expression in practice penalized by the law, it
continues to exercise the same influence, though perhaps
to a less extent. It has acquired a new value as a
recourse against injustices brought about by European
innovations. Whether it is at all effective in securing
the observance of obligations which have no longer any
other sanction, or merely relieves the feelings of the
injured party, I do not know.

OTHER SUPERNATURAL SANCTIONS

One last type of supernatural belief must be mentioned—the belief in punishment for certain specific offences which bring down an automatic retribution on the person who commits them. The belief in such supernatural penalties, which are set in motion by the act itself without the intervention of any personal agency, human or superhuman, is a familiar feature of primitive cultures. Among the Baganda their sphere of application is not wide, but there are certain rules of conduct for whose observance in particular circumstances they provide the sanction.

Such retribution attends several different types of action, and each is visited with its appropriate penalty. One is eating the totem animal of one's clan. Each clan has two totems ; that after which it is named and another which is more strictly respected. Any one who eats the latter will be punished with instant death, but the former only brings out a rash, for which remedies are known. The next is violation of the rules of avoidance between relatives-in-law. This brings on the palsy, which is ascribed to this cause only ; Musisi, the god of earthquakes, is said to have suffered from it.

The third class comprises breaches of sexual regulations in certain special circumstances. Adultery meets with supernatural punishment if committed on occasions when it is regarded as particularly reprehensible—in the case of a wife while her husband is at war and, possibly, on a journey of any kind ; of a husband while his wife is suckling a child ; of a mother with a child at the breast when she is away from home—while adultery which leads to pregnancy either kills mother or child at birth or causes the child to die later.

It is remarkable that, in most of these cases, the person who is believed to suffer is not the one who commits the offence. It is the husband whose death is caused by his wife's unfaithfulness during his absence, or the child that dies through its parent's adultery ; moreover, the event which brings down the calamity is often not the offence itself, but the performance of some action which only an innocent person can do safely—the formal testing of the child's legitimacy, or the offering of water to the husband to drink on his return home. This is the case, too, with the punishment which attends those who break the rule of sexual abstinence when in mourning for a near relative. What kills them is eating the meat which is their due share of the feast when the mourning is concluded. In these cases, therefore, the worst results of the offence can be avoided, but only in a manner which publicly proclaims the offender's guilt, so that the belief is actually effective in an indirect manner through its result in exposing the guilty person to public disapproval.

Thus these beliefs, too, have their place, along with the anger of the spirits and the power of sorcery, in reinforcing the accepted moral code. These three forces cannot, however, be said to form part of a closely connected whole. Each has its own sphere of influence, and there is no overlapping among them, nor is there any idea whatever that the punishments which form the last group are incurred because they offend some super-natural being, either *muzimu* or *lubale*. The answer to questions on the subject is always the same : " It is the sin itself which kills."

Nor is it necessary to postulate as an alternative to a belief in personified superhuman agencies the conception that these and other magical effects must be produced by some mysterious impersonal force. Such a conception is assumed as the foundation not only of magic but of all religion by Marett, who bases his theory on Cod-rington's interpretation of the Melanesian word *mana* as " a force altogether distinct from physical power, which acts in all kinds of ways for good and evil, and which it is of the greatest advantage to possess or control ". This force is described elsewhere as " that invisible power *which is believed by the natives* to cause all such effects as transcend their conception of the regular course of nature " ; and Marett, referring to Codrington's interpretation of all Melanesian religion in terms of *mana*, says : " We may well suspect some such truth as this to have long been more or less inarticulately felt by the Melanesian mind." [1] Mr. Edwin Smith applies a similar theory to an African people, the Ba-Ila, of whom he says, when discussing supernatural sanctions, " These deeds . . . by a kind of automatic action react upon the offender, or, *to put it more accurately*, they release the spring which sets the hidden mechanism of nature in action." [2] Sir James Frazer, in his exposition of the principles of magic, deduces by a similar process that a rather different explanation of its effects is " tacitly assumed " by the practitioner, and goes on to affirm that it is the duty of the student " to trace the train of thought which underlies the magician's practice ".[3]

Such statements involve a type of interpretation which seems to me to be neither permissible for a scientific inquirer nor necessary in order to account for the facts. Codrington ascribes to the Melanesians not a belief which they expressed to him, but one which, if they did hold it, would make it possible to reduce the many different uses of the word *mana* to a single primary meaning. Edwin Smith first tells us what the Ba-Ila do explicitly believe, but he then goes on to describe the situation more accurately in terms of a mechanism which would explain it. Sir James Frazer makes such explanation a matter of duty. I do not believe the anthropologist is justified in thus crediting the peoples whom he is studying with explanations of their beliefs which they do not themselves offer, simply because, without some such explanation, there appears to us to be a flaw in the process of reasoning. The Baganda are content to say that such an action produces such a result ; they do not inquire into

---

[1] Marett, *The Threshold of Religion*, pp. 118 ff.
[2] Smith and Dale, *The Ba-Ila*, vol. i, p. 347. Cf. also vol. ii, pp. 82 ff. The italics are mine in this case, and on page 255.
[3] Frazer, *The Golden Bough*, I, The Magic Art, vol. i, p. 53.

the means or attempt to account for what happens by an analogy with physical processes. This indifference to the logical consequences of one's assertions is a universal characteristic of minds untrained to abstract speculation ; there is no need to go to Africa or the South Seas to find it. Modern theologies are the product of the minority of intellectuals who wish to reduce their religious beliefs to a logically coherent system, but the ideas of the supernatural which are current among the simpler adherents of modern religions are as innocent of such questionings as are those of the Baganda.

CHRISTIANITY IN RELATION TO THESE BELIEFS

What is the relation between this system and the new religion which is now, formally at least, accepted by the whole Baganda people ? Of course it is officially disowned ; the public cult of the *lubale* has vanished, and with it have gone the temples and priesthood which enshrined it—" The temples have fallen down and the *lubale* just wander about," as it was put to me. The wars for which the king depended most upon their guidance are a thing of the past, as are the national dangers against which they warned him, and the royal welfare is now invoked in the liturgy of the Anglican Church. The one fragment that survives is at the tombs of dead kings— of Mutesa at the capital, where his many surviving widows still live, and of Kalema, the short-lived nominee of the Moslems, who drove out Mwanga ; here the dead kings' spirits still manifest themselves, though only now for such undignified purposes as the complaint that the spears which adorn their temples are not kept polished. Nor is there any open cult of the ancestors.

But the beliefs as to the existence and behaviour of the *lubale* and *mizimu* remain unshaken, and though some natives say that *lubale*, prophets and all magical practices, and even *mizimu*, are " of Satan ", others ascribe the powers of the *mulogo* to Katonda (the name used for the

s

Christian God). The latter point of view does not, of course, indicate a metaphysical theory ascribing to God responsibility for the works of the Devil. What it does show is the accommodation, in the native mind, of the new doctrine with the old. Katonda is now taken for granted, though it would be extraordinarily interesting to know how he is conceived—whether, for example, Katonda is thought of as being the same *lubale* whom the Baganda had always known, without realizing his importance or the cult which he desired. He is undoubtedly now the central figure in Baganda theology ; he is the protector and giver of blessings *par excellence*, and phrases like " May Katonda protect you ! " or " That is Katonda's affair ", of any matter of uncertain outcome, are constantly used, and probably with a more literal significance in native language than they have in ours. But Katonda has by no means replaced the other divinities, and, in cases of specific need, it is to them that many natives would first appeal. " Katonda gives you children," said one, " but if you have none you go to the prophet of Mukasa." Another, comparing old times with new, said : " The *lubale* answered prayer directly, but Katonda only answers you after you are dead."

I have described the beliefs in magic, good and evil, in the present tense because they are as much alive to-day as they ever were. There may be a few educated natives who really have been reasoned out of such ideas ; there are certainly some who have been convinced by the rational explanation of some particular phenomenon, say an epidemic of plague, and have ceased to ascribe it to supernatural causes, but it would be most unsafe to assume that the corollary of such a conviction in one instance must be the rejection of all magical beliefs. An instance of their tenacity is a remark made by my boy when we were discussing sorcery as the cause of disease. I asked what was the opinion of his father, who is the senior native assistant in Mengo Hospital—a very responsible position involving considerable medical knowledge and skill. His reply was devastating : " **My** father has worked in a hospital for thirty-five years and he *knows* how many diseases Europeans cannot cope with."

While such beliefs exist the practices to which they give rise cannot die, and the private prophets, though their numbers may be less, still play their part in Baganda life. There are native doctors in every village, who are consulted partly because their medicines are more drastic, and therefore to native ideas more effective, than those dispensed by Government and mission hospitals, but also because of the firm conviction that European medicines are useless against the visitations alike of spirits and sorcerers. The secrecy with which the proceedings have nowadays to be carried on has meant a certain alteration in the proportions of their various elements. There can now be no public display of offerings, no festive gathering of suppliants. The business-like way in which the up-to-date prophet cuts the preliminaries and comes to the business of dispensing his remedies appears in the account appended to this chapter ; but the preliminaries of invocation and possession are still an integral part of the whole performance. The second account, which describes a much less sophisticated person, is probably more typical—allowances made for the artificial element introduced by my being the only consultant—of what could be seen in any village.

The mechanism of control provided by magic over matters that are of intense importance to the individual but uncontrollable by him in any other way—recovery from illness, the fidelity of a wife, a debtor's solvency, success in business—is something for which Christianity does not provide a complete substitute. How far it provides a substitute at all must depend upon whether the natives have any idea of spontaneous prayer. Dr. Audrey Richards tells me that she met Babemba women coming out of the churches who would tell her : " I have been praying for a child " ; and that, when the rains were anxiously awaited, people would go noticeably more often both to the churches and spirit huts to pray. The Protestant Baganda do not pray individually in church ; at Matale where I lived next door to the Catholic church I constantly saw women and girls go in to say a prayer. They always used the same phrase, " We are going to say a rosary," and it did not occur to me to ask what the object of the prayer might be. But I had the impression that, for the Baganda, prayer was confined to the set formulae which they had been taught, and that its value to them was more in the region formerly covered by the type of rite that I have described as exercising a generally beneficial, protective influence, than in that of recourse for aid in an emergency.

There is one class of beliefs that have been directly destroyed by Christianity—those relating to the automatic supernatural punishments, and, in particular, to the punishments for unchastity. Here we are concerned with ideas which, unlike the beliefs in magic, have consequences that run counter to normal human desires, so that the readiness with which they are abandoned is as easily explicable as the tenacity with which the magical beliefs are cherished. It will be remembered that, in most cases, the guilty person used to be believed to die if faced with some kind of test. The general decline of native ceremonial, as a result of the scorn for everything " heathen " which has been inculcated by some European and much native Christian teaching, has meant that occasions for such trials as the legitimacy test now seldom occur. There has also been express disapproval of any belief in supernatural causes of death, which has meant either that such rites as the distribution of the goat among the relatives at the end of mourning has been given up or that it is no longer regarded as an ordeal to be approached with awe. Whether it is for the same reason that the efficacy of the belief in *makiro* has lost its force I do not know ; for it is possible that here what has destroyed its deterrent effect is the discovery of counter-magic.

Regarded strictly in its religious aspect, as a system of beliefs and practices to which man turns for reassurance in facing the unknown and confirmation of his moral standards, it is very difficult to judge how far Christianity has really been assimilated into Baganda culture. Certainly it means a great deal to them ; they know their Bibles thoroughly and unquestioningly accept the literal truth of the mythology, which they harmonize with their own in a manner that is rather amusing. Waswa's version of the coming of *Sabataka* to Buganda began with the Tower of Babel, and another man, whom I asked if any clan had a snake for its totem, replied with a rather shocked negative and referred me to the Garden of Eden. On another occasion, when I said that Europeans did not have clans, the statement that Joseph was " of the house of David " was quoted against me. To me the gospels read in Luganda sometimes took on a greater reality than they had ever had in Europe.

Men and women go to church on Sunday—women rather more than men—but attendance is not confined to such men as schoolmasters, on whom it is professionally incumbent, and the preaching would not disgrace an English service. They accept the formulae, I think, as part of the ritual—the kind of worship that is pleasing to Katonda, just as drumming and dancing pleased the older *lubale*. The differences in Protestant and Catholic ritual they sometimes compare to differences in the ceremonial of the old temples.

I have never been present at a native meal where grace was not said, nor seen Catholic natives so much as chew coffee-berries without crossing themselves. On Sunday mornings—and, in Holy Week, on weekdays, too—I used to see people sitting in their doorways reading the Bible, and I very often heard my cook's wife reading aloud to the household from both Bible and prayer-book.

This observance of forms in places far from any European supervision shows that Christianity has a very

definite importance to the Baganda ; but exactly what
it signifies to them it is extraordinarily difficult to say.
Certainly it does not mean, at this stage, the general
acceptance of a new moral code, as a result of which
actions formerly permitted meet with the spontaneous
disapproval that is aroused by those which age-old
tradition condemns. The adoption of Christian standards
of behaviour, even where they are genuinely adhered to,
involves a complicated interplay of motives which it
would need another technique than that of the anthropologist to unravel. The repudiation of their polygamous
wives by many of the chiefs who were first baptized
may have had in it an element of conviction that polygamy
was displeasing to Katonda, but a great part of its
significance must have lain in the performance of an act
which publicly differentiated them from their non-Christian
neighbours. But the outward and visible signs of
Christianity, even if they extend to behaviour in complete
conformity with Christian principles, do not necessarily
imply the presence of their inward and spiritual counterpart. Such behaviour may be adopted to please some
individual, or because it is associated with a social status
superior to that of those who do not imitate it, or because
non-conformity is penalized. The results are the same,
but they do not, in themselves, justify the assumption
that the new system of ideas has replaced the old.

As regards the recourse to magic for supernatural aid,
my impression is that with the Baganda Christianity
has neither discredited nor replaced the traditional
methods. What it has done—and this may be the reason
why its acceptance has been so widespread—has been to
supplement them where they were lacking in the promise
of a life beyond the grave, and I believe that in this lies
its main significance to the natives in the strictly religious
as distinct from the social sense. To look to heaven for
the redressing of life's injustices is not, in itself, sufficient
to the Muganda, but to be able to look forward to heaven
is a matter of great moment ; and it is probably by its

simple insistence on heaven as the good Christian's reward that the Catholic church gains a wider popularity than the Protestant with its stress on rational conviction. An old Catholic once described his crucifix as his " *tikiti* for heaven ", and agreed that, if he lost it, he would not be admitted ; and the Catholic practice of depriving the sinner of his crucifix and rosary provides a supernatural sanction for conduct of a kind which the native can appreciate. Yet, even here, the sanction is not completely effective, simply for the reason that the rules to which it is applied are not backed also by general social approval. The wife who refuses to return to her husband may or may not be induced to do so by the threat " to take away her beads ", but the bigamist who forfeits his crucifix rather than send away his second wife feels that the Fathers are unfairly using their power to penalize him.

The changes of a social nature which Christian influence has introduced have been discussed each in its context. Christian missions, both by the general education and the specialized training which they give, are doing more than any other single force towards the adaptation of the Muganda to his new life. But their general attitude towards native life, particularly in the sphere of family relations, has been to demand conformity with standards which are not really an inevitable outcome of the Christian doctrine. Because Christianity is the officially recognized religion of the English people, it is assumed that it prescribes the forms in which English life is moulded, and when it is transferred to Africa these forms are too often taken for granted as an essential part of it. The unconscious assumption that a genuine Christian must necessarily behave in all respects like an English gentleman is the product of a culture into which Christianity really has been firmly integrated ; and it might seem to follow from the interpretation of religion as a reflection of social facts, rather than as an external compelling force, that its introduction to Africa must be impossible except in the manner which was formerly regarded as the ideal, as a part of the complete system of European society. But such wholesale transformations have proved impracticable, and the idea of adaptation where adaptation is necessary has come to take the place of the older aim.

Is it not time, then, to consider the question of religious teaching scientifically, or does the very phrase symbolize an irreconcilable contradiction ? Probably no society can exist without a religion ; certainly no African society can, and there are few African societies whose indigenous religion has not been irreparably damaged by the impact of external forces, so that something must be found to take its place. This can be only Christianity ; but must it be a Christianity identical with that of any one nation of Europe ? From many of those engaged in spreading the Christian religion among primitive peoples, such a suggestion can have no hope of a hearing. But for those who hold that the most valuable content of Christianity is not a body of dogmatic statements but a system of ethics of universal validity, would it not be possible to disentangle the essential principles from the application or misapplication of them which European society represents, and to inculcate those principles in a way which would confirm and strengthen rather than disrupt the structure of native life ?

Need it be assumed that any institution which differs from those to which we are accustomed must be contrary to Christian principles, and is therefore to be disapproved, or that the virtues on which Christianity lays stress, but which, after all, have existed independently of it, can only be exercised in conditions which with us owe their existence to many other circumstances than the influence of Christian doctrine ? Is it inconceivable that the ideals of altruism in which the strength of Christianity has always lain might come to be regarded as not necessarily inseparable from a code of sexual morality which no European society has, in fact, ever followed ;

and might then be used to replace the bonds of mutual obligation which formerly grew out of the dependence of children on parents, subject on chief ? Probably it is ; for I speak as no theologian. Yet I cannot but feel that missionary effort in the direct field of religious teaching, as distinct from that of social development, would be infinitely more valuable if its emphasis was transferred from its present objects to the advocacy of ethical ideals that might counteract the self-seeking that, in Africa as elsewhere, accompanies the growth of competitive economic individualism.

APPENDIX

NOTE ON CONTEMPORARY PERFORMANCES OF PROPHETS

One of my most distinguished acquaintances was Andereya, a prophet whose fame extended all over the countryside and of whom the most fantastic tales were told. It was said that, though he acquired immense wealth by his practice, he was frequently ordered by his *lubale* to throw it into a river or to scatter it broadcast among chance passers-by. He might suddenly kill some ten goats and distribute the meat to any one who passed, and he once gave a new bicycle to a perfect stranger. My friends obtained an interview with him for me, but he would not be persuaded to let me attend a consultation. However, he allowed my boy, Ephraim, to be present, and the following is an account which he gave me immediately afterwards. I am prepared to vouch for the honesty of his intentions, though not, of course, for the accuracy of his observation.

The performance took place in the morning. This is unusual, but apparently Andereya has so many patients that he has to be prepared to see them at all times. Six of them were present, but only three could be dealt with because he was then fetched in a motor car to an urgent case. (On the day when I was there a motor car arrived with a message from the king's mother in the capital.) The prophet spread a mat on the ground and a barkcloth over it and then stood up and invoked the *lubale*, saying : " All of you from far off gather together. Come and attend to the affairs which have brought these men here, who are your friends." Then he sat down on the ground, and when he spoke again it was in a different voice and in a foreign language ; this proved to be Luziba, the language of the north-western corner of Tanganyika, of which he is a native. What he said was interpreted by a servant.

To the first patient he said : " You, I know your trouble. You have quarrelled with your brother, and he is making you blind. Go out and bring a plantain-leaf ! " When the leaf was brought he removed the midriff, struck it twice, and let the sap drip into the man's eye. Then he brought a small stick and made the patient break off a tiny piece and put it in a cup of water, which turned red. Andereya himself dipped another piece of the stick in the water and touched the sick man's tongue and eye with it, whereupon the eye turned black. The patient was then told to put his head under the bark-cloth, and the prophet put some pounded herbs along with glowing charcoal in a potsherd and thrust it in beside him. Next he washed the man's eye with a piece of barkcloth dipped in water with more medicines. He then pulled out of the eye a long piece of " something that looked like a white thread with tiny red and white specks on it ". This he put in a gourd and covered it up. The patient was told to take the gourd away and hide it for three days in the long grass, when he would find a snake in it which would tell him why his brother had poisoned his eye. He was then to kill and burn the snake and rub the ashes on his eyebrows.

It happened that the same man was there again when Ephraim went to consult the prophet on another occasion. He had actually brought a snake with him, which was duly killed and burnt. The prophet rubbed the ashes over his eye, saying : " May your eye be truly healed, for it was not you who did wrong to your brother but he to you," and ordered him to give his brother a white goat and a white fowl by way of reconciliation.

The next patient was a man who had been bewitched by an enemy urinating in his house. This man was sent to get a piece of green plantain-bark. This was laid in the barkcloth, and two coffee-berries and two seeds of the kind used for a prophet's rattle were put in it and water poured over them. The man drank the water, chewed the seeds and spat them out, and then fell to the ground as if drunk, and remained unconscious for some time. When he came to, the prophet brought a small leaf, touched his tongue with it, and said : " May all evil depart from this man and all his house, since he has come to me who pity the unfortunate." [1] Then he told the man to throw 7s. into a river near by. The man said he had not the money, so Andereya gave it him, warning him that if he used so much as a cent of it for any other purpose he would be ill. Next he made the man stand in a basin of water mixed with medicines, naked except for a loin-cloth, and washed him all over. When this was done, he said : " Take this water, and bury it along with the plantain-bark, the coffee-berries, and the seeds. When you have done this, say, ' There is no more evil upon me from that man who came to curse me, for the evil is finished.' Early next morning take the shillings to the river and say : ' I have given them you, Nabingi.' "

The third applicant wished to recover a debt of 200s. Andereya ordered him to take 100s. and throw them into the long grass. A piece of broom and a long grass with a feathery flower were brought in and laid on the bark-cloth, and the prophet beat it with a stick. A clucking sound was heard in the roof, the whole house shook, and insects began to fall from the thatch. Some mysterious creature fell from the roof with a loud noise, and before any one could see it it was jumping about under the bark-cloth. Andereya then said : " He tells you [referring, apparently, to this creature] to take the piece of broom and the grass and put them in the eaves over your door. Say ' Let my wealth come back. I have taken 100s. and given them to Nabingi. Let her return mine.' " If the money was not returned in two days he was to come back to the prophet, who would restore his 100s. with an additional 8s. by way of compensation.

At Ephraim's second visit he reported that there was a man present who had married a wife with a very high bride-price, and wished to insure against her leaving him.

[1] Andereya's native name means " He pities ".

The prescription recommended was to put a certain herb in her washing water. After she had used it a snake would come and bite her four times. There would be medicine in the bite which would produce the desired effect, so the husband was to take no notice if he heard her scream !

A less distinguished prophet, whose name I do not know, allowed me to see him perform on two occasions. He was not a member of the village, but a friend of my retainer, Zirimenya, who persuaded him to hold two séances when he happened to be visiting at Kisimula. The performances were held at Zirimenya's house, in the presence of about twenty people, including four attendants on the prophet—his two wives and two men. The duty of *Kabona* was done not by one of these but by Zirimenya, who first laid before the prophet the gourd of beer and money which I had brought, and, with some difficulty, persuaded him to accept the latter in the unusual form of two ten-shilling notes, and then called on the *lubale* in the words : " All of you, all of you *lubale*, everyone, everyone, of the lake and the dry land, of Bunyoro and Kiziba and Ankole, all of you come and see our friend, this stranger. Do not be afraid. There is no danger, there is no rope [i.e. arrest]. Here are the shillings. Come, come, come quickly ! " For some time he went on calling " Come, come ! " at intervals, and presently the prophet ordered the audience to begin singing. The songs were those especially appropriate to *lubale*, and different from those one usually hears, and were accompanied by the shaking of rattles by the prophet and his attendants.

After a little time the prophet went out and came back dressed in barkcloth and with a strip of barkcloth with bells attached to it tied round each ankle. He sat down and began to jerk backwards and forwards, and then held out his hand to the attendants, who handed him first the *lutembe* necklace and then a stick with a bunch of cowries at one end, which is the special attribute of prophets of Kaumpali. Everyone clapped their hands at its appearance, and the prophet held it first to one nostril and then the other, and then began to gather the necklace into handfuls, wave it to and fro, and beat his chest with it. Then he got up and began a dance, which ended with his seizing a handful of canes from the fire and brandishing them. After this he threw himself on the ground panting, and drank enormous draughts of beer.

He then began to speak in a high squeaky voice, jerking out one word at a time, and this was recognized as the voice of Kaumpali. Zirimenya welcomed the *lubale* in the usual words of greeting, and made remarks of the kind appropriate to set a visitor at his ease. He continued to wave the stick about, and once thrust it into the fire and then applied it to his nostrils—a proceeding which impressed the audience considerably. Next he seized one of his wives, took her on his knees, and began to wave her arms about, apparently to make her prophesy too ; this, however, she did not do. From time to time he singled out some member of the audience and ordered him to be supplied with beer ; whether or not this favoured person wanted it, the prophet insisted on his drinking, though, in my case, my cook was allowed to act on my behalf.

Next he began divining the reasons for our presence. He pointed to those of us who were wearing shoes and suggested that we had something the matter with our feet, and made other guesses of a similar kind ; one woman, he said, was possessed by a *lubale* which ought to be made to speak. All these guesses were simply received with shouts of laughter.

After more affable conversation, in which the *lubale* was treated with no sign of deference, the prophet suddenly turned upon me and asked me what I wanted. I said I had come to inquire about my friends at home, and was told that there was a child ill, and an important lawsuit going on which would soon be settled. My household were only too eager to identify the sick child among those whose photographs they had seen, and invited me in the same way to explain the lawsuit—which, by stretching several points, I could have done. Actually the prophet had simply mentioned the two most common vicissitudes of Baganda life. Other questions of the same kind were asked and received non-committal answers.

More beer was then handed round, and the stick offered to one or two people, who beat their heads with it but refused to thrust it up their nostrils. Then, with a sudden dash, the prophet demanded a piece of paper from my notebook, which he received with a shriek of joy. Zirimenya took charge of it and put it with the money I had brought. Finally he danced out backwards, while everyone raised their hands above their heads ; this was a necessary precaution against plague and was taken so seriously that I was requested to do it.

After more singing and dancing in bells by the prophet's attendants, he was possessed by Ndawula, the *lubale* of smallpox. This time he went outside and danced with a stick, making such a thunderous noise that an imaginative person might well have thought the house was shaking. Ndawula spoke in Lunyoro in a deep voice, interspersed with growls like those of a wild beast. Kaumpuli had so much disliked my spectacles that I had to remove them, but Ndawula objected even to my notebook, so that I have no record of his proceedings.

On another occasion the same man let me see him prophesy in the name of Dungu. Of this *lubale*'s prophets it is said : " He who is possessed by Dungu is possessed by a lion " (*asamira Dungu asamira mpologoma*), and in preparation for his impersonation of the lion his wives fastened on his head a crown made of a banana-leaf split into ribbons, and two big leaves across his shoulders to represent the mane. The head-dress was also of some use in the main element of the performance, whose distinguishing feature is that the prophet puts his head into the fire. After the singing had been going on for some little time, he knelt up and stared at the fire— a log fire in the corner of the house—and then made a sort of dart and bent his head over it. He repeated the process several times, a wife setting his crown straight each time. The movement was always very rapid, but he seemed to get nearer the flames each time till one smelt burning hair, and, on one occasion, he actually moved the logs with his head. In the intervals he made grunting noises and turned his head to one side or the other with sudden jerky movements as if sniffing, and with his eyes shut. This the audience said was because the lion is blind except when actually in pursuit of his prey. Occasionally, as in his previous performance, he would take a wife on his knees and jerk her head from side to side, and at one point he grasped the hands of various members of the audience in turn and butted his head against theirs with considerable force. He also uttered short roars from time to time, which were interpreted as asking who wished to consult him, but was told that we only wanted to see him put his head in the fire. The climax was reached when he crouched over the fire holding his hands very near the flames, and then suddenly plunged his head into the middle of the logs so as to scatter them, after which he fell flat on his back and I was told the *lubale* had gone. The prophet revived in a very short time, and demanded his due of beer.

CHAPTER X

CONCLUSION

WE have now completed our survey of Baganda culture as it has been modified by contact with European civilization, and it remains to attempt an estimate of the degree of success with which the necessary adaptation to new circumstances has been made and the influence which deliberate policies, governmental or other, have had upon it. When one considers all the changes that have been enumerated it seems that little of the indigenous culture can survive. Yet Buganda remains an African society which has incorporated the foreign elements into itself and has not simply been swamped by them.

THE ECONOMIC SYSTEM

Certainly the most important single factor in the maintenance of this social cohesion has been the early recognition of native rights in land. Next to this in importance has been the encouragement and assistance given to native production of commercial crops. Despite the difficulties created by this part of the Uganda Agreement—difficulties which are being avoided in the new legislation directed to the protection of native rights in the other provinces—it is this which has made it possible for the new economic development to become a part of village life, for the new pursuits to be integrated into the system of household co-operation instead of belonging, as they do in so many parts of East Africa, to an entirely separate world. Baganda do leave home to work—there is even a large Baganda population in Nairobi—but these are the adventurous spirits who want to see the world, and who hope to earn more in skilled work than they would by growing cotton. Many of these, even, so long as they do not go out of Buganda, continue to live as part of some relative's household in a village near their work. None are driven to it by sheer economic compulsion. Indeed, I remember hearing a group of natives agree that they would "rather starve" than go to work on a certain plantation whose manager was very unpopular.

The point is worth stressing, since it has been maintained by as high an authority as General Smuts, in his advocacy of European employment as the best way of civilizing the African, that all that is necessary to prevent the disintegration of native life is a system of segregation which will make it impossible for natives to live permanently anywhere outside their reserves. The aim of this proposal is to check the growth, in the territories further north, of urban native populations such as exist in South Africa, who have abandoned their old homes and settled permanently in mixed communities of many tribes, knowing no common authority save that of the police—a development with which Buganda is never likely to be faced. But its implications deserve to be discussed in their bearing on the general theory of the adaptation of native life to modern conditions. It is suggested, in effect, that the transplantation of the young men of a native community from the environment in which they have grown up, in which their place is defined by tradition, and whose standards of conduct and of value are the unconscious assumptions which regulate their behaviour, into an existence with which their previous life has no point of contact, whose organization is directed to different ends, and whose rules of conduct, depending on these aims, are enforced by different means, can automatically and without dislocation transform the whole community into a new entity adapted for participation in the world economic system. Wage-labour is to be "the thin end of the industrial wedge".[1]

[1] Smuts, *Africa and Some World Problems*, ch. iii.

The aptness of the metaphor first strikes one when one remembers that wedges are used for splitting. It is futile to suppose that a system which deliberately forces a section of an African community to lead two separate lives, only connected by the tenuous link of the material objects that the wage-earner brinks back to the reserves, can produce any constructive modification of native society. Such a system means that the contribution of Africa to the economic co-operation of the Great Society is to be made not through the adjustment of African life to new types of activity but through its subordination to the needs of European production, no less because it is only individuals, not whole families, who are to be detached from their own community. So long as the African's new economic pursuits are followed in isolation from the social environment to which the rest of his life belongs, it is meaningless to speak of an adaptation of African society.

It is by refusing to drive in any such wedge—despite the demands of the Development Commission of 1920, which recommended the creation of native reserves as an encouragement to the native population to come out to work—that administrative policy in Buganda has created the first pre-requisite for a transformation of native life which has yet left it firmly rooted in the indigenous soil.

ECONOMIC INDIVIDUALISM

It is true that many of the old social bonds no longer exist. The ties of kinship outside the individual household—never so strong with the Baganda as among the Bantu tribes—have lost most of their importance, while the household itself is a much smaller unit than it used to be. Nor is the village community any longer linked together by the bond of common loyalty to a chief who was not only the sole authority over his subjects but their one source of advancement in life. Success in life is now directly dependent upon individual economic effort;

it is no longer the reward of qualities conceived to be socially desirable. For this very reason, there is now much less of the old readiness to share the fruits of success with those kinsmen who used to consider that they had a claim upon them ; and even where wealth is the result not of personal effort but of a dispensation from above, as it is in the case of the large landowners, the possibilities of personal satisfaction which it brings are so alluring that they outweigh the attraction of a reputation for generosity. What Baganda society has most to fear is not any economic exploitation from without, but the growth among its own members of a spirit of individualistic acquisitiveness in which every man seeks to exploit his neighbour. One can see the signs of it in the younger landlords, who, free from any responsibility towards their tenants, simply regard them as a source of revenue and constantly devise new ways of interpreting the law to their advantage. At present it is only they who are in a position to exploit, and their efforts are kept in check both by government action and by the ample areas of available land. If, indeed, the goal of a land of peasant proprietors was achieved, it might be merely sentimental to regret the passing of the old obligations of mutual aid, and sufficient to look forward to the substitution for them of social services financed by the State.

Yet one cannot help wishing that European teaching did not lay quite so much emphasis on the advantages to the individual of commercializing his possessions, and that there was more place in it for the growth of a spirit of corporate loyalty, not, indeed, to church or king— that is sufficiently stressed—but to the smaller group with whom he is in constant contact in the life of the village. Where the old centre of such loyalty in the chief has gone, the village has ceased to be an entity for any other purpose than that of entry in the land register ; and though one could not lay a finger on any definite results, there was a quite tangible difference in the atmosphere of Kisimula, the village that had migrated as a body with old Bugeza, and Matale, the haphazard juxtaposition of a dozen small landlords, who had brought land from Nsubuga, and such tenants as they had collected.

The need has been realized, and the solution sought, in the development of Boy Scout troops in the schools. The Scout movement, in its concentration on practical activities and the training which it gives in intelligent observation, forms a valuable adjunct to classroom studies. But it cannot generate a spirit of co-operation which will be active in circumstances entirely different from those which gave rise to it. Loyalty is not an independent quality which, once created, will remain in existence ready to attach itself to any object which offers ; it is part and parcel of the situation in which it is formed, and dies with it. Sentiments cannot be created in one context with a view to their transference to another.

Nor can one hope for great results from the other panacea of European education—football. The enthusiasm with which native schoolboys take to football amply justifies its place in the curriculum ; but here, even less than in the Boy Scout movement, can it be assumed that the temporary association which the game creates can alter the players' outlook on social relationships in general. We are apt to forget that the phrase " team spirit " is to us a metaphor for a socially approved attitude that makes itself effective through a number of appropriate mechanisms of co-operation ; a Prime Minister or a trade union leader can appeal to it, not because the majority of his audience have ever played football, but because of a host of associations unconnected with the literal meaning of the word. We forget, too, that with us the " team spirit " is only considered to exist when it is directed to ends of which our society, as a whole, approves : a suggestion, for instance, that Russia at the present time manifests more of it than Great Britain would not meet with a wide measure of acceptance. In sum, football, as played in England, is deemed to call for the exercise of moral qualities on which English society sets a high value ; but what calls those qualities into being is the value and not the football. They cannot be created in Buganda by the reverse process.

What is wanted, then, is some positive organization for the joint pursuit of common aims, through which new ties of mutual obligation can be formed. It should be an organization co-extensive with the village community, not a group so large that the active participation of most of its members is reduced to the payment of a subscription. The village co-operative societies, which have already been successfully established in India and Java and are now beginning to be set up in East Africa, probably meet the need in the best possible way.[1] Through such societies, assisted by advice and instruction from agricultural experts, neighbours could be united by their interest in improved methods of cultivation and preparation of the produce for the market ; through them such developments might be introduced as the purchase of ploughs, which are at present beyond the means of a single family. Through them, too, it might be possible to cope with what is Buganda's chief problem at the moment—the lack of adaptability of the average cultivator, who, having acquired the habit of growing cotton and nothing but cotton, knowing what cotton requires, and having a general vague feeling that other crops are more difficult, is reluctant to change even to a crop which he is assured will be more profitable. Through them, again, thrift and foresight in planning for the future could be developed. And the principles of loyalty and regard for the interests of others, of the direction of productive effort to ends higher than mere individual gain, which are taught in church and school, could, with this field for their application, become an effective social force.

Given such a focus of village life—and assuming eventual world economic recovery—the future of Buganda should promise well. Yet there are two respects in which

[1] See C. F. Strickland, *Co-operation for Africa*, 1933.

the adjustment to modern conditions is sufficiently unsatisfactory to call for comment.

EDUCATION

One is in the educational system, which at present is directed almost exclusively to produce young men capable of doing " white-collar " jobs—teachers, native clergy, chiefs, and clerks in Government offices, plantation foremen, and the like. In the eyes of the boys and their parents the first aim of education is to qualify the pupil to earn a good income, and to earn it with the pen or typewriter rather than with the hoe. It is true that since no education, except that of the elementary vernacular or " bush " schools, is free, the number of pupils contracts in a period of economic depression, and the problem is not that of a supply of persons qualified to do clerical work which does not vary with the demand for their services. Yet, if it is assumed as the ideal that every child should receive some organized education, surely this should not consist in the general application of a curriculum devised to meet the needs of what will never be more than a minority.

An incidental disadvantage of the present system lies in the amount of time which has to be devoted to the teaching of English. Certainly a knowledge of English is an advantage to the Muganda, and there is nothing which they themselves more ardently desire. Certainly, too, if such a knowledge is to be of any value to them, it must consist of more than the memorizing of a mass of words to which their own experience provides no corresponding concept. At Budo School, by the devotion of many hours in the earlier forms to the teaching of English as a language by the most up-to-date methods, this danger is admirably avoided—but at what a cost to the balance of subjects ! The requirements of Budo, again, set the pace for the central schools from whom it recruits pupils, and in their case English teaching is often less well-directed. Of the

Catholic schools I cannot speak from first-hand observation, but with them the problem is further complicated by the fact that English is often not the native language of the teacher.

One reason for the stress on English is that the only generally recognized standard of attainment is that set by English examinations. Moreover, the Baganda are beginning to demand a university education, and, if they cannot get it on the spot, will go to Ceylon or to England for it. Schools must, therefore, enable them to qualify for entrance. During 1932 the education authorities of the three East African territories agreed to inaugurate a five-years course leading up to the Cambridge School Certificate, which would then become the entrance examination for Makerere college.

The difficulty might be lessened by greater flexibility in the demands of examining bodies at home, at any rate for those to whom the examination merely represents a standard of attainment. Those who wish to go on to a higher course of specialized study must probably, in any case, be prepared to do their work in English, for Luganda cannot be made to express the technicalities of medicine or law. But it would not then be necessary to subordinate the whole curriculum to their requirements.

But at this point arises the perennial question of vernacular textbooks. Can any African government afford to produce school textbooks in all the different languages spoken in the territory under its control ? The answer appears to be in the negative, and in Uganda the only question on which opinions differ is what foreign language shall be the medium of instruction : English or Swahili. The Government recently decided in favour of Swahili, and Swahili teaching is now required in all schools receiving government grants, outside the province of Buganda. Swahili has the advantage over English of resembling much more closely many of the native languages of the Protectorate. It is unlikely that ideas expressed in it could ever be so remote from native concepts as those of an English textbook can easily be ; the mere necessity of translation would prevent this. Yet, if it is indeed vain to hope that any African people can be given an education in which the mother tongue is the principal medium of instruction, and any other language is taught merely as a foreign language and with a view to the importance which it is likely to have in the pupil's adult life, it is vain to look forward to the development of an educational system which shall be an integral part of the social organization and not a mere excrescence upon it.

As regards the other problem, that of devising a curriculum to suit the boy who is not of a literary bent, which he can turn to account in village life and which —an essential point if education is to cease to be looked on as a means of getting away from the village—will open up to him the possibility of making a good income from his land, a scheme has just been inaugurated. The proposal is to establish an agricultural school in connection with an estate which is a paying proposition and demonstrates efficient farming in practice. The estate in question is owned by a European who is keenly interested in native development and whose activities include stock-breeding, dairying, and coffee-growing. A grant of £800 for three years has been made by Government for this purpose. If the school is successful, it could well be linked up with the development of a system of co-operative farming in the villages, in which its pupils might be expected to take a leading part.

MARRIAGE

The second case of serious dislocation lies in the sphere of sexual ethics. The standards laid down by Christian teaching are not taken for granted by the natives as they are by those who still adhere to them in Europe ; rather they are regarded as a set of arbitrary rules to be disobeyed when that can be done with impunity. The prohibition of polygamy does not cause serious difficulty, for polygamy is dying out with the passing of the economic system to which it was appropriate and the wars which reduced the number of men. But the prohibition of divorce creates a situation for which no remedy seems possible while it is maintained. Baganda marriage was a contract which could be dissolved, but which was accompanied by guarantees against its frivolous dissolution. Under Christianity it has become a theoretically indissoluble contract, and what was the pledge of its maintenance—the bride-price—has almost become an inducement to those who should be interested in its stability to encourage its repudiation. In a system which does not admit of divorce the bride-price is an anomaly, and there would be a strong case for its abolition were it not that native feeling would be outraged by the idea of marriages taking place without it. However, the likelihood of such a system becoming firmly established is so remote that this question does not arise. A solution is more likely to be found, as it has been in Europe, in the recognition of civil divorce and in provision of facilities for natives to obtain it ; but for this solution to be really satisfactory, it is essential that the refund of the bride-price should be made obligatory. If the proceedings before the Provincial Commissioner had to be terminated by the public return to the husband of his money, not only would the bride-price continue to play its former valuable part, but the reluctance to marry at all, which results from the fear of losing it, and the consequent increase of irregular *liaisons*, would be removed.

NATIVE ADMINISTRATION

It remains to estimate the success of the system of government. In one sense, the native authorities are those recognized by tradition, for they are still appointed and promoted by the king. But in another sense they are something very different, for there is no longer any personal tie between them and the people under their control, nor is their acceptability to the populace guaranteed as it used to be by the fact that they depended for their prestige on attracting and retaining a large following. On the other hand, now that the limits of their authority are set so much more narrowly than they used to be, this guarantee is not of great importance ; the modern chief is not in a position to oppress his subjects by physical violence or by demands on their services. It is conceivable that a *saza* chief might attempt to make a good thing out of the corruption of justice—though the ample salaries which they receive probably constitute the best safeguard against this—but the litigants in a *gombolola* chief's courts are so poor that this would hardly be worth his while, and certainly all those which I attended showed a most painstaking determination to get at the truth of the matters before them. Certainly there is no dissatisfaction on that score among the people at large.

Since the Baganda chiefs never derived their position, as so many native authorities do, from any belief in supernatural attributes inherent in certain individuals by virtue of their birth, there has been no violence done to popular sentiment in their conversion to a native civil service, and no reluctance to accept their authority such as is found where there exists alongside the chief appointed by government some other person who, in native eyes, is alone qualified to wield his power. The only question that has to be asked, therefore, is whether a system of government imposed, as this is, from above, satisfactorily meets the needs of the modern Baganda kingdom. There is a certain demand—not " a great and growing movement ", as Dr. Norman Leys describes it,[1] but a demand among the educated Baganda of the capital—for the introduction of popular representation into the Lukiko. I do not think the demand has ever been put forward in the shape of clearly-formulated proposals ; if what is asked

[1] Cf. Leys, *A Last Chance in Kenya*, p. 76. There is no official corroboration of Dr. Leys' statements that such a proposal was made to the king of Buganda by the British authorities and that steps in this direction are about to be taken.

is the transformation of the Lukiko into a body elected by ballot on a territorial basis, the idea to anyone who has lived in a Baganda village is fantastic. It is hard to imagine the terms in which one would explain to the electorate what they were being invited to do and why. The villagers have views, certainly, which they wish to make known to the Government ; they desire, for instance, that it should order the Indians to pay a higher price for cotton. Such views are put forward when a *saza* chief goes the round of the *gombolola* courts. It is only on the assumption that the chiefs have vested interests contrary to those of the common people that it is necessary to provide the private individual as such with a means of representation in the central government. This may be the case where the chief's career depends on co-operation in a European policy directed to the furtherance of non-native interests ; but in Buganda this danger does not have to be·guarded against.

There is no reason why a council appointed by the votes of the villagers should be any better suited to manage the affairs of the country than the present Lukiko. Presumably some qualifications would be required of a candidate for election ; and since the council would require for efficiency at least as high a standard of education as the native civil service, the only persons, other than administrative chiefs, who would be eligible, would be native lawyers and schoolmasters, with some shop assistants. The same difficulty arises with regard to the basis of the suffrage. A property qualification would weight the scales more heavily than at present on the side of the land-owner ; an educational qualification of any real value would reduce the electorate to a body very little larger than that of those eligible for election.

It is unsafe to assume, as the advocates of representative government for African societies do, either that it would in fact secure the interests or desires of the general public, or that it would give them that feeling of responsibility for their own misfortunes which is said to enable European society to bear with fortitude the consequences of its political mistakes. Conferred from above on a populace which is not aware of any desire to manage its own affairs, it can never be anything but a mechanical system, to be manipulated by a few individuals for their own ends, while the majority remain indifferent to its proceedings. To offer it, as a means of causing the government to satisfy their wishes, to people who cannot hope to understand the complicated hazards upon which the achievement of that result depends, is only to lead them to disappointment. As Lord Lugard put it recently : "Decision by a majority vote in an assembly of men selected by secret ballot on the assumption that they will represent the opinions of their constituents on every variety of question, is a form of democracy wholly alien to African thought." [1]

There is probably room—or will be in the future—for the development of channels for the representation of organizations devoted to particular interests. The Native Anglican Church, for instance, puts proposals for legislation before the Lukiko through those chiefs who are represented on its synod. There might be room for its representation in that body in its own right. Again, organizations of native producers may come to feel that their interests deserve more attention than they can get from a council of people with no experience of their special problems. Village co-operative societies, too, might then claim representation.[2] The essence of representative government, after all, is not in some particular mechanism but in the opportunity for the expression of popular opinion—where popular opinion exists. By such

[1] " Education and Race Relations," *Journal of the African Society*, January, 1933.
[2] This suggestion is contrary to the proposals of Mr. Strickland, who holds that it is essential to the success of co-operative societies to keep them out of politics. His proposals, however, are based on the experience of India, where representative government and party politics are already an accomplished fact. While I am aware of the danger of such organizations becoming mere vehicles of political agitation, I think it might be reduced by the very fact of their representation.

means as this, it might be possible to develop a system which would effectively achieve this end through what is essentially the same process as that by which European democracy grew up—the granting of a hearing to a popular voice which had something definite to ask for.

VALUE OF INDIRECT RULE

In sum, then, the history of Buganda presents a justification for the system of Indirect Rule—the preservation of native society as a basis for new developments, and its transformation only to the extent which these developments really necessitate. The serious maladjustments in modern Buganda result from the introduction of European institutions which were not called for by the need for adaptation to new conditions—the creation of a landlord class and the suppression of divorce. Though it would be going too far to state it as axiomatic that the ballot-box must produce similar dislocation, it is safe to say that not unless it meets a genuine need—and at present it certainly does not—can it be effectively incorporated into Baganda society.

It may not be out of place here to answer some of the criticisms that have recently been directed against the theory of Indirect Rule. Applied to the Baganda, it has certainly not meant their preservation in a state of picturesque antiquity [1]; nor can it have that meaning anywhere, for such preservation is impossible in the face of economic forces which no government can control. It is as a means of enabling the necessary adaptation to new conditions to take place with the minimum of disintegration that this policy is advocated, and the argument for the preservation of indigenous institutions rests not on their picturesqueness but upon their necessity for the maintenance of social stability.

Nor do those who advocate this system justify it, as

---

[1] Cf. Sir James Currie, " Present-day Difficulties of a Young Officer in the Tropics," *Journal of the African Society*, 1933.

Dr. Norman Leys asserts,[1] through any theory of the inherent inability of Africans to manage European institutions, or of differences between European and African mentality; the pre-logical savage is not, as he supposes, the latest figment of the anthropological imagination—which he himself appears to endow with mental processes different from those of the average intelligent man—but an exploded hypothesis. It is not because European institutions are unsuitable to Africans as individuals that their wholesale introduction is deprecated, but because neither African nor any other society can assimilate a complete outfit of alien institutions between to-day and to-morrow. Dr. Leys points out that we believe the early Britons to have been as intelligent as we are and to have differed from us only in " lack of opportunities ". Yet he would surely not be prepared to argue that the introduction to prehistoric Britain of mass production and manhood suffrage would have produced a result indistinguishable from the Britain of to-day. Our opportunities have included not only democracy, economic individualism, and higher education, but—up till the last century—time for gradual development. On the other hand, they have not included what it is perhaps now possible for us to offer to Africa— scientific knowledge of the structure of society as a basis for controlled development on rational lines.

There is nothing metaphysical about the statement that a human society which functions satisfactorily must be a co-ordinated whole.[2] It is not meant to convey a mysterious warning, like the danger signals on telegraph poles, against touching something you do not understand. It is intended rather to invite attention to the realities of the problem of social adaptation. What will a given

[1] *A Last Chance in Kenya*, chapter ix.

[2] General Smuts, when he suggests that what is threatened by the impact of European on African society is the native *Weltanschaung*, appears to hold such a metaphysical view (*Africa and Some World Problems*, p. 861). I have tried to show in this book that its effects are much more concrete and specific ; it is for that reason that they are amenable to scientific analysis and control.

change in native institutions produce ? The answer to that question is not : Inevitable disintegration, so make no changes. It is to be found in an examination of the institution to be modified, of its place in the society as a whole, its relation to other institutions, and the reasons why it has its peculiar characteristics, and in consideration whether the substitute which is proposed will really take its place, or whether it will leave gaps that other means must be devised to fill. It is by its ability to fulfil the needs of a given society at a given time, and not by its resemblance to the forms to which we are accustomed, that each development must be judged.

African societies have so far produced few, if any, sociologists. Consequently, the demands made by Africans, however intelligent, however highly educated, cannot be taken as decisive in determining the lines along which African development should go. The decision should be made on the results of a scientific study of the actual problems involved.

The position of the person who sets up to know what is good for somebody else is not an enviable one : his motives are always suspect. It is embarrassing to find oneself uttering, in all honesty, one of the texts which are most frequently cited by the devil for his purpose. I can only assure the reader of my honesty, and leave him to judge whether this book is a specious plea for the maintenance of the African in subjection or an objective analysis of the reaction of an African society to European civilization.

BIBLIOGRAPHY

I

UGANDA

ASHE, R. P. *Two Kings of Uganda*, 1889.
HATTERSLEY, C. W. *The Baganda at Home*, 1908.
JOHNSTON, Sir H. H. *The Uganda Protectorate*, 1902.
JONES, H. G. *Uganda in Transformation*, 1926.
LUGARD, Lord. *Rise of our East African Empire*, 1893.
ROSCOE, J. *The Baganda : their Customs and Beliefs*, 1911.
SPEKE, J. N. *Journal of the Discovery of the Source of the Nile*, 1864.
THOMAS, H. B. "An Experiment in African Native Land Settlement," *Journal of the African Society*, 1928.
TUCKER, A. R. *Eighteen Years in Uganda*, 1908.

II

COMPARATIVE MATERIAL

DRIBERG, J. H. *The East African Problem.*
EVANS-PRITCHARD, E. E. " Sorcery and Native Opinion," *Africa*, 1929.
—— " The Zande Corporation of Witch-Doctors," *Journal of the Royal Anthropological Institute*, 1932.
FIRTH, R. W. *Primitive Economics of the New Zealand Maori*, 1929.
MALINOWSKI, B. *Argonauts of the Western Pacific*, 1922.
—— *Crime and Custom in Savage Society*, 1926.
RICHARDS, A. I. *Hunger and Work in a Savage Tribe*, 1932.
SCHAPERA, I. " Customs relating to Twins in South Africa," *Journal of the African Society*, 1926-7.
Report of an Enquiry into Land Tenure and the Kibanja System in Bunyoro, 1931 (Entebbe, 1932).

society to bear with fortitude the consequences of its political mistakes. Conferred from above on a populace which is not aware of any desire to manage its own affairs, it can never be anything but a mechanical system, to be manipulated by a few individuals for their own ends, while the majority remain indifferent to its proceedings. To offer it, as a means of causing the government to satisfy their wishes, to people who cannot hope to understand the complicated hazards upon which the achievement of that result depends, is only to lead them to disappointment. As Lord Lugard put it recently : " Decision by a majority vote in an assembly of men selected by secret ballot on the assumption that they will represent the opinions of their constituents on every variety of question, is a form of democracy wholly alien to African thought." [1]

There is probably room—or will be in the future—for the development of channels for the representation of organizations devoted to particular interests. The Native Anglican Church, for instance, puts proposals for legislation before the Lukiko through those chiefs who are represented on its synod. There might be room for its representation in that body in its own right. Again, organizations of native producers may come to feel that their interests deserve more attention than they can get from a council of people with no experience of their special problems. Village co-operative societies, too, might then claim representation.[2] The essence of representative government, after all, is not in some particular mechanism but in the opportunity for the expression of popular opinion—where popular opinion exists. By such

---

[1] " Education and Race Relations," *Journal of the African Society*, January, 1933.

[2] This suggestion is contrary to the proposals of Mr. Strickland, who holds that it is essential to the success of co-operative societies to keep them out of politics. His proposals, however, are based on the experience of India, where representative government and party politics are already an accomplished fact. While I am aware of the danger of such organizations becoming mere vehicles of political agitation, I think it might be reduced by the very fact of their representation.

means as this, it might be possible to develop a system which would effectively achieve this end through what is essentially the same process as that by which European democracy grew up—the granting of a hearing to a popular voice which had something definite to ask for.

VALUE OF INDIRECT RULE

In sum, then, the history of Buganda presents a justification for the system of Indirect Rule—the preservation of native society as a basis for new developments, and its transformation only to the extent which these developments really necessitate. The serious maladjustments in modern Buganda result from the introduction of European institutions which were not called for by the need for adaptation to new conditions—the creation of a landlord class and the suppression of divorce. Though it would be going too far to state it as axiomatic that the ballot-box must produce similar dislocation, it is safe to say that not unless it meets a genuine need—and at present it certainly does not—can it be effectively incorporated into Baganda society.

It may not be out of place here to answer some of the criticisms that have recently been directed against the theory of Indirect Rule. Applied to the Baganda, it has certainly not meant their preservation in a state of picturesque antiquity [1]; nor can it have that meaning anywhere, for such preservation is impossible in the face of economic forces which no government can control. It is as a means of enabling the necessary adaptation to new conditions to take place with the minimum of disintegration that this policy is advocated, and the argument for the preservation of indigenous institutions rests not on their picturesqueness but upon their necessity for the maintenance of social stability.

Nor do those who advocate this system justify it, as

[1] Cf. Sir James Currie, " Present-day Difficulties of a Young Officer in the Tropics," *Journal of the African Society*, 1933.

INDEX

DATE DUE			